Patricia Smith's

DOLL VALUES

Antique to Modern
Series V

COLLECTOR BOOKS

P.O. Box 3009
Paducah, KY 42002-3009

The current values in this book should be used only as a guide. They are not intended to set prices, which vary from one section of the country to another. Auction prices as well as dealer prices vary greatly and are affected by condition as well as demand. Neither the Author nor the Publisher assumes responsibility for any losses that might be incurred as a result of consulting this guide.

DEDICATION

This volume is dedicated to two very special people, Nancy Young and Jean Truman, who have been a tremendous help and whose friendship we cherish and enjoy. Thank you both!

CREDITS

Thank you to the following for the use of their dolls/photographs:
Elinor Bibby, Sally Bethscheider, Richard Boss, Joanna Brunken, Doris Chandler (Bill Smith), Laura Cleghorn, Marlowe Cooper, Doll Cradle (8719 W. 50th Terr. Merriam, KS 66203), Barbara Earnshaw Cain, Debra Ekart, Esther Foss, Sally Freeman, Frasher Doll Auctions (Rt. 1, Box 72, Oak Grove, MO 64075), Maureen Fukuskima (Hawaii), Green's Doll Museum, Karen Heidemann, Phyllis Houston, Genie Jenright, Diane Kornhauser, Ruth Lane, Margaret Mandel, Jeanne Mauldin, Shirley Merrill, Jay Minter, Dora Mitzel, Pearl Pheasant, Florence Phelps, Phyllis Juhlin Park, Pat Pardon (Margaret Mandel), Ellen Peterson, Lani Pettit, Arthur Routiette, June Schultz, Henri and John Startzel, Karen Stephenson (Dora Mitzel), Sheila Stephenson, Bonnie Stewart, Joanna Stout, Pat Timmons, Turn of Century Antiques (1415 S. Broadway, Denver, CO 80220), Grace Walters and Josephine Wright.

Cover Photo: Courtesy Frasher Doll Auctions.

FOREWORD

The general idea of books is to try to help with information that may be desired by the collector. To either learn more about particular dolls that are owned, or to study dolls that one would like to own someday. If the book is a **Price Guide**, the reference will help in establishing what area these dolls may fall in and can help in evaluating one's collection for insurance coverage or, in case of damage or theft, help in recovery totals.

This book **is** a price guide and information about prices may be found on the following page, but here we would like to mention these are not prices just plucked from mid-air like a magician who appears to produce silk flowers from nowhere. The prices are **retail** (as sold by dealers/owners of doll shops or doll show dealers) and are gathered over a period of a year from doll shows, ads, auctions, doll shops, lists from mail order dealers and the general correspondence with collectors who have purchased or sold certain dolls. Auction prices cannot be totally reliable by themselves, nor can any other source completely by itself, but an overall view must be taken to arrive at an average price asked and paid. During an auction two or more people are pitted against one another to become the future owner of a certain doll and often a pre-decided upon price will fly out the window and one of them will actually pay more than planned.

At this point in time of collecting dolls, pricing is most difficult as certain dolls have fallen in prices and others have risen dramatically due to increased popularity and demand. Some of the dolls that have increased are the fine examples of closed mouth French and German, characters, dolls that have original clothing and some of the American-made cloth dolls. Prices being paid for dolls that are fine examples and all original may go way above book prices and others such as kid bodied dolls, German dolls with "dolly" faces, or modern dolls that are re-dressed may go far below book prices. When we ask a collector why they will not pay more for a kid body doll/shoulder head, the answer usually is the same, "They just stand there and I can't make them comfortable among the composition bodied ones." When asked why they no longer care for the "dolly" faced dolls, the answer generally will be, "Oh, I outgrew that period of collecting." The modern collectors who used to buy re-dressed dolls now say they have learned that they have a tough time re-selling them when they finally find the same doll with original clothes, so they just won't buy anymore in the first place as they do not want to lose money or get stuck with them.

As mentioned, quality dolls, be they French or German, are bringing higher prices and more money is being spent on the American cloth dolls such as Alabama Babies, Columbian, etc. Also the English firm of Norah Wellings has become very popular whereas the Italian Lenci dolls may have fallen off in sales slightly and continue to be hard item for dealers to sell.

In the modern field the especially great examples of composition and hard plastic dolls have risen in prices and almost all others have remained stable or have taken a slide down the price scale. It must be noted that prices on all antiques and collectables – be it dolls, furniture, glassware, art or whatever – changes with the National interest rates. When the interest rates are down, people are much more interested in purchasing large items such as a house, car, furniture or other large cost items rather than hobby items. When interest and inflation figures are lower, there is less thought about investment, which unfortunately, has became a main word in the vocabulary of the majority of collectors. In fact, during National "good times" hobbies, collectables and antiques cycle through "bad times" with many collectors changing from dolls to other things, such as the stock market, properties, etc. When these people sell their collections they often think they will pick it up again in the

4

future, but rarely do. Others lose interest and pack away their dolls, where others just stop where they are and do not pursue the hobby any further. Some lose interest altogether and find the entire hobby boring.

Another point should be made and that is the hobby of doll collecting has lost much of it's appeal to the **new** collector because the cost of getting into the hobby overwhelms them. The new collectors, very important in any field of collecting, just are not flowing into dolls as they once were and this has hurt the market tremendously. **But**, it is a buyer's market and if at all possible financially, the people who love doll collecting **are buying**, still having fun fully enjoying their hobby and their doll friends. Doll collecting **is here to stay** . . . it is not going to disappear . . . and the dolls are more available to buy right now than they have been for the past 10 years.

PRICES

This book is divided between "Antique" and "Modern" by sections with the older dolls in the first section and the newer dolls in the second section. Each section is listed by maker alphabetically or by type of material or by name of the doll. (Example: Bye-lo or Kewpie). This is done to try to make a quick reference for the reader. An index is provided for locating a specific doll. We must apologize to our readers on behalf of the publishers for omitting the valuable index tool from the fourth series of *Doll Values*.

The condition of the doll is uppermost in pricing. An all original modern doll in excellent condition will bring a much higher price than those listed in a price guide. A doll that is damaged or without original clothes, is soiled and dirty, will bring far less than the top price listed. The cost of doll repairs and clean up has soared and it is wise to judge the damage and estimate the cost of repairs before you attempt to sell or buy a damaged doll.

With antique dolls the condition of the bisque, or material the head is made from, is of uppermost importance, as is the body in that it does not need repairs and is correct to the doll. Antique dolls must be clean, nicely dressed and ready to place into a collection and have no need for repair in any way for them to bring book prices, but an all original one with original clothes, marked shoes and original wig will bring a lot more than any prices listed. Boxes are very rare, so here again, the doll will have a higher price.

It is very important to show the "retail" prices of dolls in a price guide and to try to be as accurate as possible for insurance reasons. This can be referred to as "replacement cost" as an insurance company or a postal service must have some means to appraise a damaged or stolen doll for the insuree and the collector must have some means to judge their own collections to be able to purchase adequate amounts of insurance.

No one knows your collection better than yourself and in the end, in relation to what to pay for a doll, you must ask yourself if the doll is affordable **to you** and do you want it enough to pay the price. You will buy the doll, or pass it up – it is as simple as that!

Prices shown are for dolls that are clean, undamaged, well-dressed and in overall excellent condition with many prices listed for soiled, dirty, re-dressed dolls also.

ANTIQUE AND OLDER
DOLLS SECTION

ALL BISQUE-FRENCH

Although many socket heads with swivel necks may be French, a greater amount of them are German. Among the all bisque dolls, the ones with a swivel neck are most desirable because they are rarer and **maybe** French. The French head may have a loop molded at the base of the neck. These loops are easy to identify as they look like the top of a bell: ♈

French all bisque also have kid lined joints, tiny cork pates with many being peg strung. Some French all bisque have painted eyes but most have glass eyes and well painted lashes. In the small sizes the eyes are usually set and generally blue with no pupils. As the dolls get larger, they gain the pupils and sleep.

The French style legs are much more varied, thinner and more delicate than Ger-

many made ones. Many are barefooted, although many have vertical, as well as circular ribbed stockings in many colors that can include white, blue, brown, black and yellow. The molded-on shoes can also be high top boots with pointed toes, high buttoned ones with four or more painted straps. They can be brown, pink, blue, black one strap slippers with or without heels, some with bows or even plain black with a colored bow. The legs may have painted stockings to the knees or the entire leg can be painted to give the effect of hip high stockings.

The French all bisque dolls have finely painted features with outlined lips, well-tinted bisque and feathered eyebrows. They are jointed at the neck, hips and shoulders, glass eyes, closed mouth, with good wig and nicely dressed. The doll should be in very good condition, not have any chips, cracks, breaks, nor hairlines to bring the following prices.

Swivel neck (socket head) molded shoes or boots: 4½″ – $650.00; 6″-6¼″ – $800.00.
Bare Feet: 5″-6″ – $700.00.
With jointed elbows: 5½″-6″ – $1,200.00 up.
With jointed elbows and knees: 5½″-6″ – $2,000.00.
S.F.B.J., Unis, or other late French all bisque: 5″-6″ – $350.00; 7″ – $450.00.

4″ All bisque French doll with glass eyes, closed mouth and mohair wig. Swivel neck and slim limbs. Courtesy Arthur Routiette. 4″ – $650.00 up.

8½″ All bisque French ''Wrestler'' marked: 102. Jointed neck, shoulders and hips, open mouth with two upper teeth and one lower tooth. Molded, painted white stockings. Courtesy Frasher Doll Auctions. 8″ – $1,000.00.

8

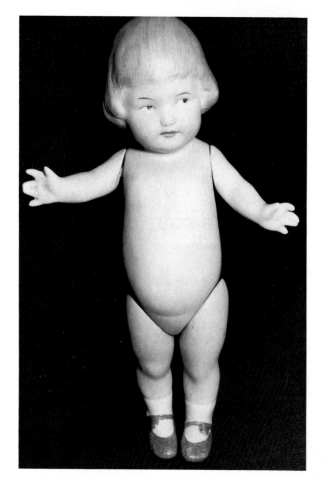

8½" German all bisque. Molded and painted hair, painted eyes to side, closed mouth, jointed at hips and shoulders only. Courtesy Frasher Doll Auctions. 8" – $225.00 up.

Swivel neck, glass eyes: Open or closed mouth, nicely dressed or original and good wig. One-strap shoes and painted socks: 4" – $225.00; 5" – $325.00; 9" – $825.00. Swivel neck, painted eyes: open or closed mouths. One-strap shoes and painted socks. Nice wig and clothes: 2" – $125.00; 4" – $160.00; 5" – $225.00; 7" – $295.00; 9" – $325.00.

One-piece body and head, glass eyes: Open or closed mouth with good wig and nicely dressed: 3" – $75.00; 4½"-5½" – $165.00; 7" – $285.00; 8"-9" – $350.00; 11" – $800.00.

One-piece body and head, painted eyes: Open or closed mouth, with good wig or molded hair and nicely dressed: 2" – $35.00; 4½"-5½" – $125.00; 7" – $185.00; 8"-9" – $225.00; 11" – $700.00.

Molded-on clothes or underwear: Jointed at shoulders only or at shoulders and hips: 4½" – $125.00; 5½" – $200.00; 6"-7" – $345.00.

With long stockings (to above knee): Glass eyes, open or closed mouth: 5½" – $425.00; 7½" – $625.00.

Molded hair: One-piece body and head; painted-on shoes and socks, painted eyes: 5" – $90.00; 6½" – $145.00.

Flapper: One-piece body and head, wig,

ALL BISQUE-GERMAN
ALL BISQUE-BABIES

painted eyes, painted-on long stockings, thin limbs, one-strap painted shoes: 5" – $265.00; 7" – $350.00. Same with molded hair: 5" – $265.00; 7" – $350.00.

Pink bisque of 1920's and 1930's: Jointed shoulders and hips with painted features and molded hair or wig: 3" – $50.00; 5" – $65.00.

Marked by maker: S&H, JDK, A.B.G., etc.: 5" – $165.00; 7" – $245.00; 8" – $325.00.

Character child marked 150: Jointed shoulders and hips, wigged or painted hair, open or closed mouth, painted-on one strap black shoes with brown soles. Glass eyes: 5½" – $200.00; Painted eyes: 5" – $145.00.

Bathing Beauty: 1920's. All bisque comes in many positions. Can be nude or be partially dressed in painted-on clothes or materials. Molded hair, cap or wig. Painted features of excellent quality, fine modeling and painting: 5½" – $300.00; 8½" – $700.00; features not well defined and medium to poor quality bisque: 4" – $65.00.

ALL BISQUE BABIES

8" All bisque baby with painted hair and eyes, open/closed mouth and on five-piece bent limb baby body. 6½" Marked: AT, in triangle. Clay-like material, painted features and molded hair, one-piece body and head, jointed hips and shoulders. Courtesy Frasher Doll Auctions. 8" – $350.00; 6½" – $185.00.

All bisque babies were made in both Germany and Japan and dolls from either country can be excellent quality or poor quality. Prices are for excellent dolls with no chips or breaks, clean and nicely dressed.

Jointed neck, shoulders and hips: Can have glass or painted eyes, wigs or painted hair: 3½" – $100.00; 6" – $200.00.

Jointed shoulders and hips only: Well painted features, free formed thumbs, molded bottles in hands, molded clothes, character faces: 3½" – $60.00; 6" – $145.00.

"Candy Babies": Generally poorly painted with high color bisque. Were given away at candy counters. 1920's: 2½" – $22.00; 4" – $35.00; 5"-6" – $65.00.

Japan Babies: Of poor to medium quality: 3½"-5" – $5.00 to 40.00; very nice quality: 3½"-5" – $15.00 to 65.00.

Pink bisque baby: Jointed at shoulders and hips, painted features and hair, bent baby legs. 1920's-1930's: 2" – $35.00; 4" – $55.00.

Toddler: Jointed neck, glass eyes: 6½" – $525.00; 9" – $675.00; 12" – $950.00.

Character baby: Jointed shoulders and hips, molded hair, painted eyes with character face. 4" – $115.00; 6" – $175.00; Glass eyes: 5" – $250.00; Swivel neck, glass eyes: 6" – $350.00.

Bye-Lo: See that section.

All bisque dolls: Top: Happifat Boy and Girl. Jointed shoulders only. Made in Germany. Lower boy and girl Bonnet dolls are in swim suits and the "Frozen Charlotte" type. Clothes and bonnets are molded on. Right is little boy made in one-piece with hands molded as if he were shouting. Courtesy Turn of Century Antiques. 5" Happifats – $245.00 each; Molded clothes, 7" – $345.00 each; Boy – $90.00.

All bisque dolls with character faces, stances or names were made in both Germany and Japan. The German dolls have finer bisque and painting of the features. Most will be jointed at shoulders, or shoulders and hips only, with very few being jointed also at the neck. They can be bare footed or have molded-on shoes and socks. No chips or breaks and clean.

Baby Bo Kaye: 6¼" – $1,300.00.
Baby Bud: Germany: 5" – $200.00; Japan: 5" – $95.00.
Baby Darling: 5" – $100.00.
Baby Peggy Montgomery: 6" – $450.00.
Bonnie Babe: 5" – $650.00; 7" – $850.00.
Bye-Lo: Jointed neck, wig, glass eyes: 6" – $650.00; Molded hair, painted eyes, one-piece body and head: 5" – $375.00.
Campbell Kids: Molded clothes: 4½" – $145.00.
Chin-Chin by Heubach: 4½" – $275.00.
Didi by Orsini: 6" – $1,150.00.
Googly: Glass eyes: 6" – $500.00-600.00.
Googly: Painted eyes: 6" – $325.00-425.00.
Googly: Glass eyes, swivel neck: 5½" – $625.00.

Googly: Elbow and knee joints: 6" – $1,600.00.
Grumpy Boy: Germany: 4" – $145.00; Japan: 4" – $75.00.
Happifats: Boy or girl: 5" – $245.00.
Heubach: Molded hair: 6½" – $250.00; molded ribbon: 6½" – $250.00; wigged: 7" – $285.00.
Heubach: Bunny Boy: 4¼" – $250.00.
Little Imp: Hoofed feet: 6½" – $275.00.
MIBS by Amberg: 3½" – $225.00; 5" – $325.00.
Mimi by Orsini: 6" – $1,150.00.
Molded-on clothes: Unjointed, painted features: 4" – $80.00.
Our Fairy: 8" – $1,200.00.
Our Mary: 4¼" – $165.00.
Peek-a-boo by Drayton: 4" – $225.00.
Peterkin: 9" – $385.00.
Peterkin, Tommy: Made for Horsman: 4" – $225.00.
Quesue San Baby: Various poses, 5" – $150.00.
Sonny: By Averill: 5" – $625.00.
Wide Awake Doll: Germany: 7½" – $275.00; Japan: 7½" – $100.00.

ALL BISQUE-NODDERS-JAPAN

"Knotters" are called "Nodders" and when their heads are touched, they "nod". The reason they are correctly called "Knotters" is due to the way they are strung, with the string tied in a knot through the head. They can also be made with cutouts on the bodies to take a tiny rod that comes out of the sides of the neck. Both styles were made in Japan and Germany.

Santa Claus: 6" - $125.00.
Teddy Bear: 6" - $125.00.

Other animals: (rabbit, dog, etc.): 3½"-5" - $30.00-65.00.
Comic Characters: Germany: 3½"-5" - $55.00-75.00.
Children/Adults: Made in Germany: 4½"-5½" - $55.00-75.00.
Japan/Nippon: 4½" - $25.00; 5½" - $35.00.
Sitting Position: Excellent quality (may be Orientals): 8" - $250.00.

4¾" Girl jointed at shoulders only, painted eyes to side, open/closed mouth and painted head band in molded hair. 4½" girl jointed at shoulders and hips, molded hair with hair bows and painted eyes. 3½" boy jointed at shoulders only, molded hair and side-glance painted eyes. Courtesy Frasher Doll Auctions. 3" – $45.00; 4" – $55.00.

JAPAN

All bisque dolls from Japan vary a great deal in quality. Jointed at shoulders (may have other joints); **good quality** bisque, well painted: 3½" – $15.00-20.00; 5" – $25.00; 6"-7" – $45.00-65.00.
Marked Nippon: With name (Baby Darling, etc.): 4" – $35.00; 6" – $80.00.
Child: With molded clothes: 4½" – $20.00; 6" – $45.00.
Nodders (elastic strung): 3" – $15.00-20.00.

Comic Characters: (See comic all bisque section).
Occupied Japan: 3½" – $8.00; 5" – $12.00; 7" – $15.00.
Figurines (no joints): Children: 3" – $10.00-$15.00; Teddy Bears – $20.00-45.00; Indians, Dutch, etc.: 2½" – $15.00; Santa Claus – $25.00; Adults – $25.00.

ALL BISQUE-COMIC CHARACTERS
ALL BISQUE-PAINTED BISQUE
ALT, BECK & GOTTSCHALCK

Mickey McGuire (copyright by Fontaine Fox, Germany) – $70.00.

Herby #C82, Japan – $35.00; Nodder – $50.00.

Mr. Peanut, Japan – 4″ – $35.00.

Johnny - Call for Phillip Morris, Germany: 5″ – $65.00.

Mickey Mouse: Walt Disney: 5″ – $65.00.

Mickey Mouse with musical instrument – $55.00.

Minnie Mouse, Walt Disney: 5″ – $65.00.

Betty Boop, Fleischer Studios, Japan: 3½″ – $45.00.

Betty Boop with musical instrument: 3½″ – $45.00.

Baby Tarzan and Mother Gorilla – $35.00.

Orphan Annie: 3½″ – $45.00; Nodder – $55.00.

Seven Dwarfs: 3½″ – $40.00.

Popeye: 3″ – $45.00.

Annie Rooney, Germany: 4″ – $135.00.

Winnie Walker, Banner, Germany: 3½″ – $65.00.

Skeezix: 3½″ – $50.00.

Dick Tracy, Germany: 4″ – $55.00.

Our Gang: 3½″ boys – $50.00; girls – $60.00.

Moon Mullins and Kayo: 4″ – $65.00.

Lady Plush Bottom, Germany: 4″ – $45.00.

Mr. Bailey, The Boss, Germany: 3½″ – $45.00.

Aunty Blossom, Germany: 3½″ – $45.00.

5″ "Skippy" all bisque, jointed at shoulders only. Marks: Skippy/Percy Crosby/made in Japan. Sticker on feet: Skippy Trademark/copyright/Percy L. Crosby/made in Japan. Courtesy Phyllis Houston. 5″ – $60.00.

ALL BISQUE-PAINTED BISQUE

Painted bisque has a layer of paint over the bisque which is not fired in. Molded hair, painted features, painted-on shoes and socks. Jointed at shoulders and hips. Can be Boy or Girl: 4″ – $25.00; 6″ – $35.00; Baby: 4″ – $30.00; 6″ – $40.00.

ALT, BECK & GOTTSCHALCK

Alt, Beck & Gottschalck produced porcelain from 1854, but it is not certain when they started to make doll heads. Their porcelain factory was located at Nauendorf, Thur, Germany. It is certain that they were producing dolls by 1893 when they displayed products at the Chicago Exhibition. This firm produced the "Bye-lo" and "Bonnie Babe" for the distributor, George Borgfeldt. The dolls will be marked:

along with a mold number.

Babies: After 1909. Open mouths, some pierced nostrils, bent leg, composition baby body and wigged. Prices will be higher if on

13

ALT, BECK & GOTTSCHALCK

Left Rear: 23″ Marked: A.B.G. made in Germany - jointed body, open mouth, pierced ears. Right Rear: 19″ Marked: S.PB, in star, H. 1909. Front: 19″ Marked: Special 4/0. Shoulder head on kid body, open mouth. Made by Adolf Wislizenus. Courtesy Frasher Doll Auctions. 23″ A.B.G. – $485.00; 19″ S-Star PB-H – $385.00; 19″ Special – $365.00.

19½″ German turned head with open mouth, kid body and bisque lower arms. Marks: 1123 made in Germany. Made by Alt, Beck & Gottschalck. Courtesy Frasher Doll Auctions. 20″ – $850.00.

20″ Marked: 639 #8. Solid dome turned shoulder/head. Made in Germany by Alt, Beck and Gottschalck. Closed mouth, kid body with bisque lower arms. Courtesy Frasher Doll Auctions. 20″ – $850.00.

toddler body, or has flirty eyes. Clean and nicely dressed, no cracks or chips to head. 12″-14″ – $350.00; 17″ – $485.00; 21″ – $695.00; 25″ – $825.00.

Child: Open mouth, wigged, sleep or set eyes and on ball jointed composition body. No cracks, chips on head, clean and nicely dressed. 14″ – $265.00; 17″ – $375.00; 21″ – $450.00; 25″ – $595.00; 31″ – $1,000.00; 36″ – $1,600.00; 40″-42″ – $2,350.00.

Turned shoulder head: Bold head or plaster pate, closed mouth, glass eyes, kid body, bisque lower arms, all in good condition with no chips, cracks or hairlines and nicely dressed. Ca. 1880's. Made for Wagner & Zetzsche. Mold numbers, such as 639, 698, 1000, 1008, 1028, etc. 16″ – $685.00; 20″ – $850.00; 24″ – $1,000.00.

Turned shoulder head: Late 1880's. Same as above, but with open mouth. 16″ – $365.00; 20″ – $425.00; 24″ – $550.00.

Character child: Ca. 1910 on. Composition jointed body, sleep or set eyes, open mouth, nicely dressed with good wig or molded hair and with no hairlines, cracks or chips. Marks:

#1322: 15" – $450.00; 19" – $600.00. #1352: 12" – $345.00; 16" – $475.00; 21" – $650.00. #1357: 14" – $500.00; 18" – $700.00. #1358: 14" – $1,100.00; 18" – $2,400.00. #1361: 12" – $345.00; 16" – $475.00; 21" – $650.00.

AMBERG, LOUIS & SONS
DOLL MAKERS and IMPORTERS

Prices for dolls in excellent condition, no cracks, chips, clean and nicely dressed. **Baby Peggy:** (Montgomery) 1924. Will be marked with the year and LA&S NY/Germany and a mold number. Closed mouth. Socket head. Mold number 973 or 972: 18" – $2,500.00; 22" – $2,800.00. Shoulder head. Mold number 983 or 982: 18" – $2,500.00; 22" – $2,800.00. All bisque, smiling closed mouth, molded hair with full bangs and "Dutch" bob hairdo. One-piece body and head, and painted-on "Mary Jane" shoes and socks: 3" – $265.00; 6" – $450.00.

Composition head and limbs with cloth body, eyes are painted and has closed smiling mouth. Hair is molded. 1923. 12" – $295.00; 16" – $450.00; 19" – $650.00. **Charlie Chaplain:** 1915-1920's. Portrait head of composition with painted features, composition hands and cloth body and legs. Black suit and white shirt. Cloth tag on sleeve or inside seam of coat. 13"-14" – $350.00.

New Born Babe: Bisque head with cloth bodies and can have celluloid, composition or rubber hands. Lightly painted hair, sleep eyes and closed mouth with protruding upper lip. 1914 and re-issued in 1924. Marks: L.A.& S. 1914/G45520 Germany. Also: L. Amberg and Son/886. Some will have "heads copyrighted by Louis Amberg". 9"-10" – $350.00; 14" – $525.00; 18" – $900.00.

New Born Babe: Open mouth version. Marks: L.A. & S. 371. 9"-10" – $300.00; 14" – $485.00.

MIBS: Marks: L.A. & S. 1921/Germany. Can have two different paper labels with one reading: Amberg Dolls/Please Love Me/I'm

13" Character Girl marked: Amberg. Pat. pending. L.A. & S. 1928. Molded and painted features. Body twist jointed waist. May be replaced arms. Courtesy Frasher Doll Auctions. 13" (with correct arms) – $325.00; 13" (without correct arms) – $125.00.

Mibs, and some without the Amberg Dolls. Molded hair with long strand down center of forehead. All bisque: One-piece body and head, jointed at the shoulders and hips. 3" – $225.00; 5" – $325.00. **Composition:** Composition head and limbs with painted-on shoes and socks. Cloth body. Painted blue eyes. 12" – $295.00; 16"-17" – $400.00.

15

AMBERG, LOUIS & SONS
AMUSCO

8" Marked: Pat. Appl'd for/L.A. & S 1926. Molded and painted features. All composition. Body twist jointed waist. Long arms with both bent at elbows mold, painted-on shoes and socks. Courtesy Glorya Woods. 8" – $165.00.

Sue (or Edwina): All composition with painted features and molded hair with waist that swivels on a large ball attached to torso. Jointed shoulders, neck and hips. Molded hair has side part with swirl bangs across forehead. Painted brown eyes. Marks: Amber/ Pat. Pen./ L.A. & S. 1928. 14" – $325.00.

Twist Bodies (Tiny Tots): 1928. All composition with swivel waist made from large ball attached to torso. Boy or girl with molded hair and painted features. Mark has attached tag on clothes: An Amberg Doll/ Body Twist/ Pat. Pend. #32018. 7½"-8½" – $165.00.

Vanta Baby: Marks: Vanta Baby-Amberg. Composition head and limbs with fat legs. Cloth body, spring strung, sleep eyes, open/closed mouth with two teeth. Made to advertise Vanta baby garments. 1927. 18" – $20.00.

Vanta Baby: Same as above but with bisque head. 18" – $675.00.

AMUSCO

20" Bisque head on composition bent baby body. Marked: Amusco 100 made in Germany. Open mouth with two teeth. Made by August Moller & Sohn. Ca. 1925 as name of AMUSCO registered by them in 1925. Courtesy Frasher Doll Auctions. 16" – $285.00; 20" – $500.00.

12″ Marked: A.M. 345 with closed mouth, painted eyes and jointed body. Courtesy Arthur Routiette. 12″ – $1,000.00.

Prices are for dolls in excellent condition, no chips or cracks, clean and nicely dressed.

Armand Marseille made the majority of their dolls after the 1880's and into the 1920's. Their factory was located in Koppelsdorf, Thur, Germany. The Armand Marseille dolls can be of excellent quality to very poor quality. The finer the bisque, which should be pale in color and not have a smeared look to it, artistically painted features, will bring the best prices. The mold number 370 means the doll is a shoulder head and the mold number 390 means it is a socket head. 1890's on.

#370: Kid body. 15″ – $225.00; 21″ – $325.00; 26″ – $475.00.

#390: Socket head. 10″ with crude five-piece body – $135.00; 10″ on good quality fully jointed body – $145.00; 14″ – $200.00; 16″ – $275.00; 18″ – $325.00; 22″ – $375.00; 24″ – $425.00; 26″ – $450.00; 28″ – $500.00; 32″ – $800.00; Some large sizes marked with "A.M." only: 36″ – $1,200.00; 38″ – $1,500.00; 42″ – $1,900.00.

Painted Bisque: 11″ – $125.00; 14″ – $165.00.

1890, 1894, 1897, 1914: Kid body. Add $50.00 for composition body. 12″ – $250.00; 15″ – $350.00; 18″ – $425.00; 20″ – $475.00; 22″ – $500.00; 26″ – $600.00; 30″ – $700.00; 36″ – $1,100.00; 40″ – $1,600.00.

Baby Betty: 1890's. 16″ – $425.00; 20″ – $545.00.

Floradora: 1890's. 9″ – $165.00; 14″ – $225.00; 16″ – $300.00; 18″ – $350.00; 22″ – $400.00; 25″ – $525.00; 28″ – $575.00; 32″ – $725.00.

Queen Louise: 1890's. 10″ – $185.00; 14″ – $350.00; 16″ – $375.00; 18″ – $400.00; 20″ – $450.00; 24″ – $500.00; 28″ – $650.00; 32″ – $800.00.

Babies: 1910 on. Can be on composition bodies or cloth bodies with curved or straight cloth legs. Add $100.00-150.00 for toddler bodies.

Babies, Newborn Types: 1924 on. #341 with closed mouth or #351 with open mouth. "My Dream Baby" for Arranbee Doll Company. Some of these #351 babies will

ARMAND MARSEILLE

24" Marked: Kiddiejoy 372 A.2.M. Shoulder head with molded hair, open mouth and sleep eyes. Kid body with bisque lower arms. (Author). 24" – $950.00.

13" Character marked: 590 A.O.M. Germany DRGM. Jointed body, sleep eyes, open mouth with two upper teeth. Courtesy Frasher Doll Auctions. 13" – $900.00.

13½" Character marked: A. 40 X M. Baby Betty DRGM. Jointed body, set eyes, open mouth. Courtesy Frasher Doll Auctions. 14" – $375.00.

10½" Marked: Baby Gloria/Germany. Molded hair, set eyes, open mouth with two teeth and cloth body and celluloid hands. Cheek dimples. Courtesy Frasher Doll Auctions. 10" – $300.00.

Twin "Tee-Wee Hand Bebes" Ca. 1927. Marked: Germany Kiddiejoy. Rare pair of pillow hand puppets, closed mouths, celluloid hands and are in original basket. (Author). $650.00 up.

be marked: *#345* - Kiddie Joy or Our Pet: 6"-7" – $165.00; 9" – $225.00; 12" – $300.00; 14" – $350.00; 16" – $475.00; 20" – $625.00; 24" – $800.00; 28" – $1,000.00. 8" Hand puppet: $265.00. Twin puppets in basket: $650.00. *#341, #351, #345* - Kiddie Joy or Our Pet with fired-in Black or Brown bisque: 6½" – $200.00; 9" – $265.00; 12" – $425.00; 16" – $525.00; 19" – $700.00; 23" – $900.00; 26" – $1,100.00. *#347* - 7½" – $135.00; 14" – $265.00.

Baby: 1910 on. Mold numbers: *326, 327, 329, 971, 985, 990, 992, 995, 996, 1330;* Add $100.00-150.00 if on toddler body. 10" – $250.00; 14" – $350.00; 16" – $425.00; 18" – $475.00; 22" – $550.00; 26" – $750.00.

Character Babies: 1910 on. Add $100.00-150.00 if on toddler body. *Mold 233:* 10" – $300.00; 14" – $450.00; 18" – $600.00; 22" – $900.00. *Mold 248:* with open/closed mouth: 14" – $1,400.00. *Mold 248:* with open mouth: 14" – $800.00. *Mold 251:* with open/closed mouth: 14" – $1,400.00; 16" – $1,550.00. *Mold 251:*

with open mouth: 16" – $950.00. *Mold 328:* 10" – $265.00; 14" – $375.00; 18" – $550.00; 22" – $700.00. *Mold 352:* 10" – $265.00; 14" – $350.00; 18" – $500.00; 22" – $700.00. *Mold 410:* two rows of teeth - some with retractable teeth; 14" – $800.00. *Mold 518:* 14" – $450.00; 18" – $550.00. *Mold 560A:* 12" – $400.00; 15" – $475.00; 18" – $550.00. *Mold 580:* has open/closed mouth; 16" – $1,300.00. *Mold 590:* has open/closed mouth; 16" – $1,300.00.

Baby Gloria: 14" – $475.00; 18" – $700.00; 24" – $950.00.

Baby Phyllis: Heads by Armand Marseille. Painted hair, closed mouth. 12" – $300.00; 16" – $475.00; 20" – $625.00.

Fany Baby: Mold number 231 along with incised "Fany". Can be on baby, toddler or ball-jointed body. With wig: 14" – $4,000.00; 18" – $5,200.00; With molded hair, *Mold #230:* 14" – $4,500.00; 18" – $5,700.00.

Melitta: Baby: 16" – $475.00; 20" – $695.00; Toddler: 20" – $875.00.

Character Child: 1910 on. They may have

ARMAND MARSEILLE

wigs or have molded hair, glass eyes or intaglio painted eyes and some will have fully closed mouths while others have open/closed mouths: *Mold 345:* 12″ – $1,000.00; 16″ – $1,600.00. *Mold 360:* 14″ – $375.00; 18″ – $625.00. *Mold 372* Kiddie Joy: (open mouth); 14″ – $525.00; 17″ – $825.00; 20″ – $900.00. *Mold 400:* 14″ – $2,500.00; 17″ – $2,800.00. *Mold 500:* 10″ – $300.00; 16″ – $500.00; 20″ – $750.00. *Mold 550:* 10″ – $500.00; 16″ – $1,800.00; 20″ – $2,800.00. *Mold 590:* (open mouth); 12″ – $350.00; 16″ – $595.00. *Mold 600:* 10″ – $700.00; 16″ – $1,500.00; 20″ – $1,900.00. *Mold 700:* 10″ – $700.00; 16″ – $1,500.00. *Mold 800:* 16″ – $800.00; 20″ – $1,900.00.

A.M.: (no mold numbers): closed mouth and intaglio eyes: 16″ – $2,000.00; 21″ – $3,000.00; 28″ – $4,000.00.

Adult Lady Dolls: 1910-1920's. Adult face and have long thin jointed limbs with knee joints above knee. *Mold 400 and 401:* closed mouth: 14″ – $1,200.00; 16″ – $1,500.00. *Mold 400 and 401* with open mouth: 14″ – $650.00; 16″ – $875.00. With painted bisque; closed mouth: 14″ – $700.00; 16″ – $950.00.

"Just Me": Mid-1920's. Bisque head on composition body and marked with name and mold number 310. Fired-in color: 9″ – $1,000.00; 12″ – $1,300.00. Painted bisque: 7″-8″ – $500.00; 12″ – $900.00. During the early 1930's the Vogue Doll Company dressed many of these "Just Me" dolls and their clothes will have the Vogue tag. *Googlies: Mold 254, 320, 210* and others with intaglio eyes: 7″ – $495.00; 12″ – $1,100.00. *Mold 253, 254, 320, 210* with glass eyes: 12″ – $1,200.00; *Mold 323* with glass eyes: most often found mold: 7″ – $625.00; 12″ – $825.00.

Child With Incised Name: Shoulder head, bisque lower arms, open mouth. 1898. Names including: Alma, Beauty, Darling, Lilly, Mabel, Rosebud, Princess, etc.: 16″ – $225.00; 18″ – $300.00; 22″ – $350.00; 25″ – $475.00.

21″ Marked: 1894 A.M. 8 DEP. Jointed body, open mouth and sleep eyes. Courtesy Frasher Doll Auctions. 21″ – $500.00.

23½″ Marked: Queen Louise. Jointed bodies, clothes and wigs in original set. Courtesy Frasher Doll Auctions. 24″ – $500.00.

9½″ "Just Me" with painted bisque. Marked: Just Me. Registered Germany A 310 5/0 M. All original in original papier mache′ egg with silver color "grass", six chicks and mohair and wood Russian Wolfhound dog, which is Marked: Made in Germany. Courtesy Frasher Doll Auctions. 9½″ in egg – $1,800.00 up.

ARNOLD, MAX OSCAR

Right: 24½″ Marked: M.O.A. Germany 200. Jointed body, open mouth and set eyes. Left: 26½″ Marked: 1894 A.M. Dep. Courtesy Frasher Doll Auctions. 24″ Max Oscar Arnold – $425.00; 26″ 1894 – $600.00.

ARNOLD, MAX OSCAR
AVERILL, GEORGENE (MADAME HENDRON)

24" Marked: M.O.A. made by Max Oscar Arnold in Germany. Has sleep eyes, open mouth and fully jointed composition body. Arnold dolls were made from 1878 to late 1920's. The factory was in Neustadt, near Coburg, Germany. 15" – $200.00; 20" – $325.00; 24" – $425.00.

AVERILL, GEORGENE (MADAME HENDRON)

Beautiful International with mask face with painted features, cloth body and original clothes. Came in 12", 14", 17" and 21" sizes. Marked with paper tag: Georgene Novelties. Childhood doll of owner Margaret Mandel. 12" – $50.00; 14" – $65.00; 17" – $90.00; 21" – $125.00; 24" – $165.00.

AVERILL, GEORGENE (MADAME HENDRON)

24″ Madame Hendron baby with composition head, lower limbs and cloth body. Marked on head. In Bunny suit: 16″ "Honey Child" and so marked. This name registered in 1926 by Bayless & Bros. & Co. Bye-lo look-a-like with painted features, all composition. 12″ "Slumbermate" by Madame Alexander. Composition and cloth. Eyes are painted in a closed, sleeping position. Courtesy Turn of Century Antiques. 24″ – $235.00; 16″ – $275.00; 12″ – $275.00.

First prices are for mint dolls. Second for crazed, chips, dirty or soiled and not original. Georgene Averill and Madame Hendron are the same person and the business names used by her were: Madame Georgene Dolls, Paul Averill Mfg. Co., Averill Mfg. Co., Georgene Novelties, Madame Hendron and the Brophey Doll Co. in Canada. Georgene Averill began making dolls in 1913 and designed a great many dolls for George Borgfeldt.

Baby Georgene or Baby Hendron: Composition/cloth: 22″ – $135.00-65.00.

Baby Yawn: Composition/closed eyes/yawn mouth: 17″ – $250.00-85.00.

Body Twist Dolls: Composition with large ball joint at waist: 15″ – $265.00-95.00.

Bonnie Babe: Bisque head/cloth body: 14″ – $750.00; 22″ – $1,200.00; Celluloid head: 15″-16″ – $450.00.

Cloth Dolls: Internationals: 12″ – $50.00-15.00; 15″ – $65.00-25.00. Children: 15″ – $100.00-40.00; 20″ – $135.00-45.00; 25″ – $150.00-55.00.

Comic Characters: 1940's-1950's; such as Little Lulu, Nancy, Sluggo, Topsy & Eva, Tubby Tom, etc. 12″ – $275.00; 14″ – $350.00.

Dolly Dingle (for Grace Drayton): 11″ – $275.00; Fangel, Maude Tousey (designer) child; all cloth. Marked: M.T.F. on tag. 12″ – $450.00.

Dolly Record: Composition/cloth with record player in back: 26″ – $425.00-150.00.

Googly: Composition/cloth: 14″ – $195.00-85.00; 16″ – $225.00-85.00; 19″ – $300.00-125.00.

Indian, Cowboy: 14″ – $195.00-85.00.

Sailor, Soldier: 14″ – $195.00-85.00.

Snookums: Composition/cloth. Character from "The Newlyweds" by George McManus. Smile face: 14″ – $275.00.

Vinyl Head, Laughing Child: With oil cloth body: 28″ – $85.00-45.00.

Whistling Dan: (boy) sailor, cowboy or policeman: 14″ – $150.00-60.00.

Whistling Rufus: (black) 14″ – $250.00-85.00.

23

BAHR & PROSCHILD

Bahr & Proschild operated at Ohrdruf, Thur, Germany from 1871 until the late 1920's. By 1910 they were also making celluloid doll heads and parts. The marks from this company are:

Character Baby: 1909 to end of production. Bent limb baby body, sleep eyes, wigged and open mouths. Allow $100.00-150.00 for toddler body. No cracks, chips or other damage and nicely dressed. Mold 585, 604, 624, 678, 619, 641: 13" – $400.00; 16" – $485.00; 19" – $575.00; 25" – $950.00. **Mold 169:** 12" – $400.00; 16" – $500.00; 20" – $600.00.
Character Child: Can be on fully jointed composition body or toddler body. Ca. 1910. Nicely dressed, no damage, chips or breaks. Molded hair or wigged: 16" – $1,800.00; 20" – $2,600.00; 23" – $3,100.00. Mold 536, 2072: Open/closed mouth: 16" – $2,550.00; 20" – $3,200.00. Mold number in 200 and 300 Series now attributed to Bahr & Proschild. Can be on French bodies. Mold numbers such as 224, 239, etc. Jointed composition bodies. Ca. 1880's. Most of these dolls had been attributed to Kestner. 15" – $475.00; 18" – $550.00; 23" – $675.00. Mold numbers 224, 239, 246, 309, 379, etc. on kid bodies: 20" – $475.00; 25" – $600.00; 29" – $875.00. Same mold numbers with closed mouths: 20" – $950.00; 25" – $1,200.00; 29" – $1,800.00.

19" Shoulder head, kid body with bisque lower arms, set eyes and solid dome. Marked: 309.8 by Bahr & Proschild. Courtesy Frasher Doll Auctions. 19" – $900.00.

20" Baby by Bahr & Proschild. Marked: 585.11. Bent limb baby body. Open/closed mouth with two upper teeth. This mold number generally has a full open mouth. Sleep eyes. Courtesy Frasher Doll Auctions. 20" – $600.00.

BAHR & PROSCHILD
BATHING DOLLS

Left: Marked: Italy 1/0. Five-piece body. Dressed in original costume of a Vatican Guard. The other three are 6½" and Marked: 250 21/0. All are original and on five-piece bodies. These three made by Bahr & Proschild. Courtesy Frasher Doll Auctions. Italy: $135.00; 6½" – $125.00 each.

BATHING DOLLS

3 Bathing Dolls. All bisque with painted-on clothes and features. Left: 3¼" reclining figure. Marks: Germany 3689. Center: 3" standing marked: Germany 5722. Right: 3½" reclining with blue head band. Marks: Germany 6399. 1920's. Courtesy Frasher Doll Auctions. 3" excellent quality on bisque and painting – $150.00; 3" fair quality of bisque and painting – $55.00; 5"-6" excellent – $300.00; 5"-6" fair – $75.00; 8"-9" excellent – $650.00 up.

25

BELTON-TYPE
BERGMANN, C.M.

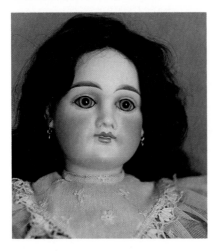

21" "Belton" with concave top and holes. Very pale bisque, closed mouth with area of white between lips, large paperweight eyes. Courtesy Sally Freeman. 21" – $2,200.00.

So called "Belton" dolls are not marked or are marked with only a number. They come on French style bodies and most have almost white bisque with a pink wash over the eyes and many have wide open/closed mouths with the area between the lip left white. "Belton" dolls have a concave flat top to the solid uncut head with one to three holes for stringing and plugging in wigs. These dolls differ from the "dome", "bald" and "ball" heads that are German. The German heads are solid shaped and completely round on top and some may have one or two holes for stringing or wigs. 1875 on.

Prices for "Belton" dolls with French excellent quality bisque heads and bodies with straight wrists, nicely dressed and with no damage to head nor body are: 8" – $625.00; 10" – $995.00; 12" – $1,150.00; 15" – $1,500.00; 18" – $1,900.00; 20" – $2,100.00; 23" – $2,400.00; 26" – $2,900.00.

BERGMANN, C.M.

The Charles M. Bergmann firm operated from 1889 at both Walterhausen and Friedrichroda, Germany. He made dolls in kid, as well as ball jointed bodies with the bisque heads being made for him by such companies as Simon and Halbig, Armand Marseille, Kestner and others.

Marks on Bergmann dolls very often carry the full name C.M. Bergmann, but at times will have the name or initials of the makers of the head, along with his initials C.M.B.

Child Doll: 1880's into early 1900's. On fully jointed body and with open mouth. 18" – $375.00; 21" – $465.00; 24" – $500.00; 27" – $650.00; 30" – $800.00; 34" – $1,200.00 up; 40" – $2,100.00 up.

Character Baby: 1909 and after. Socket head on five-piece bent limb baby body. Open mouth. 12" – $395.00; 16" – $495.00; 20" – $650.00. 612 - open/closed mouth: 16" – $825.00; 20" – $1,000.00.

Lady Doll: Adult style body with long thin limbs of the "flapper" type: 14" – $850.00; 17" – $1,200.00; 21" – $1,700.00.

34" Marked: C.M. Bergmann/Simon Halbig 14½". Jointed body open mouth and sleep eyes. Head made by Simon & Halbig for Bergmann. Courtesy Frasher Doll Auctions. 34" – $1,200.00 up.

26" Marked: B.12 L. Closed mouth, original wig and may be original dress. Jointed body. Most likely made by Alexandre Lefebvre before 1890's. Often referred to by collectors as Bebe Louve, which is not confirmed. Courtesy Frasher Doll Auctions. 16" – $2,200.00; 19" – $2,800.00; 23" – $3,400.00; 26" – $3,600.00.

BLACK OR BROWN DOLLS

Black or brown dolls can have fired-in color or painted bisques; they can range from pure black to very light tan. The quality of these dolls differs greatly and prices are based on excellent quality of color. These dolls were also made by both the German and the French. All in excellent condition.

Armand Marseille 341 or 351: 14" – $475.00; 18" – $750.00.

Armand Marseille 390: 15" – $395.00.

Armand Marseille 390N: 16" – $425.00; 21" – $650.00.

Armand Marseille 518: 16" – $650.00; 20" – $725.00.

Armand Marseille 1894: 14" – $425.00; 17" – $600.00.

Bahr & Proschild 277: Open mouth. 14" – $675.00; 17" – $900.00.

Bru Jne: 17" – $13,000.00; 21" – $15,000.00.

Bru, Circle Dot or Brevette: 17" – $14,000.00.

French, unmarked. Closed mouth: 14" – $1,600.00; 18" – $2,000.00.

French, unmarked. Open mouth: 12" – $475.00; 16" – $1,000.00; 21" – $1,600.00.

German, unmarked. Closed mouth: 6½" – $285.00; 9" – $495.00; 14" – $600.00.

German, unmarked. Open mouth: 12" – $325.00; 16" – $475.00; 19" – $700.00.

Handwerck, Heinrich: Open mouth: 16" – $500.00; 20" – $725.00.

Hanna, Schoenau & Hoffmeister: 12" – $385.00; 16" – $495.00.

Heubach, Gerbruder: Mold 7668 with wide smiling mouth: 12" – $1,500.00; 14" – $1,900.00.

Heubach, Gebruder (Sunburst mark – 7671): 8" – $900.00; 12" – $1,400.00; 14" – $1,800.00.

Heubach, Gebruder (Sunburst mark) boy, eyes to side: 11" – $1,000.00.

Heubach Koppelsdorf 399: Allow more for toddler. 9" – $350.00; 12" – $400.00; 16" – $600.00. Celluloid: 12" – $250.00; 18" – $550.00.

Heubach Koppelsdorf 463: 10" – $550.00; 14" – $750.00.

Heubach Koppelsdorf 444: 10" – $500.00; 14" – $700.00.

BLACK OR BROWN DOLLS

28″ Brown bisque marked: S&H 939. Large set eyes, open mouth with four teeth, original black curly human hair wig and jointed body with straight wrists. Courtesy Frasher Doll Auctions. 17″ – $2,200.00; 20″ – $2,800.00; 28″ – $3,400.00 up.

21″ Marked: 34-29. by S.F.B.J. Open mouth, glass eyes and on French jointed body. Courtesy Frasher Doll Auctions. 15″ – $3,000.00; 21″ – $4,800.00.

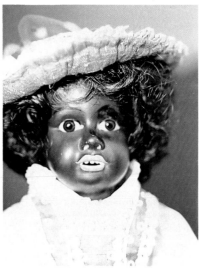

16″ French type girl incised: 5. Very black bisque, set eyes, open mouth, ears pierced into head, jointed body. Courtesy Frasher Doll Auctions. 16″ – $1,500.00 up.

20″ Marked: K star R/Simon & Halbig 126. Five-piece compositon body, open mouth. Bear, Ca. 1920's. Courtesy Frasher Doll Auctions. 20″ – $875.00 up.

16" Mark: S, PB in Star, H 1909. Jointed body, open mouth. Made by Schoeneau & Hoffmeister. Courtesy Frasher Doll Auctions. 16" – $485.00.

10½" Baby by Herm Steiner. Marked: 11 HS Germany. Cloth body and celluloid hands. 13" cloth "Mammy" style with adult shaped body and sewn-on high heeled shoes, fingers separately stitched and has quill nails. Courtesy Frasher Doll Auctions. 10½" – $285.00; 13" cloth – $165.00.

Heubach Koppelsdorf 458: 12" – $400.00; 16" – $600.00.
Heubach Koppelsdorf 1900: 13" – $450.00; 16" – $600.00.
J.D. Kestner 245, 237 Hilda: 15" – $3,700.00; 17" – $4,000.00.
Jumeau: Open mouth: 12" – $1,700.00; 16" – $1,950.00; 21" – $2,400.00.
Jumeau: Closed mouth: 12" – $3,000.00; 16" – $4,000.00; 21" – $5,000.00.
Jumeau: Marked: E.J.: 12" – $3,400.00; 16" – $4,400.00.
K Star R 100: 16" – $1,200.00; 18" – $1,500.00.
K Star R 116A: 16" – $2,400.00; 18" – $2,700.00.
K Star R 126: 16" – $600.00; 18" – $800.00. Toddler: 12" – $500.00; 16" – $750.00.
Kestner: Marked: 10" – $465.00; 14" – $595.00.
Kestner: 134: 14" – $525.00.
Paris Bebe: 16" – $2,500.00.
Recknagel: Marked: R.A. 14" – $500.00; 20" – $1,400.00.
Schoenau & Hoffmeister 1909: 14" – $465.00; 17" – $550.00.
Scowling Indian: 10" – $325.00; 13" – $465.00.

Simon & Halbig 939: 17" – $2,200.00; 20" – $2,800.00. Mold 949: 17" – $1,700.00; 20" – $2,200.00.
Simon & Halbig 1039: 14" – $500.00; 17" – $700.00.
Simon & Halbig 1358: 14" – $3,300.00; 17" – $4,000.00.
S.F.B.J. 301: Open mouth: 15" – $365.00; 17" – $525.00.
S.F.B.J. 235: Open/closed mouth: 14" – $1,800.00.
S.F.B.J. 34-29: 21" – $4,800.00.
Steiner, Jules: Open mouth: 14" – $2,500.00; 17" – $3,000.00.
S & Q 251: 10" – $465.00; 14" – $595.00.
Unis 301 or 60: 12" – $300.00.
Mammy Doll: by Tony Sarg. Composition, cloth body: 18" – $475.00.
Cloth: American made, embroidered or painted features, in overall good condition. 1930's style: 15" – $165.00; Mammy style: 15" – $175.00; WPA with molded face: 21"-22" – $500.00.

BLACK OR BROWN DOLLS
BONNIE BABE

Composition Dolls: Made in Germany. Can have wig or molded hair, glass eyes (may be flirty), nicely dressed and in overall excellent condition: 14" – $500.00; 18" – $650.00; 22" – $800.00; 26" – $1,000.00.

Sitting: 17" Brown bisque head with sleep eyes, pierced nostrils, open mouth and pierced ears. Bent limb baby body. Marked: 98/7 and attributed to Hertel Schwab & Co. Standing: 18" German composition girl marked: K.W.G. A mark attributed to Keramische Werke Grafenhain, successor to Simon & Halbig. Sleep eyes, open mouth. Courtesy Frasher Doll Auctions. 17" – $635.00; 18" – $650.00.

BONNIE BABE

The "Bonnie Babe" was designed by Georgene Averill in 1926. The bisque heads were made in Germany by Alt, Beck & Gottschalck. The bodies are cloth and arms and legs of composition or cloth body and legs. They are marked: Copy, by/George Averill-/Germany and/or marked with a number 1005/3652. Open smiling mouth with two lower teeth. 1926.

Measured by head circumference: 12"-13" – $750.00; 14"-15" – $1,000.00.
All bisque: 5" – $850.00; 7" – $975.00.
Celluloid head: Head circumference: 8"-9" – $425.00.
All bisque: Also see all bisque section.

Right: 17" "Bonnie Babe" marked: copy: Georgene Averill/Germany/1005/3652. Open smiling mouth with two lower teeth. Left: 17" Kestner 226 with open mouth. Both have painted hair. Courtesy Turn of Century Antiques. 17" Bonnie Babe – $1,000.00; 17" 226 – $575.00.

Right: Marked G.B. Germany - made for George Borgfeldt, importer. Jointed body, open mouth, set eyes. Left: 21" Marked: Majestic 8 Germany. Open mouth, set eyes and jointed body. Made for Ernst Steiner, Sonneberg, Germany. Courtesy Frasher Doll Auctions. 20" – $425.00; 25" – $575.00; Majestic: 21" – $450.00; 26" – $600.00.

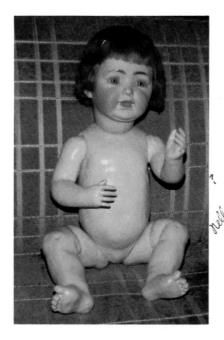

26" Baby on five-piece bent limb body, sleep eyes, open mouth and marked: G.B., on head. Made for George Borgfeldt, importer. Courtesy Jeanne Mauldin. 20" – $585.00; 26" – $800.00.

Four Palmer Cox "Brownies" of lithograph on wood. 13" and all are marked: "Copyrighted 1892 by Palmer Cox" with title of figure and verse on backs. 7½" "Brownies". All printed cloth and marked same as others. 1892-1927. Courtesy Frasher Doll Auctions. 13" wood – $75.00 each; 7½" cloth – $95.00 each.

BOUDOIR DOLLS

In the 1920's some of the American makers of Boudoir-Bed dolls were Unique Novelty, Sterling Doll Co., American Stuffed Novelty Co., Fred K. Braiting, Charles Blomm, Inc., Gerling Toy Co. and many others. Very rarely is a doll of this type found with marks of makers.

Called "Flapper" or "Vamp" dolls due to the time period they were popular in, which was 1920's into early 1930's. Not all Boudoir dolls were expensive, nor even well made. The least expensive had composition heads and shoulder plates made into two pieces or with front half glued to cloth. Most had heavily painted features, with rest of doll cloth; some had composition or celluloid lower limbs. If they had hair or bonnets, these were generally stapled on.

There were some expensive Boudoir dolls and most were imported from France. They have the more classic beauty, often with faces painted on stiffened, shaped cloth-like buckram. Hair is better and the cloth fingers are individually sewn.

Boudoir/Bed Dolls: With excellent quality and finely painted features and excellent quality clothes: 28" – $145.00 up; 32" – $195.00 up. Dolls with composition heads, stapled on wigs and composition limbs: 28" – $85.00; 32" – $95.00.

Smoking Dolls: All composition: 25" – $200.00; All cloth: 25" – $250.00 up.

Close-up of Smoking Bed Doll of the 1920's. Long heavy eyelashes and painted hair.

28" Smoking Bed Doll. All cloth with old painted face mask. Stitched fingers and completely original. 28" – $250.00 up.

16" Marked with a circle and dot and Bru Jne 4. Shoulder plate marked: 4. Open/closed mouth with molded teeth, kid body with bisque lower arms. All original except shoes, which are old. Courtesy Frasher Doll Auctions. 16" – $8,500.00.

22" Bru Jne 7 on shoulder plate. Circle and dot on head. Open/closed mouth with slightly parted lips with painted teeth. Kid body with wooden lower arms. Courtesy Frasher Doll Auctions. 22" – $14,000.00.

Bru dolls will be marked with the name Bru, Bru Jne, Bru Jne R, and some will have a circle dot (⊙), or a half circle and dot (⌒). Some will have paper labels on bodies (see below). Bru dolls are found on all kid bodies with bisque lower arms, on kid over wood, all wood or on all composition/wood jointed bodies. When there is a bisque shoulder plate, it too will be marked with Bru and a number over the edge of the shoulder. Prices are for beautifully dressed dolls with no damage any place and very clean.

Closed Mouth Dolls: Bru: All kid body, bisque lower arms. 16" – $6,500.00; 18" – $7,400.00; 21" – $8,300.00.
Bru Jne: Ca. 1880's. Kid over wood, wood legs, bisque lower arms. 12" – $5,800.00; 14" – $6,600.00; 16" – $8,500.00; 20" – $10,000.00; 25" – $14,500.00.
Bru Jne: All wood body. 16" – $7,800.00; 18" – $8,800.00.
Circle Dot or Half Circle: Ca. 1870's. 16" – $8,500.00; 19" – $12,500.00; 23" – $15,000.00.
Brevette Be'be': Ca. 1870's. 17" – $8,600.00; 20" – $10,000.00.
Open Mouth Dolls: Bru Jne R. 1890's. Jointed composition body. 1st price for excellent quality bisque and 2nd price for poor quality of bisque. 14" – $3,200.00-2,400.00; 17" – $4,800.00-3,200.00; 22" – $5,500.00-4,000.00; 25" – $6,200.00-4,600.00; 28" – $7,000.00-5,200.00.
Walker body, throws kisses. 18" – $3,800.00; 22" – $4,200.00.
Nursing Bru: 1878-1899. Operates by turn-

Left: 17" "Belton" the three holes in concave top of head, set eyes and a more unusual closed mouth than most Beltons. Composition jointed body. Right: Bru Brevette with bisque swivel head on bisque shoulder plate and kid body with bisque lower arms. Set eyes and closed mouth. Courtesy Turn of Century Antiques. 17" Belton – $1,800.00; 17" Brevette – $8,600.00.

15" Bru Jne 4. Bisque shoulder plate, closed mouth, kid body with bisque lower arms, kid over wood upper arms and wooden legs. Body labeled: Be'be' Bru BTE S.G.D.G. original clothes. Courtesy Frasher Doll Auctions. 15" – $6,600.00.

ing key in back of head. Early, excellent quality: 12" – $3,400.00; 15" – $6,500.00; 18" – $7,200.00. Not as good quality: 12" – $2,100.00; 15" – $3,700.00; 18" – $4,700.00.

High Color, late S.F.B.J. type: 12" – $1,200.00; 15" – $2,200.00; 18" – $2,800.00.

Shoes: Marked Bru Jne shoes: 12"-17" (doll height) size – $125.00 up; 20" (doll height) size – $250.00 up.

15″ Bru Jne 3. Bisque shoulder plate, kid body bisque over wood upper arms, wooden body. Original clothes, replaced wig. Courtesy Arthur Routiette. .15″ – $6,600.00.

17½″ Marked Bru Jne R 7. Open mouth with four teeth. Jointed composition body. Courtesy Frasher Doll Auctions. 17″ – $4,800.00.

BYE-LO BABY

The Bye-Lo baby was designed by Grace Storey Putnam and distributed by George Borgfeldt in 1922. Several German manufacturers produced the bisque heads including J.D. Kestner, King and Alt, Beck & Gottschalck. The celluloid heads were made by Karl Standfuss of Germany and the all bisque Bye-lo's made by J.D. Kestner. Composition heads were made by the Cameo Doll Co. of New York. Bodies for the Bye-lo were made by K & K Toy Co. of New York. An unauthorized Bye-lo in wood was made by Schoenhut. The cloth bodies have curved "frog" legs, although there are some with straight legs, and the early dolls have celluloid hands. Later dolls as well as the composition head doll have composition hands. The doll's head will be marked with the date and designer and the cloth bodies are often stamped with the same information. The all bisque dolls will be marked with a number on the back and have a round paper label on front (often missing): Bye-Lo Baby/ Germany/ Copr.

by/G.S. Putnam. Prices are for clean, nicely dressed dolls with no damage.

All Measured By Head Circumference Except All Bisque.

Bisque Head: 10″ – $385.00; 12″ – $485.00; 15″ – $850.00; 18″ – $1,400.00.

Smiling Mouth: (Very rare) 14″ – $4,400.00 up.

Socket Head: (Bisque) on five-piece bent leg baby body: 14″ – $1,200.00; 17″ – $1,500.00.

Composition Head: 10″ – $225.00; 12″ – $350.00; 15″ – $475.00.

Painted Bisque: Head with cloth body, composition hands: 10″ – $250.00; 13″ – $365.00; 15″ – $550.00.

Wood by Schoenhut: Cloth body, wood hands: 13″ – $1,450.00.

Celluloid Bye-Lo: all celluloid: 6″ – $165.00.

All Bisque: Jointed only at hips and shoulders, painted eyes: 4″ – $265.00; 5″-6″ – $385.00. Jointed at neck, shoulder and hips. Glass eyes: 6″ – $650.00. Cut

BYE-LO BABY

Pate with wig, glass eyes, jointed shoulders and hips: 6″ – $675.00. Painted eyes, immobile, in different positions: 3½″ – $325.00. Vinyl of early 1950's: Cloth/stuffed limbs. Marked: Grace Storey Putnam on head: 16″ – $300.00.

Honey Child: Bye-Lo look-a-like made in 1926 by Bayless Bros. & Co. of U.S.A. 16″ – $275.00; 20″ – $400.00.

Set of composition head Quintuplets in original box with undies, dresses and bonnets in box top - Black & White photo shows Shirley Temple with same set of five babies. Courtesy Elinor Bibby. Set in original box and all in mint condition – $1,800.00 up.

Rear: 15″ Circumference bisque head Bye-Lo marked: copr. by G.S. Putnam, made in Germany. Cloth body with celluloid hands. 11½″ head circumference composition head Bye-Lo with cloth body and composition hands. Courtesy Frasher Doll Auctions. 15″ Bisque – $850.00; 11½″ Composition – $250.00.

Right and left: Bye-Lo's. All bisque with one having wig and glass eyes and other painted hair and eyes. Center: 6″ all bisque with one-piece body and head, molded hair and painted features. Courtesy Turn of Century Antiques. 4″ Glass Eyes – $425.00; 4″ Painted Eyes – $265.00; 6″ – $185.00 up.

CATTERFELDER PUPPENFABRIK CELLULOID DOLLS

These dolls were made by Catterfelder Puppenfabrik at Catterfeld in Germany from 1902 until late 1920's. Some of the bisque heads may have been made by Kestner for them. The dolls will be marked: C.P. or with the full name Catterfelder Puppenfabrik and some with a mold number also. Prices for clean, nicely dressed dolls with no damage. **Child Doll:** Ca. 1900's. Composition jointed body. Nicely dressed, no chips, cracks or hairlines: 14" – $200.00; 17" – $375.00; 20" – $475.00; 25" – $595.00.
Child Doll: Composition jointed body. Open mouth, Mold #264, or marked C.P.: 17" – $565.00; 23" – $725.00.
Character Child: 1910 & after. Composition jointed body. Boy or girl. Closed mouth and very character faces: Mold 215: 15"-16" – $2,800.00; Mold 207: 15"-16" – $2,500.00.
Babies: 1909 & after. Wig or molded hair, five-piece bent limb baby body, glass or painted eyes: Mold 263: 15" – $450.00; 20" – $600.00; 25" – $895.00; Mold 200, 201: 16" – $475.00; Mold 208, 209, 262, 263: 14" – $425.00; 18" – $575.00; 22" – $650.00; 26" – $800.00 up.

26½" Marked: C.P. 61 Germany. Jointed body, open mouth with four teeth and sleep eyes. Courtesy Frasher Doll Auctions. 26½" – $595.00.

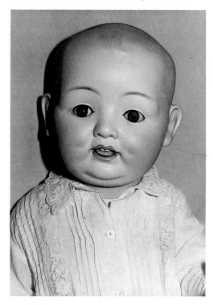

27" With 18½" head circumference. Marked: C.P. 208 G5S Deponiert. Bent limb baby body, sleep eyes, open mouth with two upper teeth and wobble tongue. Courtesy Frasher Doll Auctions. 27" – $800.00 up.

CELLULOID DOLLS

Celluloid dolls were made in Germany, Japan, France, USA and Italy. They can date from the 1880's into the 1940's when they were made illegal as they can burn/explode if placed near an open flame or heat. Some are all celluloid, or can have celluloid heads on kid, cloth or ball jointed bodies. Some of the major German companies who used celluloid are: Kammer & Reinhardt, Kestner, Kathe Kruse, Bruno Schmidt and Cuno & Otto Dressel. These companies often ordered the heads made by celluloid factories. Prices are for clean, nicely dressed dolls with no damage. 1895 into 1940's. Marks: Turtle in a diamond: Rheinische Gummi and Celluloid Fabrik Co. (Germany).

CELLULOID DOLLS

Large V with co, in circle and USA: Victoria Toy Co. Minerva with helmet mark: Buschow & Beck (Germany). SNF mark: Societe Nobel Francaise (France). Eagle mark: Petitcolin (France). 3 M's mark: E. Maar & Sohn. (Germany). Animal with spread wings and a fish tail, in square: Adelheid Nogler Innsbruck Doll Co. (Germany). Jumeau mark: Unis. (France) 1950's.

All Celluloid Baby: Inset or painted eyes: 14" – $115.00; 16" – $135.00; 19" – $175.00; 22" – $200.00; 26" – $245.00.

All Celluloid Dolls: (Germany) jointed at neck, shoulders and hips: 5" – $25.00; 9" – $75.00; 12" – $95.00; 16" – $175.00; 18" – $225.00. Jointed only at shoulders or at neck and shoulders only: 5" – $15.00; 7" – $18.00; 9" – $50.00.

All Celluloid: With molded-on clothes, jointed at shoulders only: 6" – $40.00; 8" – $62.00; 10" – $75.00.

Celluloid Shoulder Head: Germany, molded or wigged hair and **painted eyes**; open or closed mouth, kid or kidaleen bodies, cloth bodies and can have any material for arms: 14" – $125.00; 17" – $165.00; 20" – $200.00.

Celluloid Shoulder Head: Germany, but with **glass eyes**: 14" – $165.00; 17" – $195.00; 20" – $245.00.

Celluloid Socket Heads: Germany. Glass eyes (allow more for flirty eyes). Ball jointed bodies or five-piece bodies. Open or closed mouths: 15" – $200.00; 18" – $250.00; 22" – $325.00; 25" – $400.00.

Kathe Kruse: All original: 14" – $400.00; 17" – $650.00.

Kammer & Reinhardt: (K star R): *Mold 700* baby: 14" – $495.00. *Mold 701:* 12" – $675.00. *Mold 714:* 12" – $695.00. *Mold 715:* 15" – $675.00. *Mold 717:* 20" – $600.00; 25" – $950.00. *Mold 728:* 15" – $495.00; 19" – 600.00. All celluloid – Japan: 5" – $15.00; 8" – $25.00; 12" – $35.00; 16" – $85.00; 19" – $150.00; 22" – $185.00; 26" – $225.00.

Konig & Wernicke: (K & W) – Toddler: 14" – $350.00; 20" – $500.00.

Heubach Koppelsdorf: Mold 399: 12" – $250.00; 18" – $550.00.

18½" Celluloid with molded hair, open mouth and set eyes. Marks: Turtle Mark/150, on both back and head. Courtesy Genie Jinright. 18½" – $175.00.

12" All celluloid. Toddler and jointed neck, shoulders and hips. Marked with Turtle Mark. Made for Heubach Koppelsdorf, mold number 399. Courtesy June Schultz. 12" – $250.00.

Right: 20″ Celluloid shoulder head. Marked with Turtle Mark by Rheinische Gummi. Sleep eyes/lashes, open mouth with four teeth. Kid body with composition arms and legs. Left: 16″ marked 5600 S.P.B. in star, H. Jointed body, open mouth and sleep eyes. Courtesy Frasher Doll Auctions. 20″ Celluloid – $200.00; 16″ 5600 – $300.00.

All original and all celluloid HITLER youth group boy with arm band. Painted features. Turtle mark. Courtesy Grace Walters. 15″ – $200.00.

Right: 14″ Chad Valley "Duke of Kent". All cloth, felt face velvet body, glass eyes and painted features, mohair wig. Original with "Made in England" tag. Left: 14″ "'Duchess of Kent" all original, glass eyes and made same as the Duke. Courtesy Frasher Doll Auctions. 14″ – $1,000.00 up.

CHAD VALLEY
CHARLIE CHAPLAIN

Chad Valley: Label or paper tag: Chad Valley Made in England. Dolls made of cloth and velvet, jointed neck, shoulders and hips. Can have painted or glass eyes and mohair wigs. First price is for dolls in mint condition and the second price for dolls that are dirty, soiled and worn.

Child with painted eyes: 12" – $175.00-45.00; 16" – $325.00-55.00; 18" – $425.00-75.00.

Child with glass eyes: 14" – $250.00-60.00; 16" – $450.00-75.00; 18" – $550.00-100.00.

Child representing Royal Family (Four in set: Princess Elizabeth, Princess Margaret Rose, Prince Edward, Princess Alexandria and all have glass eyes) Prince Edward as Duke of Kent: 15" – $1,000.00 up; As Duke of Windsor: 15" – $1,000.00 up; Others: 15" – $800.00 up.

Left: 17" Chad Valley boy, all cloth with felt face, glass eyes. Velvet body in original Guard Costume of wool and felt. Glass eyes. Right: Chad Valley boy made like Guard. Glass eyes and in original felt and cotton suit. Courtesy Frasher Doll Auctions. 17" Guard – $600.00 up; 17" Boy – $550.00 up.

16" Portrait "Charlie Chaplin". Marked: A.D. Co. composition head and lower arms. Cloth body and legs. Original clothes, painted features. 1915. Courtesy Frasher Doll Auctions. 16" – $300.00. (Also see Cloth Doll Section).

CHASE, MARTHA
CHINA DOLLS

Martha Jenks Chase of Pawtucket, Rhode Island, began making the Chase dolls in 1893, and they are still being made by members of her family. They all have oil painted features and are made of stockinette and cloth. They will be marked "Chase Stockinet" on the left leg or under the left arm. There is a paper label (often gone) on the backs with a drawn head:

The older Chase dolls are jointed at the shoulders, hips, knees and elbows, where the newer dolls are jointed at the shoulders and hips only with straight arms and legs. Prices for very clean dolls with only minor scuff.

Older Dolls: Babies: 16" – $525.00; 20" – $625.00; 24" – $725.00.

Child: 12" – $350.00; 16" – $750.00; 20" – $875.00.

Lady: 16" – $1,200.00; 24" – $1,800.00; Life size – $2,200.00.

Man: 16" – $1,300.00; 24" – $2,000.00; Life size – $2,400.00.

Black: 24" – $2,800.00; 28" – $3,500.00.

Newer Dolls: Babies: 14" – $165.00; 16" – $195.00. Child, boy or girl: 14" – $185.00; 16" – $225.00.

Portrait of George Washington: 22"-25" – $2,800.00.

Portrait of Women: 22"-25" – $2,200.00-2,800.00.

20" Stockinette, molded face with oil painted features. Applied ears, treated limbs, rough-stroked hair. Cloth body. Press jointed at shoulders, hips, elbows and knees. Ca. 1890's. Courtesy Frasher Doll Auctions. 20" – $875.00.

CHINA DOLLS

Almost all china dolls have black hair, but during the 1880's, blondes became more popular and by 1900, one out of three of the "common" type chinas were blonde. China dolls with brown hair (or eyes) are rarer than others. Prices for clean, nicely dressed dolls with no cracks or repairs.

Adelina Patti: 1860's. Center part, roll curl from forehead to back on each side of head and "spit" curls at temples and above partly exposed ears: 14" – $300.00; 18" – $425.00; 22" – $565.00.

Biedermeir or Bald Head: Ca. 1840. Has bald head, some with top of head glazed black: Takes wigs: 14" – $500.00; 20" – $900.00. Early heads: 16" – $1,000.00 up.

Bangs: Full across forehead. 1870's. Black hair: 16" – $250.00; 20" – $400.00; 26" – $650.00. Blondes: 16" – $285.00; 20" – $450.00; 26" – $700.00.

Brown Eyes: (Painted). Can be any hairstyle and date: 16" – $650.00; 20" – $900.00; 25" – $1,200.00.

Bun: China head with bun, braided or rolled and pulled to back of head. Pink luster tint. 1830's & 1840's. Cloth body, nicely

CHINA DOLLS

dressed and undamaged: A 16″ doll can run from $900.00 up to $3,000.00 depending on rarity of hairdo.

Common Hairdo: Called "lowbrow" or "Butterfly". After 1905. Black or blondes. Wavy hairdo, center part with hair that comes down low on forehead: 8″ – $65.00; 12″ – $100.00; 16″ – $165.00; 19″ – $185.00; 23″ – $225.00; 27″ – $300.00.

Covered Wagon: 1840's to 1870's. Hair parted in the middle with flat hairstyle and has "Sausage" shaped curls around head: 12″ – $325.00; 16″ – $450.00; 20″ – $595.00; 24″ – $700.00.

Curly Top: 1845-1860's. Ringlet curls that are loose and over entire head: 16″ – $450.00; 20″ – $595.00.

Dolly Madison: 1870-1880's. Loose curly hairdo with modeled ribbon and bow in center of the top of the head. Few curls on forehead: 14″ – $250.00; 18″ – $385.00; 21″ – $450.00; 24″ – $565.00; 28″ – $625.00.

Flat Top: 1850-1870's. Black hair parted in middle, smooth on top with short curls around head: 17″ – $200.00; 20″ – $285.00; 24″ – $325.00.

Glass Eyes: Can have a variety of hairstyles. 1840-1870's: 14″ – $1,300.00; 18″ – $2,300.00; 22″ – $2,800.00; 26″ – $3,200.00.

Japanese: 1910-1920's. Can be marked or unmarked. Black and blonde hairdo. Can have "common" hairdo, or have much more adult face and hairdo: 14″ – $100.00; 17″ – $145.00.

Man or Boy: Excellent quality, early date. Painted eyes, side part hairdos: 14″ – $595.00; 16″ – $900.00; 20″ – $1,200.00 up. Glass eyes: 14″ – $850.00; 17″ – $1,200.00; 20″ – $1,500.00.

Pet Names: 1905. Same as "common" with molded shirtwaist with name on front: Agnes, Bertha, Daisy, Dorothy, Edith, Esther, Ethel, Florence, Helen, Mabel, Marion, Pauline: 8″ – $115.00; 12″ – $165.00; 16″ – $200.00; 19″ – $245.00; 23″ – $295.00; 27″ – $375.00.

Pierced Ears: Can have a variety of hair

20″ All original china with early spoon hands. Hair is brush stroked completely around face. Back of hair is in a snood with molded head band over top. Ca. 1860's. Courtesy Barbara Earnshaw-Cain. 20″ – $700.00.

23½″ Brown-eyed china and thirteen sausage curls, cloth body with replaced lower arms. Courtesy Frasher Doll Auctions. 24″ – $1,100.00.

styles: 14" – $450.00; 18" – $700.00. More must be allowed for rarity of hairdo.

Snood, Combs: Any applied hair decoration: 14" – $400.00; 17" – $600.00.

Spill Curls: With or without head band. Many individual curls across forehead and over shoulders with forehead curls continued to above ears: 14" – $300.00; 18" – $585.00; 22" – $650.00.

Wood Body: Peg wooden body, wood or china lower limbs, china head with early unusual hairdo. Fine quality and in excellent condition: 16" – $2,500.00.

Wood Body: Articulated with slim hips, china lower arms. 1840's-1850's: 12" – $850.00. Same with covered wagon hairdo: 7" – $800.00; 12" – $850.00; 15" – $1,800.00.

23½" "Adelina Patti" China. Brush marks around face, cloth body with china limbs. Courtesy Frasher Doll Auctions. 24" – $650.00.

25" Black curly hairdo china with black head band and bow in front. Called "Dolly Madison". Cloth body and china limbs. 28" "Mary Todd Lincoln". Pink luster china, cloth body with china limbs. Courtesy Frasher Doll Auctions. 25" – $565.00; 28" – $625.00.

38" China "Flat Top" with curls at temples, cloth body with china limbs. 38" china with full beaded cape, cloth body and china limbs. Courtesy Frasher Doll Auctions. 38" – $800.00.

CHINA DOLLS

28″ China with boy or girl hairdo, exposed ears, cloth body and china limbs. Courtesy Turn of Century Antiques. 28″ – $500.00.

29″ China by Kling with cloth body and china limbs. Courtesy Frasher Doll Auctions. 29″ – $650.00.

Left to right: 16″ China with "Agnes" on shoulder. Black hair "Agnes" that is 16″. Foreground has head only that is 6″ and in back is 9″. All have "Butterfly", "Lowbrow" or "Common" style hairdos. Courtesy Turn of Century Antiques. 16″ – $165.00; 9″ – $70.00; Head only – $25.00.

Prices are for clean dolls with only minor scuffs or soil.

Alabama Indestructible Doll: All cloth with head molded and painted in oils, painted hair, shoes and sockings. Marked in torso or leg: Pat. Nov. 9, 1912 Ella Smith Doll Co. or Mrs. S.S. Smith/Manufacturer and dealer/The Alabama Indestructible Doll/Roanoke, Ala./Patented Sept. 26, 1905 (or 1907).: 18" – $850.00; Black: 18" – $1,400.00.

Arnold Print Works: "Brownie" dolls designed by Palmer Cox. Copyrighted in 1892. Printed on cloth and sold by the yard. Twelve dolls per yard: Canadian, Chinaman, Dude, German, Highlander, Indian, Irishman, John Bull, Policeman, Sailor, Soldier and Uncle Sam: Yard-uncut – $250.00; Made-up: 8" – $90.00.

Art Fabric Mills: See printed cloth dolls.

Babyland: Made by E.I. Horsman from 1904 to 1920. Marked on torso, or bottom of foot. With oil painted features or printed features. With or without a wig. All cloth, jointed at shoulders and hips. First prices for early dolls that are oil painted and second prices for most of later ones are printed: 12" – $450.00-325.00; 16" – $650.00-400.00; 24" – $850.00-600.00; 30" – $1,400.00-900.00; Black: 12" – $500.00; 18" – $800.00; 26" – $1,200.00.

Bruckner Cloth Dolls: Neck band label: Bruckner Doll/Made in U.S.A., or in shoulder: Pat'd July 8th, 1901. Stiffened mask face with oil painted features. Cloth body and limbs. Child: 12" – $165.00 up; 16" – $265.00 up. Black: 12" – $225.00 up; 16" – $350.00 up. Two-headed doll. One Black and one White. (Topsy-Turvy): 12"-12½" – $325.00.

Charlie Chaplin: Made by Amberg & Sons and marked on bottom of foot: 17" – $350.00.

Chase, Martha Jenks: See that section.

Chad Valley: Also see that section. Label or paper tag: Chad Valley-Made in England. Cloth with velvet body, jointed neck, shoulders and hips. Painted or glass eyes, mohair wigs; Child with painted eyes: 12" – $175.00; 16" – $325.00; 18" – $425.00. With glass eyes: 14" – $250.00; 16" – $450.00; 18" – $550.00. Child representing Royal family (four in set - Princess Elizabeth, Princess Margaret Rose, Prince Edward, Princess Alexandria - all have glass eyes). Prince Edward as Duke of Kent: 15" – $1,000.00 up. As Duke of Windsor: 15" – $1.000.00 up. Other: 15" – $800.00 up.

Columbian Doll: Marked before 1900: Columbian Doll/Emma E. Adams/Oswego Centre/N.Y. After 1905-1906: The Columbian Doll/Manufactured by/Marietta Adams Ruttan/Oswego, N.Y. All cloth with hand painted features: 19" – $1,500.00 up in excellent condition. 19" in fair condition.

Drayton, Grace: Dolly Dingle: 1923 by Averill Mfg. Co. Cloth with printed features: Marked on torso: 11" – $325.00; 14" – $350.00.

Chocolate Drop: 1923 by Averill Mfg. Co. Brown cloth with painted features and three tufts of yarn hair: 11" – $300.00; 14" – $385.00.

Hug Me Tight: By Colonial Toy Mfg. Co. in 1916. One-piece printed cloth: 11" – $225.00; 14" – $275.00.

Farnell's Alpha Toys: Marked with label on foot: Farnell's Alpha Toys-Made in England. Child: 14" – $265.00; 16" – $325.00; King George VI: 16" – $365.00. Palace Guard/-Beefeater: 16" – $285.00.

Georgene Novelties: Marked with paper tag with both Georgene Averill and Madame Hendron. All cloth mask face and painted features. Yarn hair. Foreign costumes: 13" – $65.00; 18" – $85.00; 24" – $145.00. Children: 13" – $115.00; 17" – $175.00. Tear Drop Baby, has one tear drop painted on cheek: 16" – $265.00.

Comic Characters: 14" – $300.00-350.00.

Kewpie Cuddles: Marked with cloth label sewn to seam: Made by Kreuger, Inc. Pat. #1785800. Fat, all cloth body, painted mask face, has tiny wings: 10" – $125.00; 13" – $195.00.

Lenci: See that section.

Liberty of London Royal Dolls: Marked with cloth or paper tag. Flesh colored cloth faces with stitched in and painted features. All cloth bodies. 1939 Royal Portrait dolls are 8"-10" and included are Queen Elizabeth, Queen Mary, Queen Victoria and King George VI: $85.00. Other historical dolls: 10" – $80.00.

Kamkins: By Louise Kampes. 1928 to 1934. Marked on back of head or foot, also has

CLOTH AND FELT DOLLS

13" Bruckner, shoulder mask face, molded open/closed smile mouth with painted teeth. All cloth and all original. Painted features. Courtesy Henri and John Startzel. 13" – $250.00 up.

16" Columbian doll with painted features, stitch jointed knees and upper arms. Treated limbs. Courtesy Henri and John Startzel. 16" Excellent Condition – $1,200.00; 16" Fair Condition – $500.00 up.

15" All printed cloth. Marked: Reg'd in England. Pat. July 5, '92/and Oct. 4, '92. Courtesy Henri and John Startzel. 15" – $350.00 up.

16" Printed cloth with printed-on undies, shoes and socks. Ca. 1930's. Courtesy Henri and John Startzel. 16" – $165.00 up.

14″ Printed cloth Indian, excelsior stuffed. Commercially made and portrait type. Maker and date unknown. Ca. 1910's. Courtesy Frasher Doll Auctions. 14″ – $295.00 up.

21″ German cloth with stockinette face with well sculpted features, glass eyes, applied mohair wig, mustache and beard. All original - maker unknown. Courtesy Frasher Doll Auctions. 21″ – $200.00 up.

paper label, heart-shaped, on chest. All cloth with molded face mask and painted features, wigs and as boy or girl: 19″ – $900.00; 24″ – $1,500.00.

Kathe Kruse: Made in Germany from 1910. Modeled muslin heads, painted in oils and on jointed cloth bodies which are marked: Kathe Kruse, on sole of foot, and also may have the word Germany and a number. Later Kruse dolls will have a paper tag attached by a string also. Early cloth dolls: 15″-16″ – $1,100.00-1,400.00. Later dolls (1930's) with wigs. U.S. zone and in good condition: 15″-16″ – $700.00 up.

Madame Hendron: See Averill this section.
Mammy Style Black Dolls: All cloth with painted or sewn features. Ca. 1910's: 14″ – $225.00; 17″ – $275.00. Ca. 1930's: 14″ – $125.00.

Mollye: Made from 1920 into 1950's. Designed and made by Mollye Goldman, International Dolls Co. Marked with paper tag. Children. All cloth, painted face mask, mohair or yarn wigs: 17″-18″ – $110.00; 24″ – $135.00 up. Internationals. All cloth with face masks: 13″ – $65.00; 17″ – $100.00; 20″ – $125.00.

Philadelphia Baby: Also called "Sheppard

CLOTH AND FELT DOLLS

Doll" as was made by J.B. Sheppard in late 1890's and early 1900's. Stockinette covered body with painted cloth arms and legs. Head is modeled and painted cloth. Excellent condition: 21"-22" – $1,400.00; Good condition: $750.00.

Photographic Face Doll: 16"-17" – $350.00.

Printed Cloth Dolls: Advertising dolls to be cut out and stuffed such as: Rastus, the Cream of Wheat Chef: 18" – $95.00. Aunt Jemima, set of four dolls: $85.00 up each. Dolls with printed on underwear: Cut: 6" – $65.00; 15" – $145.00; 18" – $160.00; Uncut: 6" – $75.00; 15" – $155.00; 18" – $170.00. Girls and boys with printed outer clothes: 6" – $85.00; 15" – $150.00; 18" – $195.00. Uncut: 6" – $95.00; 15" – $165.00; 18" – $225.00.

Black Boy or Girl: 18" – $150.00 up.

Rollinson Dolls: Molded cloth with painted features, head and limbs. Wigged or molded hair. Designed by Gertrude F. Rollinson and made by Utley Doll Co. Holyoke, Ma. Marks: stamp of doll in a diamond and around border: Rollinson Doll Holyoke, Ma. Molded hair: 17"-18" – $750.00; Wigged by Rollinson: 17"-18" – $950.00.

Smith, Mrs. S.S.: See Alabama in this section.

Steiff: Made in Germany early 1900's. All felt with jointed neck, shoulder and hips. Head seam runs straight down center of face. Can have glass or painted eyes. Painted hair or wigged. Metal button in ear and stamp on body: Steiff-trademark. Made in Germany: Child: 14" – $875.00; Adult Characters (Military, etc.): 18" – $2,200.00; U.S. Zone, Germany: 12"-13" – $685.00.

WPA Cloth Dolls: Made 1935 into 1940's. Stockinette stuffed and stiffened head with cloth body with features painted in oils. Yarn hair glued on. Marks: location and number where made, such as #506, Elsworth, Kns. 18" – $365.00; 22"-23" – $475.00.

Homemade group of cloth dolls. Ca. 1930's. Two Black adults and four children. Two portrait style white adults. Stockinette faces with embroidered features on Black dolls. Courtesy Frasher Doll Auctions. Black: Set of 6 – $145.00; White: Pair – $55.00.

Walker, Izannah: Made in 1870's and 1880's. Modeled head with painted features in oils. Ears are applied. Cloth body and limbs. Hands and feet are stitched or can have painted-on boots. Mark: Patented Nov. 4, 1873. Brushstroke hairdo. In fair condition: 16″ – $3,800.00; In very good condition: 16″ – $9,000.00 up. With two vertical curls painted in front of ears. In fair condition: 18″ – $3,800.00; 24″ – $4,600.00. In very good condition: 18″ – $11,000.00; 24″ – $14,000.00.

Wellings, Norah: See that section.

18″ All cloth roller skater with removable skirt that is lined. May be commercially made or a cut and sew pattern. Ca. 1940's-1950's. 18″ – $25.00.

COMPOSITION DOLLS-GERMANY

Almost all the known German makers made dolls in other materials besides bisque with many making them with composition heads. Some of the makers were Armand Marseille, Kammer and Reinhardt and others. Composition dolls were made in Germany before World War I, but the majority were made in the 1920's and 1930's. They can be all composition or have a composition head and limbs with a cloth body.

Child Doll: All composition with wig, sleep/flirty eyes, have an open mouth or a closed one and will be on a jointed composition body: 14″ – $100.00; 18″ – $200.00; 22″ – $300.00; 25″ – $425.00.

Baby: All composition with open mouth and on all composition bent limb baby body: 16″ – $175.00; 19″ – $275.00; 24″ – $450.00; Toddler: 18″ – $275.00; 24″ – $375.00.

Baby: Composition head and limbs with cloth body, open mouth and sleep eyes: 14″ – $95.00; 18″ – $185.00; 25″ – $325.00; Painted eyes: Child: 14″ – $85.00; 18″ –

$150.00; Baby: 16″ – $100.00; 24″ – $285.00.

27″ German composition child. Composition ball-jointed body, tin sleep eyes, open mouth. Unmarked. Courtesy Frasher Doll Auctions. 27″ – $350.00.

COMPOSTION DOLLS-GERMANY
CRECHE FIGURES

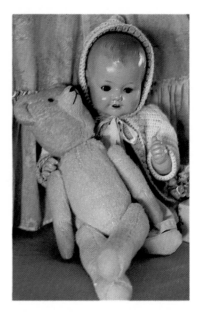

32″ Composition-type material marked: F.S. & Co. Germany. Head circumference is 20″. Flange neck, flirty eyes/lashes, open mouth and molded hair. Toddler body with cloth torso and jointed arms and legs. Courtesy Frasher Doll Auctions. 32″ – $500.00.

24″ German composition marked: A.M./2549. Made by Armand Marseille. Cloth body with composition limbs, open mouth with two upper teeth, sleep eyes/lashes and fingers curled in palm. Courtesy Frasher Doll Auctions. 24″ – $375.00.

CRECHE FIGURES

35″ Creche figure. All wood and hand carved, inset glass eyes. One hand replaced. Courtesy Frasher Doll Auctions. 35″ – $1,200.00.

Creche figures became very popular during the last part of the 1700's to the mid-1800's. Wealthy people commissioned well known artists and sculpturers to make figures for their scenes. The scenes did not just stop with major, basic figures but included entire street scenes of people and animals, as well as items such as fruit for market scenes and children, selling stalls, buckets, baskets and a number of items that fit into the scene.

The early Creche figures were gesso over wood head and limbs, a wire frame, fabric covered body. These figures have extremely fine detailed heads with carved hair or in scale finely curled wigs. They have inset glass eyes and the modeling of the features and limbs are truly a work of art. The later figures have a terra-cotta head and limbs and a wire formed body that is fabric covered. The eyes are painted with only a few having glass eyes, and detail workmanship is not as outstanding as early figures. **Older Creche:** Early gesso over wood or all wood: Lady: 13" – $395.00; 20" – $795.00; Man: 13" – $595.00; 20" – $895.00. Child: 11" – $295.00; 14" – $400.00. **Later Creche:** Terra-cotta: 13" – $195.00; 16" – $295.00.

DEP

23" Marked: DEP/10. Sleep eyes, open mouth, pierced ears, French style jointed body. Courtesy Frasher Doll Auctions. 23" – $1,200.00.

31" Marked: DEP/14. Set eyes, open mouth, French style jointed body. Courtesy Frasher Doll Auctions. 31" – $1,900.00.

Many dolls, both French and German, bear the mark DEP, as part of the mold description, but the dolls referred to here are marked ONLY with DEP and a size number, are on a French body that sometimes bears the Jumeau sticker or stamp. Some of these DEP or marked heads will also have the red stamp: Tete Jumeau and/or the artist "check" marks. The early DEP marked dolls will have a closed mouth and be of extremely fine quality in bisque and art work, and from the 1880's. Dolls

DEP

with this mark of the 1890's into 1900 will still have fine quality bisque and the later they become the higher the face color. They will have painted lashes under the eyes only and most will have hair eyelashes over the eyes. The early dolls will have outlined upper lips and the later ones will not.

It is almost certain that a great many of the DEP marked heads were actually made in Germany by either Simon & Halbig, the most likely candidate or by Kestner. Prices for nicely dressed, clean dolls with no damage. Sample mark: **DEP 10**

21″ Marked: DEP/8. French jointed body, sleep eyes/lashes, open mouth, pierced ears. Courtesy Frasher Doll Auctions. 21″ – $1,000.00.

Open mouth DEP: 14″ – $700.00; 18″ – $925.00; 25″ – $1,500.00; 30″ – $1,900.00; 34″ – $2,100.00.
Closed mouth DEP: 14″ – $1,200.00; 18″ – $1,800.00; 25″ – $2,600.00; 30″ – $3,000.00.
Walking, kissing, open mouth DEP: 14″ – $950.00; 18″ – $1,200.00; 22″ – $1,500.00; 26″ – $1,800.00.

22″ Incised: DEP on French walker body and as legs move, the head turns from side to side and she throws a kiss. Open mouth. Courtesy Turn of Century Antiques. 22″ – $1,500.00.

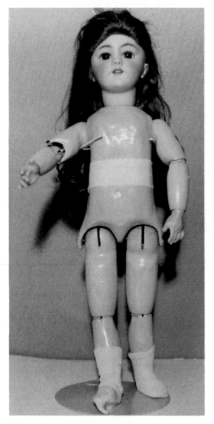

Doll House Man or Lady: with molded hair/wig and painted eyes: 6"-7" – $150.00-165.00.
Man or Women with Glass Eyes/Wigs:

6"-7" – $300.00-400.00.
Grandparents or Molded-on Hats: 6"-7" – $165.00-195.00.

6½"-7½" Doll House dolls. Man has molded, painted mustache, lady in center with wig marked: S.H. All have cloth body with bisque limbs. Courtesy Arthur Routiette. 6½"-7½" – $165.00; Man – $185.00.

DRESSEL, CUNO & OTTO

The Dressel firm was founded in 1700, but very little is known of them until 1863. They were located in Sonneberg, Thuringia, Germany and Cuno and Otto were the sons of the founder. The Dressel firm was listed as dollmakers by 1873 and they produced bisque head dolls with jointed kid or cloth bodies as well as the ball jointed composition/mache' bodies. Some of their heads were made for them by Simon & Halbig. In 1906 they registered the trademark for "Jutta" and by 1911 they were also making celluloid dolls. Prices for clean, undamaged and nicely dressed dolls. Sample marks:

  C.O.D

"Holz Masse"

Babies: Marked C.O.D., but without the word "Jutta": 14" – $365.00; 18" – $465.00; 24" – $685.00.
Child: On jointed composition body; open

mouth: 15" – $265.00; 18" – $325.00; 22" – $400.00; 25" – $525.00; 30" – $700.00.
Child: Open mouth and on kid, jointed body: 14" – $225.00; 18" – $300.00; 24" – $475.00.
Jutta: 1910-1922. Baby, open mouth and five-piece bent limb body: 14" – $425.00; 17" – $550.00; 20" – $700.00; 24" – $950.00; 26" – $1,100.00. Toddler body: 14" – $585.00; 17" – $700.00; 20" – $995.00; 24" – $1,100.00; 26" – $1,300.00. Child marked with or without the S&H. #1914, 1348, 1349, etc.: 14" – $425.00; 18" – $495.00; 24" – $725.00; 27" – $950.00; 32" – $1,250.00.
Lady Dolls: 1920's with adult face, closed mouth and on five-piece composition body with thin limbs and high heel feet. Mark: 1469: 14" – $1,300.00; 16" – $1,500.00.
Character Dolls: 1909 and after. Closed mouths and painted intaglio eyes: 12" – $1,200.00; 14" – $2,100.00; 17" – $2,500.00.

DRESSEL, CUNO & OTTO

Left: 25″ Marked: A.1770 M. C.O.D. 7 DEP. made in Germany. Shoulder head with kid body, bisque lower arms. Right: 25″ Marked: made in Germany 63. Jointed body. Open mouth. Maker unknown. Courtesy Frasher Doll Auctions. 25″ C.O.D. – $525.00; 25″ Unknown – $500.00.

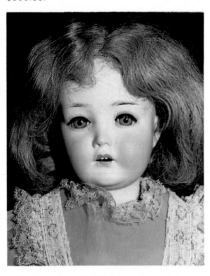

23″ Marked: C.O.D./Germany. Jointed body, sleep eyes/lashes, open mouth with four teeth. Courtesy Frasher Doll Auctions. 23″ – $425.00.

Composition: Shoulder head of 1870's. Can have glass or painted eyes, molded hair or wig and on cloth body with composition limbs with molded-on boots. Will be marked with Holz-Masse:

With wig: 14″ – $285.00; 17″-18″ – $350.00; 24″ – $450.00. Molded hair: 17″-18″ – $325.00; 24″-26″ – $400.00. **Portrait Dolls:** 1896. Such as Uncle Sam, Farmer, Admiral Dewey, Old Rip. Portrait bisque head, glass eyes, composition body. Some will be marked with a "D" or "S". Heads made for Dressel by Simon & Halbig. Original dressed, perfect dolls; Military dolls: 14″-15″ – $1,800.00; 20″ – $2,800.00. Old Rip and Witch: 12″ – $1,300.00; 15″ – $1,600.00. Uncle Sam: 14″ – $1,500.00; 20″ – $2,400.00.

16" Marked: Jutta 1914, five-piece bent limb baby body, open mouth with two teeth. Courtesy Frasher Doll Auctions. 16" – $525.00.

22" Marked: JuttaBaby/Dressel/Germany/-1922. Open mouth with two teeth and on five-piece bent limb body. Courtesy Frasher Doll Auctions. 22" – $800.00.

33" Marked: E.D. Closed mouth and paperweight eyes. Original wig and wears actual child's dress of same period, which was cut down exactly to fit by Sally Freeman. 33" – $4,200.00.

E.D. BE'BE'
EDEN BE'BE'

E. Denamur of Paris made dolls from 1885 to 1898. After 1875 his business was known as "le Maison de Bambin". The E.D. marked dolls seem to be accepted as being made by Denamur, but they may have also been made by E. Dumont, Paris. Composition and wood jointed bodies. Prices for nicely dressed, clean and undamaged dolls.

E.D. marked child: closed mouth: 14" – $2,100.00; 18" – $2,500.00; 22" – $2,800.00; 25" – $3,300.00; 29" – $3,900.00.

E.D. marked child: open mouth: 16" – $1,400.00; 20" – $1,900.00; 25" – $2,400.00.

33" Marked: E.D.14 DEPOSE. Closed mouth, composition and wood jointed body. Maybe original wig. 33" – $4,200.00.

25" Marked: E.D.11 DEPOSE. Wood and composition jointed body, pierced ears, open mouth. Courtesy Frasher Doll Auctions. 25" – $2,400.00.

EDEN BEBE

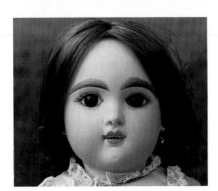

23" Eden Be'be' Paris 9. Open mouth, heavy feathered eyebrows. On French walker body. Courtesy Arthur Rouliette. 23" – $2,100.00.

EDEN BE'BE'
ELLIS, JOEL

Fleischmann & Bloedel of Paris, Furth and Bavaria. Founded in 1873 and joined S.F.B.J. in 1899. Marks: Eden Be'be'/Paris. Eden Be'be' with closed mouth and open mouth will be found on composition jointed bodies. Prices for nicely dressed, clean and undamaged dolls.

Eden Be'be': Open mouth: 15" – $1,000.00; 18" – $1,500.00; 22" – $2,000.00.

Eden Be'be': Closed mouth: 15" – $1,600.00; 18" – $2,300.00; 22" – $2,700.00.

Walking, Kissing Doll: Ball jointed body with walking mechanism, head turns and arm throws kisses. Heads by Simon & Halbig with mold 1039. Bodies and assembly by Fleischmann & Bloedel. Price for perfect, working doll: 21" – $950.00 up.

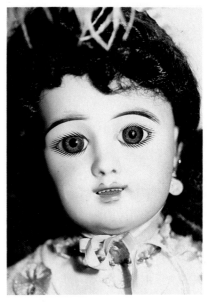

23" Marked: Eden Be'be'/Paris 10 DEPOSE. Paperweight eyes, pierced ears, open mouth and outlined lips. Courtesy Frasher Doll Auctions. 23" – $2,100.00.

ELLIS, JOEL

12½" Joel Ellis 1874 doll. All wood, fully jointed with metal hands and feet. Courtesy Turn of Century Antiques. 12" – $825.00.

ELLIS, JOEL
FARNELL, ALPHA

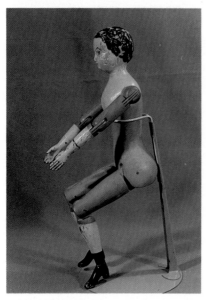

Made in 1873 and 1874 these dolls are also called "Springfield's" as Joel Ellis made the dolls under the name Co-operative Manufacturing Co. Springfield, Vermont. All wood, with tenon and mortise joints and have metal hands and feet. Painted features and molded hair. Doll in overall good condition and does not need to be dressed. 12" – $825.00; 15" – $995.00; 18" – $1,400.00.

16" Joel Ellis 1874 doll. All wood with metal hands and feet. Fully articulated. Has sausage curls around head. Courtesy Henri and John Startzel. 16" – $1,000.00.

FARNELL, ALPHA

14" Alpha Farnell boy and girl. All cloth with felt face, painted features, side glancing eyes, mohair wigs. Label on clothes: Farnell's Alpha Toys. Made in England. 1930's. Courtesy Frasher Doll Auctions.

These "adult" style dolls were made by a number of French firms from about the 1860's on into 1930's. Many will be marked only with a number or have a stamp or sticker on the body (some of these will be stamped or labeled by the store in which they were sold and not by the maker). Of all the ladies of fashion the most desirable are the Huret and Rohmer. Next in desirability is the fully articulated wood or blown kid body dolls. Some of these dolls will have bisque lower arms and/or legs, or metal limbs. The most available seems to be the F.G. marked Fashions. Prices are for dolls in perfect condition with no crack, chips nor repairs and in beautiful old or newer, appropriate clothes.

Articulated Wood or blown kid bodies and limbs (some have bisque lower arms): 16" – $2,900.00 up; 20" – $3,500.00 up.

Articulated with bisque lower legs and fine feet detail: 16" – $3,600.00; 20" – $4,300.00.

Marked Huret or Rohmer: 16" – $4,200.00; 20" – $5,400.00.

Huret Portrait Lady: 18" – $9,800.00 up.

Marked Jumeau body/number on head; portrait style face. 14" – $2,100.00; 18" – $3,200.00; 24" – $4,400.00; 28" – $5,000.00.

Marked F.G.: All kid body with swivel neck: 14" – $1,200.00; 17" – $1,500.00; 21" – $2,000.00.

Marked: F.G.: All kid body. One-piece shoulder and head: 12" – $625.00; 15" – $985.00; 18" – $1,400.00.

Marked F.G.: Gesland cloth covered body with bisque hands and lower legs: 14" – $2,600.00; 17" – $3,200.00; 21" – $3,600.00.

Marked F.G.: On Gesland cloth covered body with composition or papier mache' hands and legs: 14" – $1,800.00; 17" – $2,400.00; 21" – $2,800.00.

Smiling "Mona Lisa": With kid body with leather arms and stitched fingers or bisque lower arms. Marked with letter on head: 13" – $1,400.00; 17" – $2,700.00; 21" – $3,200.00.

Unmarked with numbers only: With one-

14" Fashion with bisque head on bisque shoulder plate, wood articulated body. Mark: E, on shoulder. Courtesy Turn of Century Antiques. 14" – $2,500.00.

16½" Fashion marked: E.9 DEPOSE B. on front of shoulder plate. Attributed to E. Barrois (1846-1852). Kid body, bisque lower arms. Cork pate and human hair wig. Courtesy Frasher Doll Auctions. 17" – $1,500.00 up.

piece head and shoulder: Extremely fine quality: 12″ – $900.00; 16″ – $1,400.00; 20″ – $1,800.00.

Unmarked with numbers only: With swivel

neck and extremely fine quality: 14″ – $1,500.00; 18″ – $2,100.00; 22″ – $2,600.00 up.

17″ Jumeau Fashion. Marked: 5, on head and shoulder plate. Swivel head on bisque shoulder plate, glass eyes and closed mouth on all kid marked body. Courtesy Frasher Doll Auctions. 17″ – $2,700.00.

12″ Fashion Marked: F.G. on shoulder and 2/9, on head. By Francois Gaultier. Swivel neck, kid body with bisque lower arms. Courtesy Frasher Doll Auctions. 12″ – $1,000.00.

15″ Fashion with swivel head on bisque shoulder plate, kid body with kid limbs. Courtesy Arthur Rouliette. 15″ – $1,400.00.

F. Gaultier (earlier was spelled Gauthier) is the accepted maker of the F.G. marked dolls. These dolls are often found on the cloth covered or all composition marked Gesland bodies. The Gesland firm was operated by two brothers with one of them having the initial F. 1887-1900. The dolls will be marked F.G., along with a number, or the F.G. in a scroll:

F.G.

Child With Closed Mouth: Excellent quality bisque, no damage and dressed ready for a collection: 14″ – $2,500.00; 16″ – $2,800.00; 19″ – $3,000.00; 22″ – $3,300.00; 25″ – $3,800.00.

Child With Closed Mouth: but high face color, no damage and well dressed and ready to display: 14″ – $1,600.00; 16″ – $1,800.00; 19″ – $2,100.00; 22″ – $2,400.00.

Child With Open Mouth: Excellent quality, no damage and dressed ready to display: 14″ – $1,000.00; 16″ – $1,300.00; 19″ – $1,600.00; 22″ – $1,900.00.

Child With Open Mouth: With high face

12½″ Marked: F. 5/9 G. French wood and composition jointed body with straight wrists, closed mouth. Courtesy Frasher Doll Auctions. 13″ – $2,200.00.

13″ Child by Gaultier and marked: F.G. in scroll. French jointed body, closed mouth and pierced ears. Courtesy Frasher Doll Auctions. 13″ – $2,200.00.

8″ and 10″ Dolls by Gaultier. 10″ marked: F.G. in scroll. Bisque shoulder heads, molded hair and painted features, closed mouths. Cloth bodies with earthenware limbs. Both original and represent Boulogne Fisherwomen. Courtesy Frasher Doll Auctions. 8″ – $225.00; 10″ – $300.00.

F.G. BE'BE'
FORTUNE TELLER
FRENCH BE'BE', MAKER UNKNOWN

color, very dark lips, no damage and dressed ready to display: 14" – $600.00; 16" – $700.00; 19" – $900.00; 22" – $1,000.00. **Marked F.G. Fashion:** See "Fashion, French" section.

Child on Marked Gesland Body: Bisque head on stockinette over wire frame body with composition or bisque lower limbs. Closed mouth: 16" – $2,600.00; 19" – $3,400.00; 25" – $4,400.00. Marked F.G. on 22" Gesland body. Open mouth: 15" – $1,200.00; 18" – $1,900.00.

FORTUNE TELLER

23" "Fortune Telling" doll incised: 5. Body is composition with one-piece arms and legs, set eyes, open mouth with four teeth, pierced ears. Original clothes with overskirt of fan-like paper folds which contain different messages written in French. Courtesy Frasher Doll Auctions. 23" – $2,200.00.

FRENCH BE'BE', MAKER UNKNOWN

A variety of French doll makers produced dolls that are unmarked from about 1880 into the 1920's. These dolls may only have a head number, or be marked with: Paris or France. Many of the French style dolls that have a number are now being attributed to German makers and it will be a questionable area for sometime.

Unmarked French Be'be': Will have a closed mouth or open/closed mouth, paperweight eyes, excellent quality bisque and painting and be on a French body. Prices are for dolls that are nicely dressed, wigged and need no repairs.

Very early face: 14" – $2,800.00; 18" – $4,200.00; 24" – $4,900.00.
Jumeau style face: 14" – $1,900.00; 18" – $2,300.00; 24" – $2,900.00.
Excellent quality: 15" – $2,000.00; 22" – $2,400.00; 26" – $3,000.00.
Medium quality, which may have poor painting or/and blotches to skin tones: 17" – $1,400.00; 22" – $1,800.00; 26" – $2,400.00.
French Be'be' with open mouth: 1890's. Will be on French body. Excellent quality. 14" – $1,200.00; 17" – $1,500.00; 21" – $1,700.00; 24" – $2,000.00.

FRENCH BE'BE', MAKER UNKNOWN

1920's: Will have high color bisque and may be on five-piece papier mache' body. Open mouth: 16″ – $650.00; 21″ – $750.00; 25″ – $950.00.

12″ French child marked: P.4. Maker unknown. Closed mouth and on French jointed body. Courtesy Frasher Doll Auctions. 12″ – $1,600.00.

18½″ Marked: 136. Maker unknown. Closed mouth with white space between lips, French jointed body with straight wrists. Courtesy Frasher Doll Auctions. 18½″ – $2,200.00.

19″ French doll marked: X6. Maker unknown, but probable Jumeau. Jointed French body, open mouth. Courtesy Frasher Doll Auctions. 19″ – $1,600.00.

FRENCH BE'BE', MAKER UNKNOWN
FREUNDLICH, RALPH

21" French child marked: 136. Paperweight eyes and open/closed mouth with white area between lips. On French jointed body with straight wrists. Courtesy Frasher Doll Auctions. 21" – $2,400.00.

14" French doll marked: Sweetheart. On French composition jointed body. Open mouth and set eyes. Courtesy Turn of Century Antiques. 14" – $450.00.

FREUNDLICH, RALPH

16½" Marked: Baby Sandy, on head. All composition, fully jointed body, molded hair, sleep eyes and clothes are replaced. 17" Patsy-type all composition. Unmarked. Painted eyes to side. Original clothes. Courtesy Frasher Doll Auctions. 16" – $300.00; 17" Unmarked – $85.00.

Ralph Freundlich of the Freundlich Novelty Co. made dolls in New York and began operating in 1923. His dolls will be all composition or cloth and composition. Most will bear a cardboard tag and doll will be unmarked or will have the doll's name on the head, but no manufacturer name.
Baby Sandy: 1939-1942. All composition with molded hair, sleep or painted eyes. Marked: Baby Sandy, on head. Original clothes, excellent condition composition with no chips, cracks or crazing: 8" – $125.00; 11" – $175.00; 14" – $225.00; 19" – $400.00. With light crazing and nicely re-dressed: 8" – $85.00; 11" – $95.00; 14" – $100.00; 19" – $200.00.
Dummy Dan: See photo for description. Original and no chips, cracks or crazing: 21" – $275.00. Light craze: $150.00.
General Douglas MacArthur: Ca. 1942. Portrait doll of all composition, painted features and molded hat. Jointed at shoulders and hips. Excellent condition and original. 18" – $200.00 up. Clothes dirty and light craze: 18" – $95.00.
Military Dolls: Ca. 1942. All composition with painted features and molded hats. Can be man or woman. In excellent condition, original and no crazing: 15" – $135.00 up. Light craze and clothes in fair condition: 15" – $85.00.

18" General Douglas MacArthur. All composition. Tag on clothes: General MacArthur. The man of the Hour by Freundlich Novelty Corp. Molded on hat. 15" "Wave" all composition. Tag: Wave by Freundlich Novelty Corp. Molded on hat. Courtesy Frasher Doll Auctions. 18" – $200.00 up; 15" – $135.00 up.

FROZEN CHARLOTTE

It is not known which came first, the ballad or the doll, but in 1865, the ballad about "Young Charlotte" was most popular. The ballad is about a vain young lady who goes to the ball, with her friend Charles, in a very light cape as she does not want to muss up her gown. The night is cold and as the sled moves through the snow young Charlotte freezes and Charles dies of a a broken heart. The entire ballad appears on Page 107 of *Antique Collector's Dolls*, Vol. I.

Frozen Charlotte and Charlie figures can be all china, partly china, such as the hair or boots, stone and fine quality porcelain. They can have molded hair, painted bald heads or take wigs. The majority have no joints with hands extended and legs separate but unjointed. They generally came without clothes and they can have painted-on boots, shoes and socks, or be bare footed.

It must be noted that in 1976 a large amount of the 15½"-16" "Charlies" were reproduced in Germany and are excellent quality. It is almost impossible to tell these are reproductions.

Prices are for dolls/figures without any damage. More must be allowed for unusual hairdos or molded eyelids.
All China: Glazed with black or blonde hair and excellent quality of painting and unjointed: 1"-2" – $25.00; 4"-6" – $65.00; 8"-10" – $135.00; 12" – $250.00. Bald

FROZEN CHARLOTTE
FULPER

head with wig, unjointed: 7" – $175.00; 10" – $235.00. Charlie: Unjointed, molded hair, pink flesh tones to head: 13" – $265.00; 16" – $375.00; 18" – $525.00.

China or "Parian": (untinted bisque): Molded hair, jointed at shoulders. Not damaged and excellent quality: 4" – $110.00; 8" – $250.00; 11" – $365.00; 14" – $500.00.

Stone Bisque: Unjointed, molded hair. No damage and medium to excellent quality of painting: 4" – $30.00; 8" – $55.00.

Stone Bisque: Jointed shoulders, molded hair and not damaged: 4" – $45.00; 8" – $70.00.

Black Charlotte or Charlie: Unjointed and no damage: 3" – $50.00; 6" – $70.00; 8" – $90.00. Jointed shoulders. No damage: 3" – $70.00; 6" – $90.00.

Molded-on Clothes or Bonnet: Unjointed, no damage and medium to excellent quality: 6" – $125.00; 9" – $165.00.

Dressed: In original clothes: Unjointed Charles or Charlotte. No damage with figure and clothes in excellent condition: 6" – $125.00; 8" – $165.00.

Jointed at shoulders: Original clothes. No damage and in excellent condition: 6" – $165.00; 8" – $260.00.

8½" Frozen Charlie. China glaze with flesh tones to head and slightly beyond neck. 13" marked Heinrich Handwerck/Halbig 2/o. Jointed body and open mouth. Courtesy Frasher Doll Auctions. 8½" – $165.00; 13" – $325.00.

Frozen Charlottes, both 3½" tall and china glazed. Blonde has finer modeling and has painted-on shoes and socks. Black hair – $65.00; Blonde – $95.00.

FULPER

The Fulper Pottery Co. made doll heads from 1918 to 1921. The heads were developed for the Horsman Doll Co. and the heads were socket heads with composition jointed bodies or they were shoulder heads with jointed kid bodies. Since the Fulper dolls are all American-made with American materials, they are sought after by the collectors of Americana, even if the quality of the heads does not match those made in Germany and France. Sample marks:

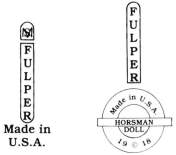

Made in U.S.A.

21″ Marked: Fulper/made in U.S.A. Five-piece bent limb baby body, open mouth with two teeth. Shown with 24″ Teddy Bear. Ca. 1920's. Grey mohair, all straw stuffed. Courtesy Frasher Doll Auctions. 21″ – $695.00; Bear – $300.00 up.

Child: Fair to medium quality bisque head painting. Open mouth. No damage, dressed ready to place into collection: Composition body: 14″ – $365.00; 16″ – $435.00; 21″ – $525.00. Kid body: 16″ – $395.00; 21″ – $495.00.

Child: Poor quality bisque (white chalky look, crooked mouth and poorly painted): Composition body: 16″ – $200.00; 21″ – $325.00. Kid body: 16″ – $185.00; 21″ – $300.00.

Baby: Bent limb baby body. Fair to medium quality bisque. Open mouth. No damage, dressed well. Good artist work on features: 18″ – $525.00; 25″ – $825.00.

Toddler: Same as for baby, but on toddler straight leg body: 18″ – $550.00; 25″ – $850.00.

Baby: Poor quality bisque and painting: 18″ – $200.00; 25″ – $450.00.

Toddler: Poor quality bisque and painting: 18″ – $250.00; 25″ – $500.00.

GANS & SEYFORTH

21½″ by Gans Seyforth. Threaded paperweight eyes, open mouth with six teeth, pierced ears, kid body with bisque lower arms. Courtesy Frasher Doll Auctions. 22″ – $395.00.

GANS & SEYFORTH
GERMAN DOLLS, MAKER UNKNOWN

Dolls marked with G & S or G.S. were made by Gans and Seyforth of Germany who operated from 1909 through the early 1930's. Some of the doll heads will be marked with their full name.

Child: Open mouth, composition jointed body. Good quality bisque, dressed and needs no repairs: 16″ – $285.00; 20″ – $350.00; 22″ – $395.00; 26″ – $450.00.
Baby: Bent limb composition baby body. In perfect condition and nicely dressed: 18″ – $495.00; 23″ – $650.00.

GERMAN DOLLS, MAKER UNKNOWN

20″ Fashion type. Marked: 912 8. Solid dome head, closed mouth, kid body with separate stitched fingers. Set eyes and original wig. Courtesy Frasher Doll Auctions. 20″ – $1,700.00.

Some of these "unmarked" dolls will be marked with a mold number and the head size number or be marked: Germany, with others marked with both.

Closed mouth child: 1880-1890's. Composition jointed body, nicely dressed and bisque head in perfect condition: 12″ – $1,000.00; 16″ – $1,400.00; 21″ – $1,800.00; 25″ – $2,000.00.

Closed mouth child: On kid body with bisque lower arms or may have cloth body: 12″ – $500.00; 16″ – $700.00; 21″ – $900.00; 25″ – $1,000.00.

Open mouth child: Late 1880's to 1900. Excellent quality pale bisque, jointed composition body and can be on kid body with bisque lower arms. Glass eyes, nicely dressed and in over all very good condition with no need for repairs: 16″ – $400.00; 21″ – $500.00; 25″ – $650.00; 29″ – $900.00.

Open mouth child from 1900 to 1920's: Composition jointed body or kid body with bisque lower arms. Excellent quality: 16″ – $275.00; 21″ – $375.00; 26″ – $575.00. Medium quality bisque and may be on papier mache′ body: 12″ – $125.00; 16″ – $225.00; 20″ – $300.00; 24″ – $375.00; 28″ – $500.00.

Babies: Solid dome or wigged, five-piece bent limb baby body, open mouth, nicely dressed and not damaged: 13″ – $425.00; 16″ – $485.00; 20″ – $600.00; 24″ – $800.00.

Tiny unmarked doll: Head is bisque and may have number or be marked Germany. On five-piece composition body, open mouth and nicely dressed: 6″ – $150.00; 10″ – $250.00. Same, but on fully jointed body: 6″ – $225.00; 10″ – $350.00.

Turned shoulder head: Cut pate or solid dome, glass eyes, kid body with bisque lower arms: Closed mouth: 18″ – $700.00; 24″ – $900.00. Open mouth: 18″ – $425.00; 24″ – $550.00.

12" Gibson Girl Fashion with bisque head, composition limbs and cloth body. Marks: "72" in green, a slight tilted "0" and a "5". Maker unknown, date Ca. 1910. Courtesy Turn of Century Antiques. 12" – $950.00 up.

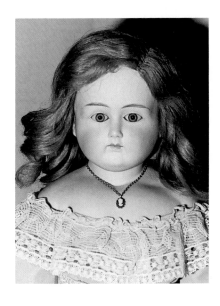

24" Slightly turned head with original wig. Her head is a dome or solidly round with not cut out pate. Closed mouth and set eyes. Unmarked. Kid body with bisque lower arms. 24" – $900.00.

18" "Gladdie" with painted ceramic head. Open/closed mouth, sleep eyes and molded hair. Marks: Gladdie/copyright by/Helen W. Jensen. 1928-1929. Ceramic painted head: 17"-18" – $975.00; Fired-in color bisque head: 17"-18" – $2,800.00 up.

GOEBEL
GOOGLY

The Goebel factory has been in operation since 1879 and is located in Oeslau, Thur, Germany. The interwoven W.G. mark has been used since 1879. William Goebel inherited the factory from his father, Granz Detley Goebel. About 1900, the factory only made dolls, doll's heads and porcelain figures. They worked in both bisque and china glazed items. The Goebel marks are:

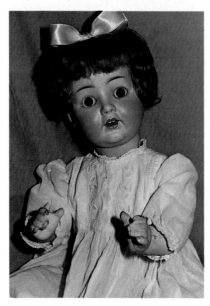

24" Marked with a crown and W over G, B5-11 ¾, Germany. Sleep eyes, open mouth with two upper teeth and on five-piece bent limb baby body. Courtesy Frasher Doll Auctions. 24" – $650.00.

Child Doll: 1895 and later. Open mouth, composition jointed body, sleep or set eyes with head in perfect condition, dressed and ready for a collection: 16" – $295.00; 20" – $395.00; 24" – $450.00.

Character: After 1910. Molded hair that can be in various styles, with or without molded flowers or ribbons, painted features and on five-piece papier mache' body. No damage and dressed to go into a collection: 6" – $325.00; 8" – $400.00.

Character Baby: After 1909. Open mouth, sleep eyes, on five-piece bent limb baby body, nicely dressed and not damaged: 14" – $365.00; 17" – $450.00; 21" – $550.00; 25" – $675.00.

GOOGLY

Bisque head with glass sleep or set eyes to side, closed smiling, impish or watermelon style mouth, original composition body. Molded hair or wigged. 1911 and after. Not damaged in any way, nicely dressed:

Armand Marseille: 200: 11" – $2,200.00. 240: 11" – $2,000.00. 241: 12" – $2,500.00. 253: 8" – $725.00; 12" – $950.00. 258: 8" – $850.00; 12" – $1,300.00. 310: Fired-in color: "Just Me": 7"-8" – $1,000.00; 12" – $1,300.00. 310 Painted bisque: 7"-8" – $500.00; 12" – $900.00. 323: 6½" – $500.00; 8" – $625.00; 12"-14" – $875.00.
Demalcol: 8" – $500.00; 11" – $650.00; 14" – $800.00.
Heubach Einco: 14" – $6,000.00.

Heubach (marked in square): 8" – $850.00; 12" – $1,400.00.
Heubach Koppelsdorf: 318: 9" – $1,200.00; 14" – $2,000.00. 319: 12" – $1,100.00. 417: 12" – $800.00.
Kestner: 165 This number now attributed to Hertel & Schwab: 12" – $3,300.00; 16" – $5,300.00. 172 & 173: attributed to Hertel & Schwab: 16" – $5,400.00. 221: 12" – $3,600.00; 16" – $5,300.00; 18" – $6,200.00.
Kammer & Reinhardt (K star R): 131: 12" – $4,000.00; 15" – $6,600.00.
P.M. (Otto Reinecke): 950: 8" – $850.00; 12" – $1,400.00.
S.F.B.J.: 245: 8" – $1,000.00; 14"-15" – $5,000.00.

Steiner, Herm: 8" – $625.00; 12" – $850.00.

All Bisque Googlies: Jointed at hips and shoulders, painted-on shoes and socks. Molded hair or wig, glass eyes, closed mouth. In perfect condition with no chips, cracks or hairlines. Nicely dressed: One-piece body and head, swivel neck, glass eyes: 5" – $625.00. Swivel neck, painted eyes: 5" – $395.00 up. Jointed knees and elbows: 5" – $1,600.00.

Composition Face: Very round composition face mask or all composition head with wig, glass eyes to side and closed impish watermelon style mouth. Body is stuffed felt. In original clothes and all in excellent condition with no crazing: 6½" – $345.00; 10"

– $525.00; 12" – $725.00. Fair condition, crazing and few cracks: 6½" – $150.00; 10" – $200.00; 12" – $350.00.

Painted Eyes: Composition or papier mache' body with painted-on shoes and socks. Bisque head with painted eyes to side, closed smile mouth and molded hair: Not damaged and nicely dressed: 8" – $400.00; 12" – $600.00.

Disc Eyes: Bisque socket or shoulder head with molded hair (can have molded cap), closed mouth and inset celluloid discs in large googly eyes: 10" – $650.00; 12"-13" – $745.00.

Molded on Hat: Marked Elite: 12" – $1,800.00.

12" Googly with molded hat. Incised: DEP. Elite U.S.1. This is "Uncle Sam" caricature in a series of WWI personalities. Glass eyes. Courtesy Frasher Doll Auctions. 12" – $1,800.00.

Front Left: 13" Googly marked: DEP. Elite. Socket head with molded military helmet with molded eagle design and point on top. Glass eyes. Center: See all bisque section. Right: 12" Googly marked: DEMALCO/-Germany. Glass eyes. Back: 19" Kestner shoulder head with closed mouth, kid body and bisque lower arms. Courtesy Frasher Doll Auctions. 12" – $650.00 up; 13" – $1,800.00; 19" – $850.00; All Bisque – $225.00.

GOOGLY

11" Googly marked: 165 2/0. Bisque head on jointed body. This googly mold has always been attributed to Kestner, but recently to Hertel & Schwab Co. by The Coleman's and the Ciesliks of Germany. 11" – $3,300.00.

12" Marked: G.B. 252/Germany/A.O.M./-DRGM. Intaglio eye googly. Mold hair in top knot. Original outfit with original price on back which was $1.25. Courtesy Henri and John Startzel. 12" – $1,400.00.

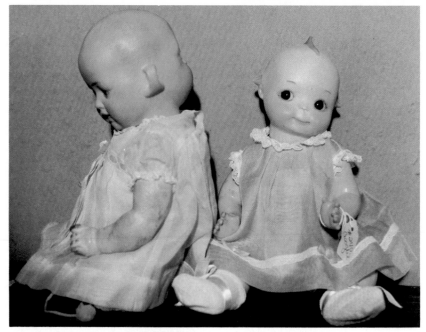

12" Two-faced bisque head baby that is unmarked. One side of head is smiling with glass eyes and other side is somber expression with painted eyes. Both sides have open/closed mouths. Painted hair and bent limb baby body made by Kley & Hahn. Right: 12" Googly with mold number 240, glass eyes and molded, tuffed hair. Courtesy Turn of Century Antiques. 2-faced doll – $765.00; 12" – $2,000.00.

7″ Googly marked: 320 A.11/0 M. Germany. Made by Armand Marseille. Intaglio eyes, closed mouth and painted hair. Toddler body with painted-on shoes. 11″ composition Rabbit by Effanbee and on a Patsy style body. Courtesy Frasher Doll Auctions. 7″ – $575.00 up; Rabbit – $185.00 up.

5½″ Black bisque Kewpie type googly. Marked: 4-0. Jointed shoulders and original. Two small child half dolls with one on right being a googly. Right: 6½″ all celluloid boy Marked: Cellbra celluloid-Warenfabric (one word). Symbol of winged mermaid. Courtesy Frasher Doll Auctions. 5½″ – $575.00 up; 6½″ – $45.00; Half dolls: Left – $100.00; Right – $250.00.

8″ Googly all composition, jointed at shoulders only. Painted hair with molded top knot. Original ribbon with label "Maiden America" and sticker on feet: Des.Pat. 8-24-15. 1915. Kate Silverman. Courtesy Sally Freeman. 8″ – $125.00.

GREINER
HALF DOLLS (PINCUSHION)

The Greiner marked dolls were made by Ludwig Greiner of Philadelphia, PA, U.S.A. These dolls were made from 1858

32" Marked: Greiner's Improved Patent Heads, Pat. March 30, 1858. Molded hair, painted features, cloth body with leather arms. Original clothes. Courtesy Frasher Doll Auctions. 32" – $1,900.00.

into the 1880's. The heads are made of papier mache' and they can be found on various bodies, such as all cloth, which are very often homemade, have leather arms and some were on the Lacmann bodies that have stitched joints at the hips and knees and are very wide at the hip line. These bodies will be marked J. Lacmann's Patent March 24th, 1874, in an oval. The Greiner heads will be marked: Greiner's Patent Doll Heads/Pat. Mar. 30 '58. Also: Greiner's/Improved/Patent Heads/Pat. March 30, '58. Also: Greiner's Patent Doll Heads/Pat. Mar. 30 '58. Ext. '72.

Greiner Doll: Can have black or blonde molded hair, blue or brown painted eyes, be on a nice homemade cloth body with cloth limbs, or a commercial cloth body with leather arms. Dressed for the period and clean with head in perfect condition with no paint chips and not repainted: With '58 label: 18" – $800.00; 22" – $1,100.00; 25" – $1,300.00; 28" – $1,600.00; 31" – $1,900.00; 35" – $2,200.00; 38" – $2,600.00. With '72 label: 18" – $425.00; 22" – $600.00; 28" – $800.00; 30" – $950.00. With either year label, head chips or repainted or small chips and not dressed well: 18" – $350.00; 23" – $575.00; 25" – $685.00; 28" – $650.00; 30" – $750.00; 35" – $900.00.

HALF DOLLS (PINCUSHION)

Half dolls can be of china, bisque, composition, papier mache' or terra-cotta. Not all were used as pincushion dolls, but for such items as lamps, cosmetic or clothes brush, tea cozies, candy boxes, powder boxes and perfume bottle tops.

Most date from 1900 on into the 1930's with the majority being made in Germany, but many made in Japan. Generally they will only carry the mark of country and/or a number. The most desirable will be marked with the company, such as William Goebel: $\underset{W}{\heartsuit}$

or Dressel, Kestner & Co.:

Company-marked half dolls often will have

the marks on the underside of the figure. (Inside).

The most desirable half dolls will have both arms molded entirely away from the body so the hands are not touching the figure at all, jointed shoulders, bald head with wigs, with animals and those of children or men.

Arms/Hands: Completely away from figure: China or bisque: 5" – $125.00; 8" – $195.00 up; 12" – $700.00 up.

Arms Extended: But hands attached to figure: China or bisque: 3" – $55.00; 5" – $62.50; 8" – $80.00. Papier mache' or composition: 4½" – $20.00; 6½" – $50.00.

Common Figures: With arms and hands attached to figure: China: 3" – $22.50; 5"

– $32.50; 8″ – $45.00. Papier mache' or composition: 3″ – $12.00; 5″ – $20.00. **Jointed Shoulders:** China, bisque: 5″ – $75.00; 8″ – $90.00; 12″ – $125.00. **Papier Mache':** 4″ – $27.50; 7″ – $65.00. **Wax over papier mache':** 4″ – $37.50; 7″ – $85.00.

Children or Men: 3″ – $35.00; 5″ – $55.00; 7″ – $85.00. Jointed shoulders: 3″ – $55.00; 5″ – $80.00; 7″ – $125.00. **Lady with Animal:** Any material: 5″ – $75.00; 8″ – $145.00. **Japan Marked:** 3″ – $15.00; 5″ – $27.50; 7″ – $40.00.

Half doll on brush made in Germany. Pierrot head with ruff around shoulder on original powder puff. 3″ Bald head with wig. 2¼″ child with molded bonnet and 5″ marked: 14753. Has both hands molded away from body. All made in Germany. Courtesy Frasher Doll Auctions. Brush – $60.00 up; Powder puff – $50.00 up; Bald head – $55.00 up; Child – $35.00 up; 5″ – $125.00.

Rear: 4″ low cut white bodice and has had yellow ribbons attached to hair. Front Left: 3¼″ large molded hat and carries a draw string purse. Right: 3½″ molded bonnet, green flowers and ribbon tie under chin, holds rose in one hand and fan in other. Incised with Goebel mark. Courtesy Frasher Doll Auctions. 3½″-4″ Arms away from body – $100.00 up; Others – $60.00 up.

HALF DOLLS (PINCUSHION)

4½" and 8½" Overall bald doll pincushion with full length legs. Arms both molded away from body. Original skirt and slip. Made in Germany. $195.00 up.

Rear Left: 3½" with hair ribbon and flowers, lavender bodice. 3½" Auburn hair and has cloth flowers attached to shoulders. Front Left: 3½" pink flowers in hair, both arms molded away from body. 3¼" pink bow in grey hair, green and white bodice, one arm molded away from body. Courtesy Frasher Doll Auctions. Arms away from body – $100.00 up; Others – $60.00 up.

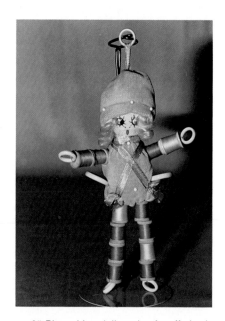

Half doll that is 3½" tall (doll only) with molded-on bonnet, flowers and gown. Marks: Germany. Is on a rolled cylinder body and dressed. 3½" – $60.00 up.

6" Pincushion doll made of stuffed velvet and tiny spools of thread. Painted face mask and mohair, celluloid rings for hands and feet. Two rings on sides held thimble and scissors. $25.00 up.

Heinrich Handwerck began in business in 1876 and located at Gotha, near Walterhausen, Germany. The company made dolls and doll bodies. Many of their heads were made by Simon & Halbig and other companies.

As early as 1891, Heinrich Handwerck had registered an 8-point star as a trademark and had registered, in Germany, such dolls as "Be'be' Cosmopolite" (1895), Be'be' Re'Clame" (1898), and "Be'be' Superior" (1913). The 1913 "Be'be' Superior" was actually made by Kammer & Reinhardt as they bought the Handwerck factory at the death of Heinrich in 1902, but continued to use the Handwerck trademarks.

In 1897 Heinrich Handwerck patented (in Germany) a ball jointed body #100297 and some of the doll bodies are so marked.

Some mold numbers from this company are: 12x, 19, 23, 69, 79, 89, 99, 100, 109, 119, 124, 125, 139, 152, 189, 199, 1200, 1290. A large number of their dolls will be marked with the makers name and no mold number. Marks used by Heinrich Handwerck are:

Child: After 1885. Open mouth, sleep or set eyes, on ball jointed body. Bisque head with no cracks, chips, good wig, nicely dressed and ready to display: 16″ – $300.00; 19″ – $425.00; 23″ – $525.00; 25″ – $600.00; 27″ – $725.00; 30″ – $900.00; 33″ – $1,300.00; 36″ – $1,700.00; 39″-40″ – $2,500.00; 42″ – $2,900.00.

42″ Heinrich Handwerck with blue sleep eyes, open mouth, pierced ears and on fully jointed composition body. Courtesy Turn of Century Antiques. 42″ – $2,900.00.

31″ Marked: 109 DEP. Handwerck. Set eyes/lashes, open mouth and on jointed body. Courtesy Frasher Doll Auctions. 31″ – $950.00.

HANDWERCK, HEINRICH
HANDWERCK, MAX

29" Marked: Handwerck 119, Germany Halbig. Sleep eyes, pierced ears, open mouth, jointed body. Courtesy Frasher Doll Auctions. 29" – $900.00.

25" Marked: Germany Heinrich Handwerck/Simon Halbig. Jointed body, open mouth, sleep eyes. Shoes marked: H. H., on soles. All original in original box. Courtesy Frasher Doll Auctions. 25" – $600.00; Original with box – $850.00.

HANDWERCK, MAX

31" Marked: Max Handwerck. Jointed body, open mouth, sleep eyes. Courtesy Frasher Doll Auctions. 31" – $1,100.00.

26½" Marked: Max Handwerck. Germany 4½. Jointed body. Sleep eyes, open mouth. Courtesy Frasher Doll Auctions. 26" – $600.00.

HANDWERCK, MAX
HARTMANN, CARL
HERTAL, SCHWAB & CO.

Max Handwerck did not enter the doll field until 1900 and his factory was located at Walterhausen, Germany. In 1901 he registered "Be'be' Elite" with these heads made by William Goebel. As for the marks on his dolls, the full name: Max Handwerck, generally was used, but some will be marked: M.H.

Child: Bisque head in perfect condition, sleep or set eyes, open mouth and on jointed composition body, dressed nicely: 16″ - $350.00; 20″ - $425.00; 24″ - $500.00; 28″ - $700.00; 32″ - $1,200.00; 36″ - $1,500.00; 40″ - $2,300.00.

Be'be' Elite: Bisque head with no cracks or chips, sleep or set eyes, open mouth, flange neck on cloth body with composition limbs: 17″ - $425.00; 21″ - $625.00. Socket head on jointed composition body: 17″ - $475.00; 21″ - $600.00.

Left: 26″ Marked: 30 K/H 3 Germany. Jointed body, set eyes, open mouth. Made by Carl Hartmann. Right: 24″ Kestner mold #154. Carl Hartmann manufactured and exported dolls from 1914 to 1926. His factory was located in Stockheim, Bavaria. Courtesy Frasher Doll Auctions. 26″ K.H. - $525.00; 24″ 154 - $600.00.

13½″ Marked: 151. Painted hair, set eyes and open mouth with molded tongue. Five-piece jointed body. This doll has always been attributed to Kestner, but now is being attributed to Hertel, Schwab & Co. Courtesy Frasher Doll Auctions. 13″ - $350.00; 17″ - $525.00.

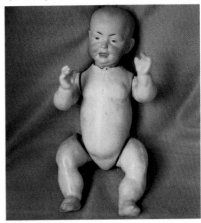

13″-14″ Bent limb baby with bisque head. Painted eyes, open/closed smiling mouth and lightly molded hair. Marks: 159-1. Made by Hertel, Schwab & Co. in 1911. This baby also comes in a two-faced version with a crying face on the other side. Courtesy Pearl Pheasant. 13″ - $325.00; 17″ - $475.00.

HEUBACH, GEBRUDER

The Heubach Brothers (Gebruder) factory was located at Lichte, Thur, Germany. The factory ran from 1863 into the 1930's. The date they initially began making dolls is not known, but it was approximately 1910 when they started producing character dolls. The company gained respect for manufacturing fine porcelain bisque pieces.

The Gebruder Heubach factory produced some very character dolls and babies with every imaginable expression that reflects almost every mood. They are generally small dolls. The Heubach dolls are often found on rather crude, poor quality bodies, but the character of the heads make up for the bodies. Marks:

Some Gebruder Heubach mold numbers: 28, 30, 37, 43, 45, 56, 58, 60, 63, 66, 68N, 69, 70, 71, 73, 74, 76, 77, 77G, 78, 79, 81, 83, 86, 87, 90, 91, 93, 94, 95, 101, 119, 122, 165, 750, 892, 0716, 0746, 1063, 1602, 3774, 4660, 5636, 5730, 5777, 6662, 6692, 6736, 6773, 6789, 6836, 6894, 6896, 6970, 7043, 7054, 7066, 7072, 7118, 7143, 7246, 7345, 7602, 7604, 7616, 7622, 7644, 7650, 7711, 7788, 7802, 7850, 7856, 7877, 7977, 8004, 8191, 8192, 8193, 8232, 8306, 8412, 8578, 8774, 9355, 9558, 9573, 10542, 10633, 96643.

Character Dolls: Bisque heads, open/closed or closed mouths, intaglio painted eyes, on kid, papier mache' or jointed composition bodies. Molded hair or wigs: **Allow more for glass eyes.** No damage to head, nicely dressed and ready to add to a collection: **5636:** Laughing Child. Intaglio eyes, jointed body: 12″ – $900.00. Glass eyes: 12″ – $1,000.00; 14″ – $1,200.00.

5689: Open mouth, smiling. 16″ – $1,400.00; 18″ – $1,600.00.

5777 & 9355: "Dolly Dimples". Ball jointed body: 16″ – $1,300.00; 22″ – $2,300.00; 24″ – $2,600.00.

5730 "Santa": Incised "Santa": 20″ – $2,500.00.

6692: Shoulder head, smiling, intaglio eyes: 15″ – $450.00.

6736: Laughing child, wide open/closed mouth, molded lower teeth: 10″-12″ – $800.00; 16″-17″ – $1,500.00.

6896: Pouty, jointed composition body: 19″ – $795.00.

6969, 6970, 7246, 7407, 8017, 8420: Pouty boy or girl (allow more for glass eyes). Composition jointed body: 12″ – $1,600.00; 16″ – $2,200.00; 20″ – $2,700.00. Toddler body: 20″ – $2,900.00.

7602: Painted hair, intaglio eyes, long face pouty, closed mouth: 16″ – $2,400.00; 20″ – $2,800.00 up.

7604: Laughing Child. Jointed body, intaglio eyes: 12″ – $400.00.

7616: Open/closed mouth with molded tongue. Socket or shoulder head. Glass eyes: 12″ – $1,000.00; 15″ – $1,400.00.

7622: Molded hair boy, intaglio eyes, closed mouth and light cheek dimples: 12″ – $650.00; 16″ – $1,000.00.

7634: Crying, squinted eyes: 14″ – $850.00.

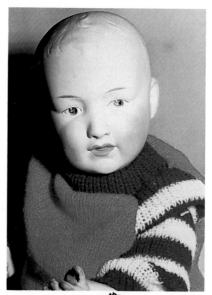

12″ Marked: 7623 H over G. Intaglio eyes, open/closed mouth and on five-piece bent limb baby body. Courtesy Frasher Doll Auctions. 12″ Baby – $650.00; 16″ Jointed body – $1,000.00.

7644: Laughing Child. Socket or shoulder head. Intaglio eyes: 14" – $500.00.

7711: Open mouth child, jointed body: 12" – $325.00; 16" – $485.00; 20" – $625.00; 24" – $850.00.

7788: "Coquette" tilted head, molded hair, can have modeled ribbon in hairdo: 12" – $700.00.

7925, 7926: Adult: 16" – $2,600.00.

7977 or 7877: "Stuart Baby". Modeled bisque bonnet: 12" – $1,100.00; 14" – $1,400.00; 16" – $1,600.00. Glass eyes: 12" – $1,500.00; 14" – $1,600.00; 16" – $1,800.00.

8191: Smiling openly, jointed body: 12" – $750.00; 14" – $875.00.

8192: Open/closed smiling mouth and molded tongue between teeth: 15" – $1,000.00; 22" – $1,900.00.

8192: Open mouth: on five-piece body: 9" – $375.00; 14" – $525.0. On jointed body: 14" – $625.00; 17" – $750.00.

8420: Glass eye pouty: 14" – $525.00; 17" – $650.00.

8774: "Whistling Jim". Eyes to side and mouth modeled as if whistling: 12" –

$900.00; 16" – $1,200.00.

9355: Shoulder head: 16" – $650.00; 22" – $1,500.00.

10586 or 10633: Child with open mouth. Jointed body: 16" – $400.00; 20" – $600.00; 25" – $825.00.

10532: Open mouth. Jointed body: 12" – $325.00.

Child with "dolly" type face: (non-character): open mouth, glass sleep or set eyes, jointed composition body, bisque head with no damage and dressed nicely and ready to place into a collection: 16" – $425.00; 19" – $595.00; 24" – $750.00.

Googly: Marked with a Heubach mark. Glass eyes: 8" – $825.00; 12" – $1,350.00.

119: Braids coiled around ears of molded hairdo, intaglio eyes: 16" – $2,200.00.

Indian Portrait: man or woman: 13" – $2,600.00.

Babies or Infants: Bisque head, wigs or molded hair, sleep or intaglio eyes, open/closed "pouty" type mouths and on bent limb bodies. May have mold numbers 7602 or 6898. 8" – $325.00; 10" – $365.00; 14" – $475.00.

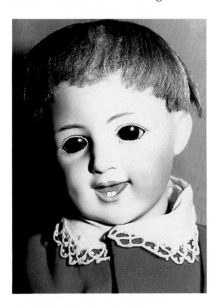

19" Marked: 6½ Heubach Sunburst mark, DEP. Germany. Open mouth with molded tongues and two lower teeth, dimples and on jointed body. Sleep eyes. Courtesy Frasher Doll Auctions. 19" – $1,700.00.

Left: 12½" Marked: 0.77 Germany. Shoulder head on kid body with open/closed mouth. Right: 14" Marked: 0 Germany 7172. Shoulder head on kid body, molded hair, closed mouth. Courtesy Frasher Doll Auctions. 12" – $700.00; 14" – $850.00.

HEUBACH, GEBRUDER

18" Marked: 5689 7 and Heubach Sunburst mark, DEP. Sleep eyes, open mouth with four teeth and on jointed body. Shown with two Heubachs marked 7602 and Heubach in square. One on sled is a candy container with cardboard body. Smaller one has painted eyes and other two have glass eyes. Courtesy Frasher Doll Auctions. 18" – $1,600.00; 12" – $475.00; Candy container – $165.00.

9½" Gebruder Heubach laughing boy with open/closed mouth and molded lower teeth, painted hair and on body with bellows to operate arms. Wire and wood lower arms and papier mache' legs. Courtesy Turn of Century Antiques. 9½" – $850.00.

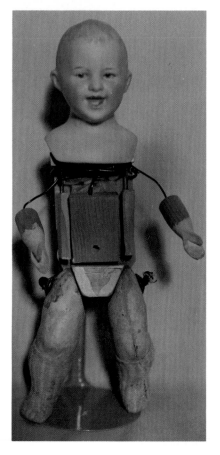

10" Marked: 7246 Germany 2 and Heubach Sunburst mark. Closed pouty mouth, painted hair and on five-piece bent limb baby body. Courtesy Frasher Doll Auctions. 10" – $325.00.

HEUBACH, GEBRUDER
HEUBACH KOPPELSDORF

12½" Marked: Heubach mark, DEP. 3 Germany 7603. Intaglio eyes, closed mouth and painted hair. Courtesy Frasher Doll Auctions. 12½" – $425.00.

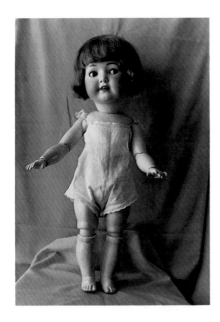

21" Marked: Heubach Koppelsdorf 321.7 Germany. Jointed toddler body, flirty eyes with tin eyelids, open mouth with two teeth, pierced nostrils. Childhood doll of Josephene Wright of Austria. 1920's. Photo by Sally Freeman. 21" – $675.00.

37" Marked: Heubach Koppelsdorf 312 SUR Germany. Sleep eyes, open mouth and on jointed body. Courtesy Frasher Doll Auctions. 37" – $1,200.00.

HEUBACH KOPPELSDORF

This company began in 1887 in Koppelsdorf, Germany. Marks from the Ernst Heubach of Koppelsdorf firm will be: E.H., the full name: Heubach Koppelsdorf or:

Some mold numbers of Heubach Koppelsdorf: 27X, 87, 99, 230, 235, 236, 237, 238, 242, 250, 251, 262, 271, 273, 275, 277, 283, 300, 302, 312, 317, 320, 321, 330, 338, 340, 342, 349, 367, 399, 407, 410, 438, 444, 450, 452, 458, 616, 1310, 1900, 1901, 1906, 1909, 2504, 2671, 2757, 3027, 3412, 3423, 3427, 7118, 32144.

Child: On kid body with bisque lower arms, bisque shoulder head, open mouth. No damage and nicely dressed. 14″ – $185.00; 20″ – $295.00; 24″ – $395.00; 30″ – $750.00.

Child: After 1885. Composition jointed body, open mouth, sleep or set eyes. No damage and nicely dressed. 8″ – $125.00; 10″ – $150.00; 14″ – $245.00; 20″ – $345.00; 24″ – $450.00; 30″ – $750.00; 34″ – $900.00; 38″ – $1,200.00.

Babies: 1910 and after. On five-piece bent limb baby body, open mouth with some having a wobbly tongue and pierced nostrils. Sleep eyes. No damage and nicely dressed. 9″ – $225.00; 12″ – $325.00; 16″ – $425.00; 20″ – $525.00; 26″ – $750.00.

Babies on Toddler Bodies: Same as above but with toddler body: 14″ – $525.00; 16″ – $585.00; 20″ – $650.00; 26″ – $850.00.

Infant: 1925. Molded or painted hair, sleep eyes, closed mouth, flange neck bisque head on cloth body with composition or celluloid hands. No damage and nicely dressed:

Mold 338: 12″ – $500.00; 14″ – $700.00.

399 (white only): 12″ – $285.00.

340: 12″ – $525.00; 15″ – $725.00.

349: 12″ – $450.00.

350: 14″ – $600.00.

Infant: Same as above but with fired-in tan or brown color: 12″ – $395.00; 14″ – $485.00.

Mold 452: Tan/brown bisque head and same color toddler body, open mouth and sleep or set eyes. Molded, painted hair. Ear-

25″ Marked: Heubach 302.7 Koppelsdorf/Germany. Sleep eyes, open mouth and on jointed body. Courtesy Frasher Doll Auctions. 25″ – $465.00.

24″ Marked: Heubach Koppelsdorf 320.8 Germany. On five-piece toddler body, open mouth and sleep eyes. Courtesy Frasher Doll Auctions. 24″ – $650.00.

rings. No damage and originally dressed or re-dressed nicely: 12" – $425.00.

Black or Dark Brown: Mold 320, 339, 399: Painted bisque head, on painted black or dark brown five-piece straight leg baby or toddler cut body. Sleep eyes, molded, painted hair or wig. No damage and very minimum amount of paint pulls (chips) on back of head with none on face : 10" – $350.00; 12" – $400.00; 16" – $600.00; 20" – $800.00; 22" – $1,000.00.

Character Child: 1910. Molded hair, painted eyes and open/closed mouth. No damage and nicely dressed. Mold 262, 330 and others: 12" – $425.00; 16" – $700.00.

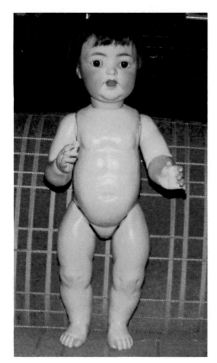

27½" Marked: Heubach Koppelsdorf 342. Five-piece toddler body. Sleep eyes and open mouth with two upper teeth. Courtesy Jeannie Mauldin. 28" – $850.00.

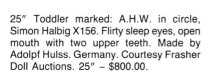

25" Toddler marked: A.H.W. in circle, Simon Halbig X156. Flirty sleep eyes, open mouth with two upper teeth. Made by Adolpf Hulss. Germany. Courtesy Frasher Doll Auctions. 25" – $800.00.

JULLIEN
JUMEAU

Jullien marked dolls were made in Paris, France, from 1875 to 1904. The heads will be marked: Jullien and a size number. In 1892 Jullien advertised L'Universal and the label can be found on some of his doll bodies.

Child: Closed mouth, paperweight eyes, French jointed composition/papier mache' body (some may have wooden parts also).

Undamaged bisque head with clean unbroken body and all in excellent condition, nicely dressed: 18" – $3,100.00; 20" – $3,300.00; 24" – $3,600.00; 28" – $3,900.00.

Child: Same as above, but with open mouth: 18" – $1,800.00; 20" – $2,000.00; 24" – $2,400.00; 28" – $2,700.00.

23" Incised: Jullien/8. Paperweight eyes with heavy painted upper and lower lashes, open mouth and on early French body with pull strings for "MaMa-PaPa" talker. Courtesy Turn of Century Antiques. 23" – $3,500.00.

JUMEAU

Te'te' Jumeau: 1879-1899 and later. Marked with red stamp on head and oval sticker on body: Be'be' Jumeau. Closed mouth, paperweight eyes, composition body with full joints or jointed but with straight wrists. Pierced ears with extra large sizes having applied ears. No damage at all to bisque head, undamaged French body, dressed and ready to place into a collection: 10" – $2,000.00; 12" – $2,000.00; 14" – $2,300.00; 16" – $2,600.00; 19" – $2,900.00; 21" – $3,200.00; 23" – $3,500.00; 25" – $3,600.00; 28" – $4,400.00; 30" – $5,100.00.

Te'te' Jumeau: Same as above but with open mouth: 10" – $995.00; 14" – $1,400.00; 16" – $1,600.00; 19" – $1,900.00; 21" – $2,100.00; 23" – $2,300.00; 25" – $2,500.00; 28" – $2,800.00; 30" – $3,000.00.

1907 Jumeau: Incised 1907 and sometimes has "Te'te' Jumeau" stamp. Sleep or set eyes, open mouth, jointed composition body. No damage and ready to display: 14" – $1,100.00; 17" – $1,500.00; 20" – $1,800.00; 25" – $2,300.00; 28" – $2,800.00; 32" – $3,200.00.

E.J. Child: Ca. early 1880's. Head incised

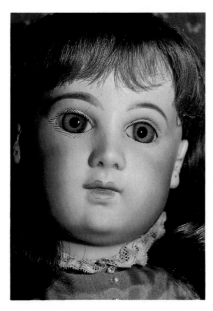

17" Marked: 8, on head and Bebe Jumeau Diplome d'Honner, on body sticker. Called a "Portrait Jumeau". Jointed body, applied ears, closed mouth. Courtesy Frasher Doll Auctions. 17" – $5,000.00.

24" "Portrait" Jumeau marked: 10, on head. Body marked: Jumeau Medaille d'or, stamped in blue. Applied ears, closed mouth, jointed body with straight wrists. Courtesy Frasher Doll Auctions. 24" – $6,200.00.

19" Te'te' Jumeau with lady body. Body stamped in blue on back. Closed mouth, pierced ears, tiny waist and pronounced derriere. Courtesy Frasher Doll Auctions. 19" – $5,000.00.

Shows back side of Te'te' Jumeau lady doll.

JUMEAU

21" "Triste" Long Face Jumeau. Marked: 10, on head and on marked Jumeau body with straight wrists. "Triste" in French means: downcast, doleful, sad which does not really describe long face Jumeau. 21" – $10,000.00 up.

24" Marked: 11, on head along with red artist marks. Jointed body marked: Jumeau Medaille d'or Paris. Closed mouth. 22" "Long Face Jumeau" (Triste Bebe) marked: 10, on head and stamped on body: Bebe Jumeau Diplome d'Honneur. Courtesy Frasher Doll Auctions. 22" – $10,000.00; 24" – $3,200.00 up.

De′pose′/E.J. Paperweight eyes, closed mouth, jointed composition body with unjointed (straight) wrists. Larger size dolls will have applied ears. No damage on head or body, excellent quality clothes: 10" – $3,900.00; 14" – $4,900.00; 16" – $5,000.00; 19" – $5,600.00; 21" – $6,200.00; 25" – $7,000.00.

De′pose′-Jumeau: (incised): 1880. Head will be incised Jumeau/De′pose′ and doll should have sticker on body: Bebe Jumeau. Closed mouth, paperweight eyes and on jointed composition body with straight wrists mostly. No damage at all and nicely dressed ready to display. 15" – $3,500.00; 18" – $4,300.00; 22" – $4,800.00; 25" – $6,000.00.

Long Face (Triste Jumeau): 1870's. Closed mouth, applied ears, paperweight eyes and on jointed composition body with straight wrists. Head generally marked with size number only and body will have label Jumeau sticker. The French word "triste" being used to describe a "Long Face" Jumeau actually means, in French, "Sad, sorrowful, mournful, downcast, moping, woeful, gloomy", etc. This would indicate a pouty, sad looking doll, which they are not, but the American slang for the same French ones would be "Long Face". So therefore the use of the word "triste" came into being. No damage to head and body and nicely dressed ready to display: 20"-21" – $10,000.00 up; 29"-30" – $13,000.00 up.

Portrait Jumeau: 1870's. Closed mouth, usually large almond-shaped paperweight eyes and jointed composition body with straight wrists. Head marked with size number only and body with Jumeau stamp or label: 12" – $4,000.00; 16" – $5,000.00; 20" – $5,600.00; 24" – $6,200.00.

Phonograph in Jumeau body: Bisque head with open mouth. No damage, working and nicely dressed ready to display: 20" – $2,800.00; 25" – $3,200.00.

Wire Eye (Flirty) Jumeau: Lever in back of head operates eyes. Open mouth, jointed composition body with straight wrists: 20" – $5,200.00; 24" – $5,600.00.

Celluloid Head: Incised Jumeau: 14" – $495.00.

Mold Number 200: Series with very character faces. Marked Jumeau. No

24″ Jumeau marked: 1907. Open mouth and body is marked with a blue Jumeau label. Courtesy Frasher Doll Auctions. 24″ – $2,200.00.

21″ Marked: Te'te' Jumeau with open mouth and on jointed composition marked Jumeau body with pull strings for "MaMa-PaPa" talker. Courtesy Turn of Century Antiques. 21″ – $2,100.00.

24″ Jumeau 1895 Walker, head turns, talker (Ma-Ma) in body, arm raises to blow a kiss. Open mouth and fully marked. Courtesy Turn of Century Antiques. 24″ – $2,400.00.

JUMEAU
KAMMER & REINHARDT

damage to bisque head or composition body: 19″ – $10,000.00 up.
S.F.B.J. or Unis: Marked along with Jumeau: Open mouths. No damage to head or composition jointed body: 16″ – $900.00 up; 20″ – $1,200.00 up. Closed mouth: 16″ – $1,400.00; 20″ – $1,700.00.
Two Faced Jumeau: Has two different faces, one crying and one smiling, heads turn with knob on top usually covered with lacy hood. Open/closed mouths, jointed composition body. No damage and nicely dressed: 14″ – $7,800.00.
Fashion: (also see "Fashion" section): Bisque shoulder head on bisque shoulder plate (jointed neck), all kid and leather body or will have bisque lower limbs. Head generally marked with size number and kid body may have a Jumeau stamp. No damage and dressed as lady and ready to display: 14″

– $2,100.00; 18″ – $3,200.00; 21″ – $4,400.00; 28″ – $5,000.00.
Composition Lady body: Marked Te'te' Jumeau on head. No damage and beautifully dressed: 18″ – $4,800.00; 21″ – $5,400.00.
Mold 221: Ca. 1930's. These small dolls (10″) will also have a paper label: Jumeau. Adult style bisque head on five-piece body and painted-on shoes. Closed mouth and set glass eyes. Dressed in original ornate long gowns. No damage to head or body: 10″ – $500.00.
Mold 306: Jumeau made after formation of Unis and mark will be: Unis/France in oval with 71 on one side and 149 on other, followed by 306/Jumeau/1938/Paris. Called "Princess Elizabeth". Closed mouth, paperweight or flirty eyes, jointed composition body. No damage and dressed ready to go into a collection: 20″ – $1,350.00.

KAMMER & REINHARDT

Kammer & Reinhardt dolls often have the Simon & Halbig name or initials along with their own mark, as a great number of heads were made for them. They were located in Walterhausen, Thur, Germany and began in 1895 although their first models were not on the market until 1896. The trademark of this company was registered in 1895. Marks:

S & H
126

Character Boy or Girl: Mold 101: Closed mouth, painted eyes, on jointed composition body or five-piece body. No damage, clean and nicely dressed: 8″-9″ – $1,100.00; 14″ – $1,800.00; 17″ – $3,000.00; 21″ – $3,300.00. *Mold 101:* Glass Eyes. Closed mouth and on fully jointed body. No damage and dressed: 16″ – $4,000.00; 21″ – $4,500.00. *Mold 102:* Very rare character child. No damage to head or body: 12″ – $8,400.00; 14″ – $8,800.00. *Mold 103 or 104:* Extremely rare. No damage to head or body: 17″ –

$14,000.00. *Mold 107:* Pursed closed mouth, intaglio eyes. No damage to head or body: 15″ – $6,400.00; 21″ – $8,600.00. *Mold 109:* Closed mouth, intaglio eyes and on fully jointed body. No damage and nicely dressed: 14″ – $5,800.00; 19″ – $7,300.00. *Mold 109:* Glass Eyes: 20″ – $12,000.00; 25″ – $18,000.00. *Mold 112, 112x, 112a:* Closed mouth, intaglio eyes, jointed body. No damage and nicely dressed: 14″ – $5,600.00; 19″ – $8,000.00; 22″ – $10,000.00. *Mold 112, 112x, 112a:* Glass Eyes: 16″ – $7,800.00; 22″ – $10,000.00 up. *Mold 114:* Intaglio eyes, painted eyes, closed mouth and on five-piece or fully jointed body. No damage and nicely dressed: 8″ – $1,200.00; 14″ – $2,600.00; 18″ – $3,900.00. *Mold 114:* Glass Eyes: 18″ – $6,000.00; 23″ – $6,500.00. *Mold 117a, 117:* Glass eyes, closed mouth, on fully jointed body or small sizes on five-piece body. No damage to head or body and nicely dressed: 14″ – $2,500.00; 16″ – $3,200.00; 18″ – $3,800.00; 24″ – $4,800.00; 28″ – $6,500.00. *Mold 117, 117x:* Open Mouth: 16″ – $1,600.00; 20″ – $2,100.00; 24″ – $2,800.00; 28″ – $3,400.00. *Mold 117n:* Open mouth and flirty eyes. Fully jointed body. No damage to head or eye mechanism, good body and nicely dressed: 16" – $900.00; 20" – $1,600.00; 26" – $2,200.00; 32" – $2,900.00. *Mold 127:* Molded hair, open/closed mouth. Toddler or jointed body: 16" – $875.00; 20" – $1,300.00. **Character Babies:** Open/closed, closed mouths on five-piece bent limb baby body. Solid dome with painted hair or wigs. No damage to head and body in excellent condition. Nicely dressed and ready to display: *Mold 100:* Called "Kaiser Baby". Intaglio eyes, open/closed mouth: 10" – $475.00; 16" – $685.00; 18" – $900.00. *Mold 100:* Glass Eyes. Wig: 16" – $1,600.00; 18" – $1,900.00. *Mold 100:* Black or tan: 10" – $950.00; 16" – $1,300.00. *Mold 115, 115a:* 15" – $2,500.00; 18" – $3,500.00; 22" – $4,000.00. Toddler body: 15" – $3,200.00; 18" – $4,200.00; 22" – $5,000.00; 26" – $6,300.00. *Mold 116, 116a:* 15" – $2,000.00; 18" – $2,300.00; 22" – $2,900.00. Toddler body: 15" – $2,400.00; 18" – $2,800.00; 22" – $3,300.00. *Mold 116, 116a:* Open Mouth: 15" – $1,300.00; 18" – $1,900.00. Toddler *mold 119:* 25"

– $3,400.00. *Mold 123, #124:* Add more for flirty eyes: 16" – $8,200.00; 20" – $10,000.00. Toddler: 16" – $9,200.00; 20" – $10,500.00. *Mold 127:* 12" – $800.00; 16" – $1,000.00; 20" – $1,300.00. **Character Babies:** Open mouth, sleep eyes on five-piece bent limb baby body. Wigs, may have tremble tongue or "mama" cryer box in body. No damage to head or body. Nicely dressed. Allow more for flirty eyes. *Mold 121:* 14" – $600.00; 18" – $850.00; 22" – $995.00. Toddler: 14" – $850.00; 18" – $1,100.00; 22" – $1,500.00. *Mold 122, 128:* 15" – $700.00; 18" – $825.00; 22" – $975.00; 26" – $1,400.00. Add more for toddler. *Mold 126:* 12" – $425.00; 15" – $500.00; 20" – $675.00; 25" – $900.00; 31" – $1,800.00. Toddler: 8" – $375.00; 15" – $650.00; 20" – $875.00; 25" – $1,400.00. *Mold 118a:* 16" – $1,600.00; 20" – $2,000.00. *Mold 135:* 16" – $1,200.00; 20" – $1,600.00. **Child Dolls:** 1895-1930's. Open mouth, sleep or set eyes and on fully jointed composition body. No damage to head or body and nicely dressed. Most often found mold numbers are 400, 403, 109, etc. Add more for flirty eyes: 16" – $500.00; 18" –

16" Large size rare glass eyes. Mold #112. Marked: K star R 112. Open/closed mouth with molded teeth on jointed body and has original wig. Courtesy Frasher Doll Auctions. 16" – $7,800.00.

8" Marked: K star R 109. Composition body, painted eyes and closed pouty mouth. Courtesy Frasher Doll Auctions. 8" – $4,000.00.

KAMMER & REINHARDT

21" Marked: K star R/Simon Halbig 117N Germany. Flirty sleep eyes, open mouth and on jointed body. Courtesy Frasher Doll Auctions. 21" – $1,700.00.

14" Marked: K star R 114. Closed pouty mouth, painted eyes with original wig and on jointed body. Courtesy Turn of Century Antiques. 14" – $2,600.00.

21" "Marie" marked: K star R 101. Painted eyes, closed pouty mouth and shown with 7½" "Marie" 101 and 7½" "Hans" boy with mold number 114. Both are in original clothes. Courtesy Frasher Doll Auctions. 21" – $3,300.00; 7½" 101 – $1,100.00; 7½" 114 – $1,200.00.

28½" Marked: Simon Halbig, K star R. Open mouth with four teeth, pierced ears and sleep eyes. 11" "Kaiser Baby" marked: K star R 100. Open/closed mouth and painted eyes. Courtesy Frasher Doll Auctions. 29" – $900.00; 11" – $485.00.

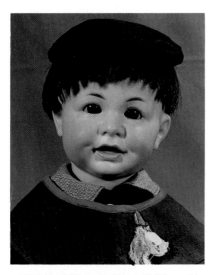

16" Marked: K star R, Simon Halbig, 116A. Open/closed mouth, sleep eyes and on toddler body. Courtesy Henri and John Startzel. 16" – $2,400.00.

22" Baby marked: K star R, Simon Halbig 22. Five-piece bent limb baby, open mouth with 2 upper teeth and sleep eyes/lashes. Courtesy Frasher Doll Auctions. 22" – $700.00.

$575.00; 22" – $725.00; 26" – $825.00; 30" – $975.00; 33" – $1,500.00; 36" – $1,900.00; 38" – $2,300.00; 42" – $2,500.00. Mold 192: Closed mouth, sleep eyes, fully jointed composition body. Nicely dressed, no chips, breaks, cracks or hairlines: 14"-15" – $1,200.00; 21" – $1,800.00. Mold 192: Open mouth, on fully jointed body with sleep or set eyes: 7" – $375.00; 16" – $575.00; 22" – $850.00; 26" – $1,100.00.

Small Child Dolls: Open mouth, sleep or set eyes and on five-piece body. No damage and nicely dressed: 5" – $225.00; 8"-9" – $325.00.

Small Child Dolls: Closed mouth: 6"-7" – $375.00; 9" – $425.00.

Googly: Mold 131. Glass eyes, closed smile mouth and on five-piece body or fully jointed body. No damage and nicely dressed: 12" – $4,000.00; 15" – $6,600.00; 17" – $7,200.00.

Celluloid: Babies will have kid, kidaleen or cloth bodies. Child doll will have fully jointed composition bodies. Open mouths. Some mold numbers: 225, 255, 321, 406, 717, 826, 828, etc.: Babies: 15" – $425.00; 20" – $600.00. Child: 16" – $475.00; 20" – $650.00.

16" Marked: K star R/Simon Halbig 126. Flirty eyes, open mouth with two teeth and on bent limb baby body. Courtesy Frasher Doll Auctions. 16" – $575.00.

KAMMER & REINHARDT
KESTNER, J.D.

18½" Baby marked: K star R, Simon Halbig 121. Open mouth with two teeth, deep dimples and sleep eyes. Courtesy Frasher Doll Auctions. 19" – $875.00.

20" Kammer and Reinhardt mold number 126. Tremble tongue, sleep eyes, original wig and has a mechanism so that when laid down the eyes can remain open. Courtesy Turn of Century Antiques. 20" – $675.00.

KESTNER, J.D.

The Johannes Daniel Kestner firm was founded in 1802 and his name was carried through the 1920's. The Kestner Company was one of the few that made entire dolls, heads and bodies. It was in 1895 that Kestner started using the trademark of the crown and streamers found on some bodies. Most Kestner dolls are marked with both a letter and a number and some of these also will have a mold number and/or the initials J.D.K. (Samples: G-11, M-16, D-8). Sample marks:

B Made in 6
GERMANY
J.D.K.
126

F Germany K

Some Kestner mold numbers: 117, 127, 128, 128x, 129, 135, 137, 139, 140, 142, 143, 144, 146, 147, 148, 150, 151, 152, 153, 154, 155, 156, 157, 158, 160, 161, 162, 163, 164, 165, 166, 167, 168, 169, 170, 171, 172, 173, 174, 176, 178, 180, 182, 183, 184, 185, 186, 187, 188, 189, 190, 193, 194, 195, 196, 200, 211, 212, 213, 214, 215, 216, 217, 219, 220, 221, 226, 230, 234, 235, 237, 238, 241, 243, 245, 249, 252, 255, 257, 259, 260, 261, 262, 263, 264, 268, 270, 272, 280, 286, 319, 518, 639, 920, 1070, 1080, 1914.

Child Doll: Ca. 1880. Closed mouth, some appear to be pouties, sleep or set eyes, composition jointed body with straight wrists. No damage and nicely dressed to add to collection: *Mold X:* 14" – $1,500.00; 17" – $1,900.00; 20" – $2,200.00; 24" – $2,500.00. *Mold XI:* 14" – $1,600.00; 17" – $2,000.00; 20" – $2,400.00; 24" – $2,800.00. *Mold 128x or 169:* 14" – $1,500.00; 17" – $1,900.00; 20" – $2,200.00; 24" – $2,500.00; 28" – $2,800.00.

Turned Shoulder Head: Ca. 1880's. Closed mouth. Set or sleep eyes, on kid body with bisque lower arms. Both head and body undamaged and nicely dressed: 17" – $800.00; 20" – $950.00; 24" – $1,200.00.

Turned Shoulder Head: Ca. 1880's. Same as above but with open mouth: 17" – $465.00; 20" – $595.00; 24" – $700.00; 31" – $1,000.00.

Character Child: 1910 and after. Closed mouth or open/closed mouth (unless noted). Glass or painted eyes, on jointed composition body. Plaster pate, good wig and no damage to head or body. Nicely dressed: *Mold 208:* Painted eyes: 12" – $1,600.00; 17" – $2,900.00. *Mold 212:* Glass eyes: 14" – $2,000.00; 17" – $3,200.00; 20" – $3,600.00. Painted eyes: 14" – $1,600.00; 17" – $2,900.00. *Mold 224:* 16" – $550.00. *Mold 241:* Open mouth, glass eyes: 16" – $2,200.00; 20" – $3,600.00. *Mold 249:* 20" – $1,200.00. *Mold 260:* On toddler body: 12" – $625.00; 16" – $750.00; 20" – $950.00.

Character Dolls: Boxed set with four heads and one body. 11"-12". Usually has one head with open mouth and three with closed mouths and painted eyes. All heads in perfect condition, no damage to body and one outfit: Boxed set: 11"-12" – $6,400.00; 16"-18" – $8,000.00. Extra heads with painted eyes on old bodies and no damage to either. *Mold numbers: 175, 176, 177, 178, 179, 180, 182, 184, 185, 186, 190, 208, 212, etc.:* 11"-12" – $1,600.00. Same mold number in larger sizes. Painted eyes, closed or open/closed mouths: 16" – $2,300.00; 18" – $3,000.00. Same mold number with Glass Eyes: 12" – $2,000.00; 16" – $2,800.00; 18" – $3,500.00.

Child Doll: Late 1880's to 1930's. Open mouth, on fully jointed composition body, plaster pate (if original), sleep eyes, some set, not damaged in any way (head or body) and nicely dressed. *Mold numbers: 129, 142, 144, 145, 146, 147, 152, 156, 159, 160, 162, 164, 166, 167, 168, 174, 195, 196, 214, 215, etc.:* 14" – $400.00; 17" – $475.00; 20" – $525.00; 26" – $700.00; 30" – $1,000.00; 36" – $1,600.00; 42" – $2,500.00. *Mold 143:* 12" – $565.00; 17" – $750.00; 20" – $975.00. *Mold 192:* 14" – $400.00; 17" – $500.00; 20" – $600.00.

Child Doll: Open mouth, sleep or set eyes, bisque shoulder head on kid body with bisque lower arms. No damage to head or body and nicely dressed. Includes *mold numbers 147, 148, 149, 166, 195, etc.* Add more for fur brow. 17" – $425.00; 20" – $500.00; 26" – $700.00; 30" – $950.00. *Mold 154 and 171:* Most often found mold numbers. Open mouth and sleep or set eyes. No damage and nicely dressed. Jointed composition body: 15" – $375.00; 18" – $450.00; 22" – $525.00; 27" – $750.00; 32" – $1,000.00; 40" – $2,100.00. Kid body with bisque lower arms: 15" – $350.00; 18" – $425.00; 22" – $500.00; 27" – $695.00; 32" – $950.00; 40" – $1,800.00.

Character Babies: 1910 and after on five-piece bent limb baby body, sleep or set eyes, open mouth and can be wigged, solid domed with painted hair or lightly molded hair. Head and body not damaged and nicely dressed. *Mold 121, 142, 150, 151, 152:* 12" – $400.00; 16" – $550.00; 20" – $650.00; 25" – $900.00. *Mold 211, 226, 260:* 10" – $350.00; 12" – $450.00; 16" – $550.00;

25" Marked: 11, closed mouth shoulder head with set eyes, kid body with bisque lower arms. Courtesy Frasher Doll Auctions. 25" – $2,500.00.

KESTNER, J.D.

20″ Marked: F made in Germany 10 169. Closed mouth, sleep eyes and on jointed body. Courtesy Frasher Doll Auctions. 20″ – $2,200.00.

32″ Marked: 14 166 K made in Germany. Kestner paper label on front shoulder plate. Cloth/kid body with bisque lower arms. Courtesy Frasher Doll Auctions. 32″ – $1,000.00.

12″ Kestner marked: G. 3. 208. Painted eyes, closed mouth and original wig. Jointed body and wears original chemise. Courtesy Frasher Doll Auctions. 12″ – $1,600.00 up.

20″ – $775.00; 24″ – $1,100.00. *Mold 220:* Baby or Toddler body: 16″ – $2,400.00; 18″ – $2,700.00. *Mold 234, 235, 238:* 16″ – $575.00; 20″ – $750.00; 24″ – $900.00. *Mold 237, 245, 1070 (Hilda)* wigged or solid dome: 12″ – $1,700.00; 16″ – $2,700.00; 20″ – $3,200.00; 23″ – $4,400.00. Toddler: 16″ – $3,300.00; 20″ – $3,700.00; 23″ – $4,600.00. *Mold 239:* 12″ – $450.00; 16″ – $575.00. *Mold 247:* 16″ – $825.00; 18″ – $1,400.00; 21″ – $1,800.00; 25″ – $2,200.00. *Mold 257:* 14″ – $485.00; 18″ – $725.00; 21″ – $800.00; 25″ – $1,000.00. Marked: J.D.K. Baby, solid domed, painted eyes and open mouth: 15″ – $775.00; 20″ – $995.00; 24″ – $1,400.00. **Adult:** Mold 162: Sleep eyes, open mouth, adult jointed composition body (thin waist and molded breasts) with slender limbs. No damage to head or body and dressed nicely as lady: 16″ – $1,000.00; 18″-19″ – $1,200.00; 22″ – $1,500.00. Mold 172: "Gibson Girl". Bisque shoulder head with closed mouth, kid body with bisque lower arms, glass eyes. Undamaged head and body. Dressed as lady and ready to display: 12″ – $1,300.00; 17″ – $2,600.00; 21″ – $3,500.00.

Oriental: Mold 243: Olive fired-in color to bisque, matching color five-piece bent limb baby body (or jointed toddler style body). Wig, sleep or set eyes. No damage to head

nor body and dressed in Oriental style outfit: 14″ – $2,400.00; 18″ – $2,900.00.

Small Dolls: Open mouths, five-piece or jointed bodies, wigs, sleep or set eyes. Dressed ready to display and no damage to head or body: 7″ – $250.00; 9″ – $325.00.

17″ "Gibson Girl" by Kestner and marked: 172. Closed mouth and sleep eyes. Adult body. Courtesy Frasher Doll Auctions. 17″ – $2,600.00.

19″ Marked: C made in Germany 129. Sleep eyes, open mouth with four teeth and on jointed body. Courtesy Frasher Doll Auctions. 19″ – $500.00.

20″ Marked: E made in Germany 9 167. Sleep eyes, open mouth and on jointed body. Courtesy Frasher Doll Auctions. 20″ – $525.00.

KESTNER, J.D.

32″ Marked: N½ made in Germany 196. Jointed body, sleep eyes, open mouth with four teeth and has fur eyebrows. Courtesy Frasher Doll Auctions. 32″ – $1,200.00.

24″ Marked: made in Germany Z.J.D.KZ. 226. Open mouth with two teeth, sleep eyes and on five-piece bent limb baby body. Courtesy Frasher Doll Auctions. 24″ – $1,100.00.

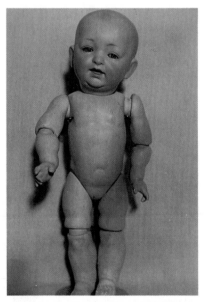

10½″ Incised: JDK toddler. Painted hair and sleep eyes. An adorable tiny size. Courtesy Turn of Century Antiques. 10½″ – $495.00.

15″ Marked: made in Germany 11-247-J.D.K. Sleep eyes, open mouth with two small upper teeth. All original. Courtesy Henri and John Startzel. 15″ – $800.00.

21″ Marked: Hilda J.D.K. Jr. 1914. ges gesch 1070. Made in Germany. Open mouth, sleep eyes and on five-piece bent limb baby body. Courtesy Frasher Doll Auctions. 21″ – $3,300.00 up.

21″ Marked: JDK 211 made in Germany. Sleep eyes, open mouth and on five-piece bent limb baby body. Courtesy Frasher Doll Auctions. 21″ – $800.00.

KEWPIE

All prices for dolls that have no chips, hairlines or breaks. (See Modern section for composition and vinyl Kewpies). Designed by Rose O'Neill and marketed from 1913. Labels:

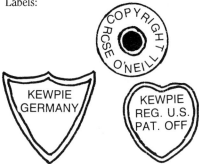

All Bisque: One-piece body and head, jointed shoulders only. Blue wings, painted features with eyes to side. 1½″ – $65.00;

2½″ – $95.00; 4″-5″ – $125.00; 6″ – $150.00; 7″ – $225.00; 9″ – $350.00.
All Bisque: Jointed at hips and shoulders: 4″ – $400.00; 9″ – $650.00.
Shoulder Head: Cloth body: 6″ – $450.00.
Action Kewpie: Confederate Soldier: 3½″ – $285.00. Farmer: 4″ – $400.00. Gardner: 4″ – $400.00. Governor: 3½″ – $350.00. Groom with Bride: 4″ – $400.00. Guitar Player: 3½″ – $300.00. Holding pen: 3″ – $350.00. Huggers: 3½″ – $200.00. On Stomach: 4″ – $400.00. Thinker: 4″ – $365.00; 6″ – $475.00. Traveler: 3½″ – $300.00. With Broom: 4″ – $350.00. With Cat: 3½″ – $350.00. With Dog (Doodle): 3½″ – $700.00. With Helmet: 6″ – $550.00. With Outhouse: 2½″ – $850.00. With Rabbit: 2½″ – $275.00. With Rose: 2″ – $265.00. With Teddy Bear: 4″ – $600.00. With Turkey: 2″ – $350.00; With Umbrella and Dog:

KEWPIE

4½" to 9" All bisque kewpies. Jointed at shoulders only. Courtesy Frasher Doll Auctions. 4½" – $125.00; 6" – $150.00 up; 7" – $225.00 up; 9" – $350.00; 10" – $400.00.

7½" All bisque "Kewpie" signed O'Neill on foot and 5" with the original sticker on chest. Both jointed at shoulders only. Courtesy Turn of Century Antiques. 5" – $125.00 up; 7½" – $225.00 up.

3" "Action Kewpie" holding pen and sitting on tray. Both tray and Kewpie are bisque. Courtesy Frasher Doll Auctions. 3" – $350.00 up.

3½" – $750.00. Kewpie soldier with nurse: 6" – $1,200.00 up. In basket with flowers: 3½" – $365.00. With draw string bag: 4½" – $425.00. Button Hole Kewpie: $165.00. Kewpie Doodledog: 1½" – $350.00; 3" – $600.00. Hottentot. Black Kewpie: 3½" – $300.00; 5" – $375.00; 9" – $850.00. Perfume Bottle: 3½" – $450.00. Pincushion: 2½" – $225.00.

Celluloid Kewpie: 2" – $32.00; 5" – $50.00; 9" – $120.00; Black: 5" – $125.00.

Cloth Body Kewpie: With bisque head, painted eyes: 12" – $1,600.00. With glass eyes: 12" – $2,500.00.

Glass Eye Kewpie: On chubby toddler, jointed body. Bisque head. Marks: Ges. Gesch./O'Neill J.D.K.: 10" – $2,300.00; 12" – $3,800.00; 16" – $6,000.00 up.

All Cloth: (made by Kreuger) All one-piece with body forming clothes, mask face: (Mint): 12" – $125.00; 16" – $165.00; 20" – $385.00; 25" – $685.00. All cloth: Same as above, but with original dress and bonnet: (Mint): 12" – $150.00; 16" – $225.00; 20" – $485.00; 25" – $785.00 up.

Composition: Jointed shoulders only: 9" – $75.00; 14" – $125.00. Jointed neck, hips & shoulders: 9" – $100.00; 14" – $200.00.

Left to Right: 3½" All bisque Kewpie Traveler signed: O'Neill. 4¾" bisque Soldier signed on foot. Arm bent and holds American flag. 3½" Kewpie Huggers. All molded in one-piece. Courtesy Frasher Doll Auctions. Traveler – $300.00; Soldier – $550.00; Huggers – $200.00.

Left to Right: 2½" Celluloid marked: 10/9. Molded in one-piece with original crepe paper clothes. 2½" Celluloid minister/priest. Molded in one-piece, painted on glasses & original. 2½" Celluloid Santa Claus & Mrs. Claus. Both marked and original. 2¾" Soldier of celluloid. Made in Japan. 4½" Celluloid with label, jointed arms and Turtle Mark on back. 9" All composition with label. Kewpie card marked: 1915 Campbell Art Co. Courtesy Frasher Doll Auctions. 2½"-3" Celluloid – $32.00-70.00; 9" Composition (Fair condition) – $75.00; Card – $20.00 up.

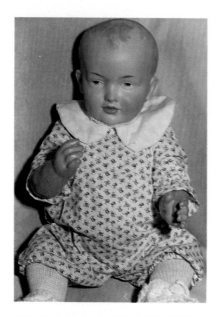

14″ Marked: K & H 151. Molded hair, intaglio eyes and closed mouth on five-piece bent limb baby body. Courtesy Frasher Doll Auctions. 14″ – $465.00.

22″ Marked: 250 K.H. Walkure. Sleep eyes, open mouth and on jointed body. Courtesy Frasher Doll Auctions. 22″ – $575.00.

Kley & Hahn operated in Ohrdruf, Germany, from 1895 to 1929. They made many different baby dolls, as well as extremely fine character children. Some of their molds are: 50, 52, 56, 66, 75, 76, 129, 130, 132, 138, 140, 141, 142, 143, 149, 150, 151, 154, 156, 157, 158, 159, 160, 162, 166, 167, 176, 179, 199, 210, 220, 250, 266, 277, 282, 331, 520, 522, 525, 526, 531, 536, 546, 549, 552, 568, 585, 680. Sample marks:

K & H   ＞K ⋠ H＜

Character Child: Boy or girl. Painted eyes, closed or open/closed mouth, on jointed composition body. Undamaged head and body and nicely dressed. Mold 520, 523, 525, 526, 531, 536, 546, 549, 552: 16″ – $2,500.00; 20″ – $4,000.00; 24″ – $4,400.00. Same mold numbers on toddler bodies: 16″ – $2,700.00; 20″ – $4,200.00; 24″ – $4,600.00. Same mold numbers on bent limb baby bodies: 14″ – $1,300.00; 17″ – $2,400.00; 21″ – $3,800.00; 25″ – $4,200.00. Same mold numbers with Glass

29½″ Marked: Walkure Germany 76. Sleep eyes, open mouth with four teeth and on jointed body. Courtesy Frasher Doll Auctions. 30″ – $950.00.

Eyes: 14″ – $1,800.00; 16″ – $2,700.00; 20″ – $4,400.00; 24″ – $4,800.00.

Character Babies: Molded hair or wig, glass sleep or set eyes or painted eyes, can have open or closed mouth. On bent limb baby body. No damage to head or body and nicely dressed. Mold numbers: 130, 132, 138, 142, 150, 151, 158, 160, 162, 167, 176, 199, 522, 525, 531, 585, 680: 12″ – $400.00; 16″ – $525.00; 20″ – $675.00. Same mold numbers on toddler bodies: 14″ – $425.00; 16″ – $575.00; 18″ – $650.00; 20″ – $775.00; 24″ – $975.00. *Mold 568:* 16″ – $650.00; 18″ – $825.00; 21″ – $950.00. *Mold 162:* with talker mechanism in head: 17″ – $850.00; 23″ – $1,150.00; 26″ – $1,800.00. *Mold 162:* With flirty eyes and clock works in head: 18″ – $1,000.00;

25″ – $2,200.00. *Mold 568:* Toddler: 20″ – $950.00; 26″ Baby: $700.00. *Mold 680:* Toddler: 16″ – $750.00; 16″ Baby: $550.00. *Mold 153, 154, 157, 169:* Child, closed mouth: 16″ – $2,200.00; 19″ – $2,700.00. Open mouth: 16″ – $675.00; 19″ – $1,100.00. *Mold 159* (two faced): 12″ – $765.00; 16″ – $1,200.00. *Mold 166:* With molded hair and open mouth: 17″ – $800.00; 19″ – $1,100.00. *Mold 166:* With molded hair and closed mouth: 18″ – $2,300.00.

Child Dolls: Walkure and/or 250 mold mark. Sleep or set eyes, open mouth and on jointed composition body. Head and body undamaged and nicely dressed: 16″ – $295.00; 20″ – $495.00; 24″ – $575.00; 28″ – $725.00; 32″ – $1,100.00.

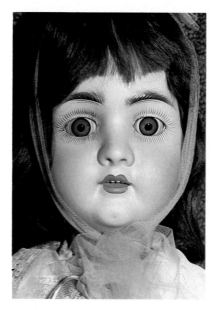

20½″ Kruse baby "Renatchen" composition head, painted eyes, closed mouth, stockinette body with moveable arms and separately stitched fingers. Fully marked with name and numbers. Courtesy Frasher Doll Auctions. 20″ – $1,600.00.

35″ Child by Konig and Wernicke. Marked: KW 4711 93 made in Germany. Set eyes, open mouth and on jointed body. Courtesy Frasher Doll Auctions. Child: 15″ – $325.00; 18″ – $500.00; 21″ – $650.00; 31″ – $900.00; 35″ – $1,100.00. Baby: 15″ – $450.00; 18″ – $545.00; 21″ – $625.00. Toddler: 15″ – $500.00; 18″ – $600.00; 21″ – $700.00. Flirty Eyes: 18″ – $625.00; 21″ – $725.00.

Founded in 1910 by Kathe Kruse, the wife of a well-known Berlin sculptor. Her

first dolls were copies of a baby of the Renaissance period and of her own children. The heads were handpainted in oils. In 1916 she obtained a patent for a wire coil doll. These dolls were Kathrinchen, a Dutch doll, Lutt Martin, Fritz, Christincen and Michel. In 1923, she registered, as a trademark, a double K with the first one reversed, along with the name Kathe Kruse.

After World War II Kathe Kruse dolls were made of plastics by the Rheinische Gummi Celluloid Fabrik Company of Germany. These plastics were first shown at the Toy Fair in Nuremberg in 1955. Marks: The early dolls had molded muslin heads that were hand-painted, jointed cloth bodies and have Kathe Kruse, in script, along with a number and sometimes Germany, on the sole of the foot.

Early Marked Dolls: In excellent condition and with original clothes: 17″ – $1,200.00; 20″ – $1,600.00. 1920's Dolls: With wigs, still have cloth bodies and oil painted heads: 17″ – $700.00; 20″ – $850.00.

U.S. Zone: Germany. 1945-1951: (Turtle Mark): 16″ – $375.00-400.00.

Plastic Dolls: With glued-on wigs, sleep eyes or painted eyes. Marked with Turtle in diamond and number on head, on back are marked: Modell/Kathe/Kruse/and number: 16″ – $350.00.

16″ "Judy" and "Karl". Ca. 1950's. Early plastic made for Kathe Kruse by Rheinische. Gummi and celluloid Fabrick Co. whose trademark is shown on tag (Turtle Mark). Sleep eyes and completely original in boxes. Courtesy Doll Cradle. 16″ – $400.00 each; 16″ Mint with box – $525.00 each.

Box ends on Kathe Kruse all original boy and girl.

Kuhnlenz made dolls from 1884 to 1930 and was located in Kronach, Bavaria. Marks from this company include: G.K. with numbers such as 56-38, 44-26, etc. Other marks attributed to this firm are:

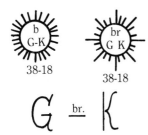

Child With Closed Mouth: Bisque head in perfect condition, jointed composition body, nicely dressed: 14″ – $875.00; 18″ – $1,000.00; 22″ – $1,300.00.

Child With Open Mouth: Bisque head in perfect condition, jointed composition body and nicely dressed: 14″ – $425.00; 18″ – $575.00; 22″ – $650.00.

Child On Kid Body with closed mouth: All in excellent condition and nicely dressed: 14″ – $650.00; 18″ – $725.00; 22″ – $850.00.

17″ Marked: GK N made in Germany. Ges. No. 205 Gesch. Trademark of Edmund Knoch. Rare character with open/closed mouth, intaglio eyes and a shoulder head with kid body and composition lower arms. Courtesy Frasher Doll Auctions. 15″ – $2,200.00; 17″ – $2,800.00; 20″ – $3,400.00.

19″ Marked: 38-27. Bold head with slightly turned shoulder, kid body with bisque lower arms. Closed mouth. Courtesy Frasher Doll Auctions. 19″ – $825.00.

15″ Made by Gebruder Kuhnlenz. Marked: DEP 44-26. French jointed body with straight wrists, paperweight eyes, open mouth with four teeth. Courtesy Pat Timmons. 15″ – $475.00.

LANTERNIER (LIMOGES)

17" Incised: J.E.Masson/S.C. Lorraine, Al & C/Limoges. Bisque head with set eyes, closed mouth with teeth and on adult composition body. Courtesy Turn of Century Antiques. 17" – $700.00.

20" Marked: JB Limoges France, sleep eyes, open mouth and nice jointed French body. Courtesy Turn of Century Antiques. 20" – $775.00.

19" Clown marked: Limoges. Set eyes with painted upper and lower lashes. Composition French body and factory original clothes. Courtesy Turn of Century Antiques. 19" – $725.00.

A. Lanternier & Cie (Company) of Limoges, France, made dolls from about the 1890's on into the 1930's. Prior to making doll heads, they made porcelain pieces as early as 1855. The doll's heads will be fully marked and will sometimes carry a name such as: Favorite, LaGeorgienne, Lorraine or Cherie. They are marked with an anchor or Fabrication/Francoise, in a square, along with an A.L. or A.L.&Cie. The dolls are generally found on papier mache' bodies, but can also be on composition jointed bodies. Marks:

FABRICATION
FRANCAISE

AL & Cie
LIMOGES

Child Doll: Open mouth, set eyes, on jointed body. No damage to head nor body and dressed nicely. Good quality bisque with pretty face: 16" – $625.00; 20" – $775.00; 23" – $900.00; 26" – $1,100.00. Poor quality bisque with very high coloring or blotchy color bisque: 16" – $400.00; 20" – $475.00; 23" – $525.00; 26" – $645.00.

Character: Open/closed mouth with teeth, smiling fat face, glass eyes, on jointed composition or papier mache' body. No damaged in any way and nicely dressed: Marked: TOTO: 16" – $695.00; 18" – $1,000.00; 22" – $1,200.00.

Lady: Adult looking face, set eyes, open/closed or closed mouth. Jointed adult composition body: 14" – $400.00; 17" – $700.00.

LENCI

Lenci dolls are all felt with a few having a cloth torso. They will be jointed at neck, shoulders and hips. The original clothes will be felt or organdy or a combination of both. The features are oil painted and usually have eyes painted to the side. Sizes can range from 5" to 45". Marks: On cloth or paper tag: Lenci Torino Made in Italy. Lenci may be written on the bottom of the foot, or underneath one arm. Mint condition rare dolls will bring higher prices.
Children: No moth holes, very little dirt on clothes, doll as near mint as possible, doll in overall excellent condition: 14" – $400.00; 16" – $575.00; 18" – $700.00; 20" – $900.00. Dirty, original clothes in bad condition or redressed: 14" – $100.00; 16" – $165.00; 18" – $250.00; 20" – $300.00.
Tiny Dolls (called Mascottes): In excellent condition: 5" – $125.00; 9"-10" – $225.00. Dirty, redressed or original clothes in bad condition: 5" – $50.00; 9"-10" – $85.00.
Ladies With Adult Faces: "Flapper" or "Boudoir" style with long limbs. In excellent condition: 24" – $800.00 up; 28" – $1,200.00 up. In poor condition, redressed or original clothes in bad condition: 24" – $300.00; 28" – $450.00.
Clowns: Excellent condition: 18" – $900.00; 26½" – $1,800.00; Poor condition: 18" – $300.00; 26½" – $500.00.
Indian or Oriental: In excellent, mint condition: 16" – $1,000.00. Dirty and poor condition: 16" – $300.00.
Golfer: Excellent, perfect condition: 16" – $950.00. Poor condition: 16" – $200.00.
Shirley Temple Type: Excellent condition: 30" – $1,200.00. Poor condition: 30" – $300.00.
Bali Dancer: Excellent condition: 22" – $1,400.00. Poor condition: 22" – $300.00.
Smoking Doll: In excellent condition, painted eyes: 25" – $1,000.00. In poor condition: 25" – $350.00. With glass eyes, in excellent condition: 16" – $1,700.00; 20" – $2,600.00. Glass eyes: poor condition: 16" – $350.00; 20" – $450.00. "Surprised Eyes", with very round painted eyes: 16" – $700.00; 20" – $1,600.00. With glass, flirty eyes: 16" – $1,200.00; 20" – $2,100.00.
Boys: Side part hairdo: 16" – $450.00; 19" – $800.00; 24" – $1,000.00.
Babies: Mint: 16" – $800.00; 20" – $1,200.00. Fair condition: 16" – $400.00; 20" – $600.00.

27" Lenci Lady. Long limbed doll with felt face and arms. Cloth torso and limbs. Painted features, original. Courtesy Frasher Doll Auctions. 27" – $1,200.00 up.

LENCI

16" Lenci baby. All felt, bent limb baby body. Jointed at neck, shoulders and hips, painted features. Organdy dress and bonnet with felt booties and flower trim. Courtesy Frasher Doll Auctions. 16" Mint – $800.00; 16" Fair – $400.00.

16" Lenci marked on bottom of foot. All felt jointed, neck, shoulders and hips. Painted features and all original. Courtesy Frasher Doll Auctions. 16" – $575.00.

Rear Left: 22" Lenci all felt, jointed at neck, shoulders and hips. Painted features. Original. Right: 21" Lenci-type. All felt, jointed at neck, shoulders and hips, painted features and original felt costume. Front Left: All felt and fully jointed, painted features. Tag: Ars. Lenci. Made in Italy. Right: 13" Lenci girl, fully jointed, painted features and original. Courtesy Frasher Doll Auctions. 22" Excellent – $900.00; 22" Fair – $300.00; 21" Lenci-type, fair – $100.00; 14" Boy, excellent – $400.00; 13" Girl, excellent – $300.00.

15″ Lenci-type "Red Riding Hood". Has all the Lenci characteristics although unmarked. All cloth with painted features, fully jointed and original costume of cotton, muslin with velvet cape. Courtesy Frasher Doll Auctions. 15″ – $400.00.

23″ "Lori Baby" marked: Lori and stamped Geschutz S&Co. Germany. Painted hair, sleep eyes and open/closed mouth. Five-piece bent limb baby body made by Swaine & Co. Courtesy Frasher Doll Auctions. 14″ – $1,400.00; 20″ – $2,200.00; 23″ – $2,800.00; 26″ – $3,400.00.

12″ Marked: D.1.P.3. and has green stamp: Geschutz S&Co. Germany. Made by Swaine and Co. Glass eyes, open/closed mouth and on five-piece bent limb baby body. Courtesy Frasher Doll Auctions. 12″ – $600.00; 15″ – $1,000.00; 20″ – $1,600.00.

MASCOTTE
MECHANICALS

Mascotte dolls were made by May Fre're's Cie from 1890 to 1897, then this firm became part of Jules Steiner from 1898 into the 1900's. Some dolls are marked: Bebe Mascotte/Paris and others are incised M, plus a number. Prices are for a doll with perfect bisque head and on nice French body. Nicely dressed: Closed mouth: Marked: Mascotte: 16" – $2,800.00; 18" – $3,200.00; 20" – $3,500.00; 22" – $3,700.00; 24" – $4,000.00.

Marked With M plus a number: 16" – $2,300.00; 18" – $2,800.00; 20" – $3,000.00; 22" – $3,200.00; 24" – $3,500.00.

24" Marked: Mascotte. Closed mouth, jointed body. Courtesy Frasher Doll Auctions. 24" – $4,000.00.

23½" Marked: M 10 and red artists marks: HX. French jointed body, closed mouth and original wig. Made by Mascotte. Courtesy Frasher Doll Auctions. 24" – $3,500.00.

MECHANICALS

A. Theroude mechanical walker patented in 1840 with papier mache' head with bamboo teeth in open mouth. Stand on three wheels, two large and one small, tin cart with mechanism attached to leg: 16" – $1,800.00.

Autoperipatetikos of 1861. Base is clocklike works and has tin feet and when wound the doll walks. Heads can be china, untinted bisque or papier mache': early china head, 11" – $1,200.00; later china hairdo, 11" – $850.00; untinted bisque head, 11" – $785.00; papier mache' head, 11" – $550.00.

Hawkins, George walker with pewter hands and feet, wood torso. Hands modeled to push a carriage, which should be a Goodwin, patented in 1867-1868. Carriage has two large wheels and one small one in front. Molded hair, doll's head will be marked: X.L.C.R./Doll head/Pat. Sept. 8, 1868: 11" – $1,400.00.

Jumeau: Raises and lowers both arms and head moves. Holds items such as a hankie and bottle, book and fan, etc. one in each hand. Key wound music box in base. Closed mouth and marked: Jumeau: 15" – $3,000.00 up; 20" – $3,800.00 up. Same

MECHANICAL METAL DOLLS

as above but with open mouth: 15" – $1,600.00 up; 20" – $2,600.00 up.

Jumeau: Marked: Jumeau standing or sitting on music box that is key wound and doll plays an instrument: 14" – $3,200.00 up; 17" – $3,800.00 up.

Jumeau: Marked: Jumeau walker with one-piece leg, arms jointed at elbows and she raises her arm to blow kisses and the head turns. Cryer box and open mouth: 16" – $1,400.00 up; 22" – $2,000.00 up.

Jumeau: Marked: Jumeau walker standing on three-wheel cart and when cart is pulled, the doll's head turns and arms go up and down: 15" – $3,400.00; 18" – $3,800.00.

Steiner, Jules: Composition upper and lower torso-chest, also lower legs and all of arms. Twill covered sections of hips and upper legs. Key wound. Cries, kicks and turns head. Open mouth with two rows teeth: 18" – $1,800.00. Same as above but with bisque torso section: 18" – $4,000.00.

German Makers: One or two figures on music box, key wound and in good working order: $950.00 up. All prices shown above are for originally dressed mechanicals and in working order. No damage to figure or any of the bisque parts. They will be a lot less if redressed or damaged in any way.

Marked: Paris Be'be' Beta Depose. Key wind and she smells flowers and fans herself and head nods. Made by Daniel and Cie. Courtesy Turn of Century Antiques. $3,800.00.

Musical automation by Schoenau & Hoffmeister. Marked: S, P.B. in star, H 4600. Bisque heads, sleep eyes and open mouths. Original. Girl plays violin and boy beats drum and cymbals. Courtesy Frasher Doll Auctions. $1,200.00.

METAL DOLLS

Dolls marked Minerva were made by Buschow & Beck. Those marked Juno were made by Karl Standfuss and ones with a Diana mark were made by Alfred Heller. All are German. Marks:

METAL DOLLS
MON CHERIE
NIPPON (JAPAN)

Doll With Any Of Above Marks: Can be on cloth or kid body and can have composition, celluloid or bisque lower arms. Many will be found on homemade bodies and these should be well done and proportioned. Nicely dressed. Molded hair, glass eyes: 16" – $135.00; 20" – $185.00. Molded hair, painted eyes: 12" – $90.00; 16" – $110.00; 20" – $125.00. Wigged and glass eyes: 16" – $150.00; 20" – $200.00.

All Metal Child: Nicely dressed, fully jointed, open or open/closed mouth and glass eyes: 17" – $250.00; 20" – $300.00.

All Metal Baby: Bent limb metal body (most are spring strung) molded hair and painted eyes. Nicely dressed: 12" – $100.00; 16" – $125.00; 18" – $195.00.

16½" Marked: Mon Cherie LP Paris. Set eyes, open mouth and on jointed French body. Made in 1920's. The doll was marketed by L. Prieur with the head probably made by Couty. Courtesy Turn of Century Antiques. Child, open mouth: 16" – $695.00; 20" – $1,100.00.

Left: 20" Marked: FY Nippon 404. Sleep eyes, open mouth and jointed body. Right: 22" marks: Morimura Bros. Japan. Sleep eyes, open mouth and on jointed body. Courtesy Frasher Doll Auctions. 20" – $295.00; 22" – $325.00.

At the outbreak of World War I, the German doll makers converted to wartime operations and Japan stepped into the doll void created. There were many obstacles for Japan to overcome in their attempt at molding and painting Western style dolls in the short time they were in production. (1918-1922). In the beginning their products were not too well done, but the quality of the dolls not only improved, but a few are excellent.

Morimura Brothers was the name of a very large Japanese import firm that imported dolls of all kinds from 1915 to 1922. In 1922, after World War I, their import section that handled dolls was taken over by Landfelder, Homma & Hayward, Inc. Morimura Brothers mark:

Another major firm in Japan was Yamato and their marks are:

ℱ𝒴

The center for celluloid, metal and rubber dolls was Tokyo. Porcelain dolls were made in Kyoto; Osaka was where the dolls of cotton and paper were made.

Nippon Marked Baby: Good to excellent quality bisque, well painted, nice body with bent limbs and nicely dressed: 11" – $135.00; 15" – $250.00; 19" – $375.00; 24" – $495.00.

Nippon Marked Child: Good to excellent quality bisque, good fully jointed body, excellent quality painted features and nicely dressed: 16" – $250.00; 20" – $295.00; 24" – $350.00.

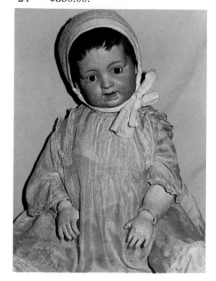

22½" Marked: 2 Morimura Bros. Japan. Bent limb baby body with jointed wrists, sleep eyes, open mouth with two upper teeth. Courtesy Frasher Doll Auctions. 23" – $450.00.

MOLDED HAIR BISQUE

The molded hair bisques are just like any other flesh-toned bisque dolls, but instead of having a wig, they have molded hair, glass set or finely painted and detailed eyes and generally they will have a closed mouth. They almost always are a shoulder head with one-piece head and shoulder plate. They can be on a kid body or cloth with bisque lower arms and some have composition lower legs. These dolls are generally very pretty.

Child: Girl: 16" – $425.00; 19" – $675.00; 21" – $900.00; 24" – $1,100.00. **Boy:** 16" – $525.00; 19" – $750.00; 21" – $950.00.

25" Molded hair bisque with glass eyes and closed mouth. Shoulder head on cloth body with bisque lower arms. Courtesy Frasher Doll Auctions. 25" – $1,100.00.

MOLDED HAIR BISQUE MOTSCHMANN

20″ and 15½″ Tinted bisque shoulder heads with molded hair, painted eyes, closed mouth, kid bodies with bisque lower arms. Courtesy Frasher Doll Auctions. 20″ – $850.00; 15½″ – $425.00.

MOTSCHMANN

Charles Motschmann made dolls from 1857 into 1860's in Sonneberg, Germany. These early dolls were babies, children and Orientals. They will have glass eyes, closed mouths and have heads of papier mache′, wax over papier mache′ or wax over composition. They can have lightly brush stroke painted hair or come with a wig. If the mouth is open, they will have bamboo teeth. The larger dolls will have arms and legs jointed at the wrists and ankles. The torso (lower) is composition as are the arms and legs, except for the upper parts which will be twill style cloth. The mid-section will also be cloth. If the doll is marked, it can be found on the upper cloth of the leg and will be stamped:

PATENT 29 APRIL
1857
CH. MOTSCHMANN
SONNEBERG

Motschmann marked or Type Baby: 14″ – $350.00; 17″ – $450.00; 21″ – $525.00; 25″ – $625.00.

24″ Motchmann Baby. Papier mache′-composition. With inset glass eyes. Painted curls at sides of head. Swivel head on shoulder plate, arms and legs are wood with upper sections of cloth. Composition hands and feet. Papier mache′ torso with bellows and squeak box. 24″ – $600.00.

Bisque dolls made in Germany by various firms. Bisque with fired-in color and on jointed, tinted yellowish bodies. Can be a child or be on a five-piece bent limb baby body. Most made after 1900. Armand Marseille: Girl or boy marked only with A.M.: 8" – $600.00; 12" – $900.00. Mold 353 baby: 14" – $1,300.00; 18" – $2,000.00. BSW (Bruno Schmidt) Mold 500: 14" – $1,600.00; 18" – $2,200.00. J.D.K. (Kestner Mold 243 baby: 15" – $4,000.00; 19" – $5,000.00. Molded hair baby: 18" – $5,000.00. S & H (Simon & Halbig) Mold 164: 16" – $2,000.00; 20" – $2,600.00. Mold 220: 18" – $2,900.00; Mold 1099, 1129, 1199: 16" – $2,400.00. Mold 1329: 16" – $2,000.00; 20" – $2,600.00. All bisque: 7"-8" – $900.00. S,PB in star H-4900: 14" – $895.00; 18" – $1,300.00.

Traditional Doll made in Japan: Papier mache' swivel head on shoulder plate, cloth mid-section and upper arms and legs. The limbs and torso will be papier mache', glass eys, pierced nostrils. The early dolls will have jointed wrists and ankles and will be slightly sexed. Early fine quality originally dressed: 1890's: 15" – $225.00; 20" – $375.00; 27" – $575.00. Early boy with painted hair: 15" – $250.00; 20" – $400.00; 27" – $600.00. 1930's or later: 13" – $65.00; 16" – $85.00.

Lady. All original and excellent quality: 1920's: 12" – $150.00; 16" – $225.00.

Japanese Baby with bisque head. Sleep eyes, closed mouth and bisque will be white. On five-piece papier mache' body. Original clothes and in excellent condition. Late 1920's: 8" – $50.00; 12" – $125.00. Glass eyes: 8" – $60.00; 12" – $135.00.

Japanese Baby made of crushed oyster shell (head) and will have papier mache' five-piece body (bent limb), glass eyes and original: 8" – $50.00; 12" – $90.00; 16" – $125.00.

Oriental Dolls that are all composition, jointed at shoulders and hips. Painted features, painted hair or can have bald head with braid of yarn hair down the back with rest covered with cap: 10" – $75.00-85.00.

17" Marked: S&H 1329 oriental with glass eyes. Open mouth and on jointed body. In Tibetan outfit. Courtesy Frasher Doll Auctions. 17" – $2,100.00.

17" Oriental marked: 25/164. Made by Simon & Halbig. Sleep eyes, open mouth and all original. Courtesy Turn of Century Antiques. 17" – $2,000.00.

ORIENTAL DOLLS

11" Oriental marked: Simon & Halbig 1329. Olive skin tones, open mouth and original clothes and wig. Courtesy Turn of Century Antiques. 11" – $1,200.00.

12" Schoenau and Hoffmeister marked: 4900 S, P.B. in star, H. 9/9. Set eyes, open mouth with four teeth. Maybe original wig, but redressed. Courtesy Frasher Doll Auctions. 12" – $750.00.

26" Tall doll is a traditional Japanese girl with inset glass eyes. Baby in Stroller and boy with cap in front are "Ling Ling" and "Ming Ming" by Quan-Quan Co. All composition with painted features. Man and woman are early Chinese opera dolls. Courtesy Frasher Doll Auctions. 26" – $575.00; Ming & Ling – $75.00; Man – $165.00.

28" Traditional doll. Painted papier mache' head, cloth upper limbs and mid-section. Inset glass eyes and all original. Courtesy Frasher Doll Auctions. 28" – $600.00.

Japanese babies with bisque heads. Left has painted eyes and right has inset glass eyes. Both are original. Courtesy Frasher Doll Auctions. 8" Painted eyes – $50.00; 8" Glass eyes – $60.00.

ORSINI

Jeanne I. Orsini of New York City designed dolls from 1916 into the 1920's. It is not known who made the heads for her, but it is likely that all bisque dolls designed by her were made by J.D. Kestner in Germany. The initials of the designer are: J.I.O. and the dolls will be marked with these initials along with a year such as 1919, 1920, 1926, etc. Since the middle initial is I., it may appear to be a number 1. The dolls can also be marked: Copr. by/J.I. Orsini/Germany.

Painted Bisque Character: Can be on cloth body with cloth limbs or a bent limb baby body of composition, toddler or baby. Flirty sleep eyes and open smile mouth. Can be wigged or have molded hair and can be boy or girl. Head is painted bisque. Mold 1429: doll in excellent condition and well dressed: 14" – $1,500.00; 18" – $1,700.00.

Bisque Head Baby: Fired-in color bisque head with sleep or set eyes, open mouth. Cloth body and has painted hair. Marks: Kiddie Joy JIO 1926: 14" – $1,200.00; 18" – $1,800.00.

All Bisque: Jointed at hips and shoulders with very character face, sleep eyes and painted-on shoes and socks. Can be marked on back: Copy. by /J.I. Orsini/Germany, or have a paper label with doll's name on front. Names are DoDo, Fifi, Mimi, Didi, Zizi, etc.: 5"-6" – $1,150.00; 7"-8" – $1,250.00.

PAINTED BISQUE
PAPIER MACHE

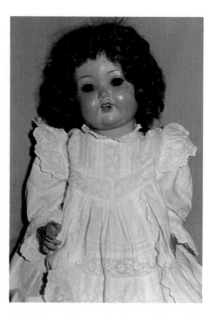

26″ Marked: Heubach Koppelsdorf 342.10 Germany. Painted bisque head, open mouth and flirty eyes. On five-piece bent limb baby body. Courtesy Frasher Doll Auctions.

23″ Painted bisque by Armand Marseille. Marked: A.M. Koppelsdorf Germany 1330 A. 12 M. Five-piece bent limb baby body, open mouth and original wig. Courtesy Frasher Doll Auctions

PAPIER MACHE′

Papier mache′ dolls were made in France, Germany, England, United States and many other countries. Papier mache′ is a type of composition in that it is moldable—made from paper pulp, wood and rag fibers, containing paste, oil or glue. Flour, clay and/or sand was added for stiffness. The hardness of papier mache′ depends on the amount of glue that is added.

Many so called "papier mache′" parts on dolls were actually laminated paper and not papier mache′ at all. Laminated paper doll heads/parts are several thicknesses of molded paper that have been bonded (glued) together, or pressed after being glued.

Papier mache′ means "chewed paper" in French, and as early as 1810, dolls of papier mache′ were being mass produced by using molds.

Marked: M & S Superior: 2015 (Muller & Strassburger): Papier mache′ shoulder head with blonde or black molded hair, painted blue or brown eyes, old cloth body with kid or leather arms and boots. Nicely dressed and head not repainted or chipped and cracked: 14″ – $300.00; 18″ – $625.00; 24″. – $800.00. Glass eyes: 20″ – $1,000.00. With wig: 18″ – $1,200.00. Repainted nicely: 14″ – $100.00; 18″ – $250.00; 24″ – $350.00. Chips, scuffs or not repainted very well: 14″ – $50.00; 18″ – $85.00; 24″ – $100.00.

French and French Type: Painted black hair with brush marks on solid dome, some have nailed on wigs. Open mouth with bamboo teeth, inset glass eyes or full closed mouth. In very good condition (shows some wear), nice old clothes. All leather/kid body: 15″ – $700.00; 20″ – $1,200.00; 26″ – $1,600.00; 30″ – $2,200.00.

18″ Early papier mache′ with glass eyes and hairdo braided bun in back. Canvas type material body and limbs. Courtesy Henri and John Startzel. 18″ Excellent, but some wear – $900.00; 18″ Fair condition – $400.00.

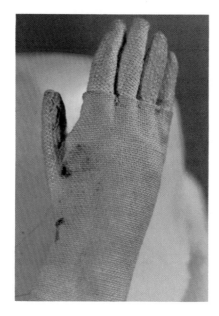

Canvas type material on early papier mache′ with unusual hand construction. Courtesy Henri and John Startzel.

12″ Ca. 1917-1920. Papier mache′ head with mohair and painted features. Cloth body and limbs. Clothing is sewn to doll. Marks: None. Courtesy Sally Freeman. 12″ – $85.00 up.

PAPIER MACHE
PARIAN-TYPE (UNTINTED BISQUE)

Early Mache': With cloth body and wooden limbs. Early hairdo with top knots, buns, puff curls or braiding. Ca. 1840's. Not restored in original or very old well made clothes. In very good condition and may show some extra wear: 10" – $400.00; 14" – $550.00; 17" – $650.00; 20" – $900.00; 24" – $1,200.00.

Marked Greiner: Dolls of 1858 on: Blonde or black molded hair, brown or blue painted eyes, cloth body with leather arms, nicely dressed and head not repainted and with only very minor scuffs: 18" – $800.00; 23" – $1,100.00; 29" – $1,600.00; 32" – $1,900.00.

Motschmann Types: With wood and twill bodies. Separate torso section and separate hip section, glass eyes, closed mouth and brush stroke hair on solid dome. Nicely dressed and ready to display: 16" – $375.00; 20" – $485.00; 24" – $550.00.

German Mache': of 1870-1900's with molded barious curly hairdo, painted eyes and closed mouth. May be blonde or black hair. Nicely dressed and ready to display. Not repainted; second price is for glass eyes: 16" – $425.00-475.00; 20" – $500.00-550.00; 26" – $595.00-625.00; 32" – $800.00.

Showing wear and scuffs, but not touched up: 16" – $185.00; 20" – $250.00; 26" – $375.00.

Turned Shoulder Head: Solid dome, glass eyes and closed mouth. Twill cloth kid body with composition lower arms. In very good condition, nicely dressed: 18" – $475.00; 22" – $725.00.

German Character Heads: These heads are molded just like the bisque heads. Glass eyes, closed mouth and on fully jointed composition body. In excellent condition and nicely dressed: 16" – $675.00; 20" – $875.00.

1920's On Mache': Papier mache' head, usually with brighter colors than the older ones. Wigged, usually dressed as a child, or in Provincial costumes. Stuffed cloth bodies and limbs, or have mache' arms/hands. In excellent overall condition: 8" – $65.00; 12" – $85.00; 16" – $125.00.

Clowns: Papier mache' head with clown painted features. Open or closed mouth, molded hair or wigged and on cloth body with some having composition or papier mache' lower arms: In excellent condition: 12" – $250.00; 16" – $400.00.

PARIAN-TYPE (UNTINTED BISQUE)

The use of the name "Parian" is incorrect for dolls, but the term has been used for so long it would be difficult to attempt to change it. The dolls are actually made of unglazed porcelain.

"Parian-type" dolls were made from the 1850's to the 1880's with the majority being made in the 1870's and 1880's. All seemed to have been made in Germany and if marked, the mark will be found on the inside of the shoulder plate. As to variety, there are hundreds of different heads and an entire collection could be made up of them. It must be noted that the really rare and unique unglazed porcelain dolls are difficult to find and their prices will be high.

"Parian-type" dolls can be found with every imaginable thing applied to head and shirt tops, from flowers, snoods, ruffles, feathers, plumes, ribbons, etc. Many have

inset glass eyes, pierced ears and most are blonde, although some will have light to medium brown hair and a few will have glazed black hair.

Some of the "parian-type" unglazed porcelain dolls and China dolls shared the same molds, and the men and boys as well as ones with swivel necks can be considered rare.

Various Fancy Hairstyles: With molded combs, ribbons, flowers, head bands or snoods. Cloth body with cloth/"parian" limbs. Perfect condition and very nicely dressed: Glass eyes, pierced ears: 17" – $1,250.00; 21" – $1,450.00. Painted eyes, unpierced ears: 17" – $750.00; 21" – $900.00.

Modeled Necklaces: Jewels or standing ruffles (undamaged): Glass eyes, pierced ears: 17" – $1,250.00 up; 21" – $1,500.00 up.

PARIAN-TYPE (UNTINTED BISQUE)

Painted eyes, unpierced ears: 17″ – $700.00; 21″ – $1,000.00.

Bald Head: Solid domes that takes wigs, full ear detail. 1850's. Perfect condition and nicely dressed: 14″ – $500.00; 16″ – $695.00; 20″ – $1,100.00.

Very Plain Style: With no decoration in hair or on shoulder. No damage and nicely dressed: 15″ – $200.00; 18″ – $325.00.

Men or Boys: Men or boy hairdos with center or side parts. Cloth body with cloth/parian limbs. Decorated shirt and tie: 15″ – $400.00; 18″ – $750.00.

Undecorated Shirt Top: 15″ – $350.00; 18″ – $700.00; 24″ – $1,000.00.

16½″ Parian-type of late 1860's. Applied bow in hair and glazed and ruffled top. Pierced ears and glass eyes. Replaced cloth body and china limbs. Courtesy Frasher Doll Auctions. 17″ – $1,250.00.

26″ Parian-type white bisque shoulder head on cloth body with bisque lower arms. This hairdo is called ''Alice in Wonderland''. Has molded head band. Courtesy Frasher Doll Auctions. 26″ – $1,000.00.

16″ Parian-type with white bisque and very ''apple red'' cheeks. Molded ribbon in hair and turned shoulder head. Cloth body with leather arms. Courtesy Turn of Century Antiques. 16″ – $350.00.

PHENIX
PIANO BABY

25" ''Be'be' Phe'nix'' marked: 9L ★ .
Pierced ears, open mouth with six teeth,
jointed body with straight wrists. Wears
original dress which has red label with gold
letters across front with her name. Made
by Henri ALEXANDRE, Paris, who made
dolls from 1889 to 1900. Dolls may be marked: PHENIX ★ 95. 16" – $1,800.00; 18"
– 1,800.00; 22" – $2,300.00; 25" –
$3,900.00.

PIANO BABY

Piano Babies were made around the 1880's on into the 1930's. They were made by various German firms with the finest quality ones apparently from the Gebruder Heubach Company, although other quality makers, such as Kestner also made them. **Piano Baby:** All bisque and unjointed, will have molded-on clothes and molded hair and painted features. They come in a great variety of positions, lying down, sitting and even on their backs. Some are with animals, flowers, etc. Excellent quality to detail of modeling and in perfect condition: 4" – $125.00; 8" – $345.00; 12" – $525.00; 16" – $675.00 up. Medium quality and may not have painting finished on back side of figure: 4" – $85.00; 8" – $225.00; 12" – $325.00; 16" – $450.00. With animal, pot, flowers or other items: 4" – $145.00; 8" – $365.00; 12" – $575.00.

Pair of German bisque Piano Babies. Marked: 2185. Intaglio eyes and excellent quality.
Courtesy Frasher Doll Auctions. 8" Long – $345.00.

Rabery & Delphieu began making dolls in 1856. The very first dolls had kid bodies and are extremely rare. The majority of the Rabery & Delphieu dolls are on French composition/wood or mache' bodies. They will be marked with: R.D. A few may be marked: Bebe de Paris.

Child With Closed Mouth: In excellent condition with no chips, breaks or hairlines to the bisque head. Body in overall good con-dition, dressed and wigged and ready to place into a collection: 14" – $1,700.00; 17" – $2,000.00; 20" – $2,600.00; 22" – $2,800.00; 25" – $3,100.00.

Child With Open Mouth: In excellent condition with same conditions for closed mouth dolls: 14" – $900.00; 17" – $1,600.00; 20" – $1,900.00; 22" – $2,000.00; 25" – $2,400.00.

21" Marked: R.1.D. open/closed mouth and on early straight wrist jointed body. Courtesy Frasher Doll Auctions. 21" – $2,600.00.

19½" Molded felt mask face with painted features, mohair wig, cloth body, jointed at shoulders and hips. Marked on soles of shoes and on necklace: Raynal. Made in France. Ca. 1925. Courtesy Frasher Doll Auctions.

RECHNAGEL OF ALEXANDERINETHAL
REINECKE

10" Marked: 21 Germany R.12A. Sleep eyes, open mouth and on five-piece body. All original in provincial costume. Courtesy Frasher Doll Auctions. 10" – $145.00.

Dolls marked with an R.A. were made by Rechnagel of Alexanderinethal, Thur,

Germany. They came also marked with a number and/or Germany. These dolls have a bisque head, composition bodies, as well as papier mache' and wood jointed bodies. R.A. marked dolls date from 1886 to after World War I and can range from excellent workmanship to very poor workmanship. Prices shown are for dolls with good artist painting (lips painted straight as well as the eyebrows), nicely or originally dressed and no damage to head nor body.

Child: Set or sleep eyes, open mouth with small dolls having painted-on shoes/socks: 7"-8" – $125.00; 12" – $165.00; 15" – $235.00; 19" – $325.00; 21" – $425.00.

Baby: Ca. 1909-1910 on. Five-piece bent limb baby body or straight leg, curved arm toddler body and with sleep or set eyes, open mouth. No damage to head or body and nicely dressed: 9" – $125.00; 12" – $185.00; 16" – $250.00; 19" – $325.00.

Character: With painted eyes, modeled-on bonnet and open/closed mouth, some smiling, some with painted-in teeth. Not damaged and nicely dressed: 8" – $350.00; 12" – $500.00.

Character: Glass eyes, closed mouth and composition bent limb baby body: 7" – $495.00; 10" – $550.00; 13" – $695.00.

REINECKE

17" Marked: P.M. 23 Germany 7½. Sleep eye/lashes, open mouth with two teeth and on five-piece bent limb baby body. 14" "Dream Baby" mold 341 by Armand Marseille. Courtesy Frasher Doll Auctions. 17" – $400.00; 14" – $375.00.

Dolls marked with a P.M. were made by Otto Reinecke of Hof-Moschendorf, Bavaria, Germany, from 1909 into the 1930's. The most often found mold number from this company is the 914 baby or toddler. The marks include the P.M. as well as a number and/or Germany.
Child: Bisque head, open mouth and on five-piece papier mache' body or jointed body. Can have set or sleep eyes. No damage to head or body, nicely dressed and ready to display: 9" – $125.00; 12" – $195.00; 15" – $285.00; 18" – $375.00; 22" – $450.00 up.
Baby: Open mouth and sleep or set eyes. Bisque head on five-piece bent limb baby body. No damage and nicely dressed: 12" – $250.00; 16" – $375.00; 22" – $500.00; 25" – $675.00.

REVALO

The Revalo marked dolls were made by Gebruder Ohlhaver of Thur, Germany from 1921 to the 1930's. Bisque heads with composition body. No damage to head or body and nicely dressed.
Child: Sleep or set eyes, open mouth: 14" – $350.00; 17" – $450.00; 20" – $525.00; 24" – $600.00.

Molded Hair Child: With or without molded ribbon and/or flowers. Painted eyes and open/closed mouth. Jointed body: 11" – $565.00; 14" – $695.00.
Baby: Bisque head with open mouth and sleep or set eyes. Five-piece bent limb baby body: 15" – $450.00; 17" – $550.00. Toddler: 15" – $500.00; 17" – $600.00.

Left: 15" Marked: Revalo. Germany 1. Sleep eyes/lashes open mouth and on jointed body. Shown with 16" marked: S.P.B. in star, H. 1800. Made by Schoenau and Hoffmeister. Courtesy Frasher Doll Auctions. 15" – $450.00; 16" 1800 – $325.00.

SCHMIDT, FRANZ

Franz Schmidt & Co. began in 1890 at Georgenthal, near Walterhausen, Thur. They obtained an extremely interesting patent (in England) during 1891 for sleeping eyes made so the upper lids moved further and faster than the lower lids. It was in 1902 they registered the trademarks of crossed hammers with a doll between and the "F.S.&Co." mark.
Baby: Bisque head on bent limb baby body.

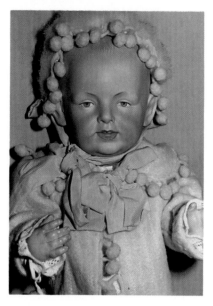

Sleep or set eyes, open mouth and some may have pierced nostrils. Not damaged in any way and nicely dressed: Mold 1271, 1272, 1297: 14″ – $450.00; 17″ – $525.00; 20″ – $645.00; 24″ – $825.00. Mold 1267: Open/closed mouth, painted eyes: 16″ – $1,500.00; 19″ – $2,400.00; Glass Eyes: 16″ – $1,800.00; 19″ – $2,800.00. Mold 1285: 16″ – $600.00; 20″ – $750.00. Mold 1295, 1296, 1310: 14″ – $425.00; 17″ – $500.00; 20″ – $600.00; 24″ – $800.00. Add more for toddler body.

Child: Mache' and composition body with walker mechanism with metal rollers on feet. Open mouth and sleep eyes. Working and no damage to head nor body. Mold 1250: 12″ – $200.00; 16″ – $525.00; 20″ – $650.00. Mold 1266, 1267 Child: Jointed body, open mouth, sleep eyes: 22″ – $1,200.00.

19″ Marked: F.S. & Co. 1267. Painted hair, painted brown eyes, open/closed mouth with two molded upper teeth. On five-piece bent limb baby body and may be wearing part of original clothes. Courtesy Frasher Doll Auctions. 19″ – $3,800.00.

16″ Marked: 1295 F.S. & Co. Sleep eyes, open mouth and on five-piece jointed baby body. Courtesy Frasher Doll Auctions. 16″ – $475.00.

23″ Marked: 1296 F.S. & Co./Simon Halbig. Sleep eyes, open mouth. On five-piece bent limb body. Courtesy Frasher Doll Auctions. 23″ – $800.00.

16" Marked: F.S. & Co. 1271/40 2. Sleep eyes, open/closed mouth with two molded upper teeth and on five-piece bent limb baby body. Courtesy Frasher Doll Auctions. 16" – $500.00.

SCHMITT & FILS

Schmitt & Fils produced dolls from 1870's to 1891 in Paris, France. They should be marked on head and body with crossed hammers in a shield. The dolls have composition/wood jointed bodies and came with fully closed mouths or open/closed mouths. Marks:

Child: Bisque head on jointed composition/wood body with closed mouth or open/closed mouth. No damage, chips or hairlines and body in excellent condition. Dressed nicely in the French styles and ready to display: 15" – $5,000.00; 18" – $6,200.00; 20" – $6,500.00; 23" – $7,500.00; 25" – $8,600.00.

23" Marked with Sch, in shield. Closed mouth and on jointed body which is also marked. 17" Smaller Schmitt-type on Schmitt body. Original. Courtesy Barbara Earnshaw. 23" – $7,500.00; 17" – $6,000.00.

SCHOENAU & HOFFMEISTER

Schoenau & Hoffmeister began making dolls in 1901 and were located in Bavaria. The factory was called "Porzellanfabrik Burgrubb" and this mark will be found on some dolls' heads. Dolls are also marked with a five-point star with the initials SH and pb inside the star. Some of their mold numbers are: 21, 169, 170, 769, 900, 914, 1800, 1906, 1909, 1923, 4000, 4500, 4900, 5000, 5300, 5500, 5700, 5800, Hanna. Mark:

Marked: Porzellanfabrik Burggrub/Princess Elizabeth with sleep eyes, smiling open mouth and on five-piece chubby toddler body. Second and third fingers molded together. Courtesy Frasher Doll Auctions. 16" – $1,900.00; 24" – $3,000.00.

Oriental: Mold 4900. Open mouth, sleep or set eyes. Bisque head on jointed olive toned composition body. No damage and nicely dressed in Oriental styles: 10" – $365.00; 14" – $895.00; 18" – $1,300.00.

Princess Elizabeth: Smiling open mouth, sleep eyes and on chubby five-piece composition body. Marked with name on head. No damage to head or body: 16" – $1,900.00; 20" – $2,400.00; 24" – $3,000.00.

Hanna: Brown or Black bisque (fired-in color), open mouth papier maché five-piece or jointed body. Sleep or set eyes. No damage and dressed in grass skirt or native print cloth gown: 8"-10" – $185.00-225.00.

Hanna Baby: Character head of bisque with open mouth and sleep eyes. On five-piece bent limb baby body. No damage and nicely dressed: 14" – $450.00; 17" – $550.00; 24" – $895.00.

Character Baby: Bisque head on five-piece bent limb baby body. Open mouth and set or sleep eyes. No damage and nicely dressed: 12" – $300.00; 17" – $525.00; 20" – $600.00; 24" – $700.00 up.

Character Toddler: Same description as babies but with a toddler body: 17" – $675.00; 20" – $750.00.

Children: Bisque head with open mouth and set or sleep eyes, composition jointed body. No damage to head or body and nicely dressed ready to go into a collection: 10" – $100.00; 15" – $300.00; 18" – $385.00; 21" – $450.00; 26" – $600.00; 30" – $950.00; 34" – $1,200.00.

27" Marked: Germany, S.PB, in Star, H. 914. Open mouth with four teeth and on jointed body. Courtesy Frasher Doll Auctions. 27" – $650.00.

33" Marked: S.P.B., in Star, H. 1906. Sleep eyes and on jointed body. Shown with baby marked: 151, which is attributed to both Kestner and Hertel & Schwab. Courtesy Frasher Doll Auctions. 33" – $1,100.00; 16" Baby – $550.00.

SCHOENHUT

The Albert Schoenhut & Co. was located in Philadelphia, PA, from 1872 into 1930's. Albert's grandfather and father were both wood carvers in Germany. It was in 1909 that Albert applied for a patent for a swivel spring-jointed doll, but did not receive that patent until 1911. It was in 1913 that he began making the infant doll with bent limbs. In 1924 the Schoenhut firm bought out the "Bass Wood Elastic Dolls" that were jointed by elastic instead of springs and were cheaper in price. Schoenhut dolls will be incised: Schoenhut Doll/Pat. Jan. 17, "11. U.S.A./& foreign countries and will have paper label with the same mark in an oval.

Child With Carved Hair: May have comb marks, molded ribbon, comb or bow. Closed mouth and spring-jointed all wood. Original or nice clothes: Excellent condition: 16" – $1,500.00; 19" – $1,900.00. Very good condition with some wear: 16" – $700.00; 19" – $850.00. Poor condition with chips and dents: 16" – $400.00; 19" – $500.00.

Baby Head: Can be on regular body or bent limb baby body. Bald spray painted hair or wig, painted decal eyes and all wood: Nicely dressed: Excellent condition: 16" – $550.00; 17" – $625.00. Good condition: 16" – $350.00; 17" – $395.00. Poor condition: 16" – $200.00; 17" – $225.00.

"Dolly" Face: Common doll: Wigged, open/closed mouth with painted teeth, decal painted eyes and spring jointed. Original or nicely dressed: Excellent condition: 17" – $550.00; 20" – $650.00. Good condition: 17" – $200.00; 20" – $250.00. Poor condition: 17" – $150.00; 20" – $195.00.

Sleep Eyes: Has lids that lower down over the eyes and has an open mouth with teeth or just slightly cut open with carved teeth. Original or nicely dressed: Excellent condition: 17" – $750.00; 20" – $900.00. Good condition: 17" – $350.00; 20" – $450.00. Poor condition: 17" – $200.00; 20" – $265.00.

Walker: All wood with one-piece legs with "walker" joints in center of legs and torso. Painted decal eyes and closed or open/closed mouth. Original or nicely dressed: Excellent condition: 14" – $550.00; 17" – $750.00; 20" – $1,000.00. Good condition: 17" – $325.00; 20" – $425.00. Poor condition: 17" – $175.00; 20" – $225.00.

SCHOENHUT

Left to Right: 16" Carved head and hair with blue ribbon. Open/closed smiling mouth with six molded teeth. 13½" Baby face pouty boy and 16" girl with carved hair and hair band. All are Schoenhuts and all have painted eyes. Courtesy Frasher Doll Auctions. Left – $1,900.00; Center – $350.00 up; Right – $1,500.00.

15" Schoenhut boy with wig. 19" Girl with carved hair with comb marks and blue bow in back. Intaglio brown eyes. Courtesy Frasher Doll Auctions. 15" – $550.00; 19" – $1,900.00.

16" Schoenhut boy with carved hair. All wood with spring jointed body. Shown with 14" "Patsy" by Effanbee. Courtesy Frasher Doll Auctions. 14" Patsy – $250.00; 16" – $1,900.00.

16" Schoenhut boy. All wood, spring jointed body. Wears boys suit with Schoenhut doll pin. Courtesy Frasher Doll Auctions. 16" – $650.00.

16" Marked: Schoenhut doll/Pat. Jan. 17, 1911/U.S.A. Mohair wig, open/closed mouth with painted teeth. Courtesy Glorya Woods. 16" – $500.00 up.

SCHUETZMEISTER & QUENDT

Schuetzmeister & Quendt only made dolls for a few short years from 1893 to 1898. The factory was located in Boilstat, Thur, Germany. Some of their mold numbers are: 101, 210, 301. Marks:

SQ   S̶Q̶   S 9

Child: Can have cut pate or be a bald head with two stringing holes. No damage and nicely dressed, open mouth: 16" – $400.00; 20" – $500.00; 24" – $600.00.
Baby: Five-piece bent limb body. Not damaged and nicely drssed. Open mouth: 14" – $350.00; 17" – $450.00; 22" – $650.00.

Right: 15" Marked: 201 S.Q. Five-piece bent limb baby body, open mouth with two teeth and sleep eyes. Left: 18" Marked: F.S. & Co. 1295. Baby made by Franz Schmidt. Courtesy Frasher Doll Auctions. 15" S.Q. – $375.00; 18" 1295 – $575.00.

SIMON & HALBIG

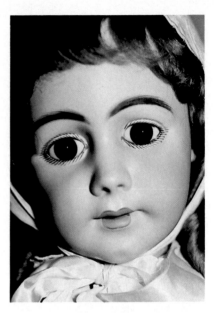

19" Marked: Simon and Halbig 949 with closed mouth and large set paperweight eyes. Fully jointed composition body. Courtesy Turn of Century Antiques. 19" – $1,800.00.

36" Very large doll marked: S&H 939. Large paperweight eyes, open mouth and on jointed composition body. Courtesy Frasher Doll Auctions. 36" – $3,500.00.

Simon & Halbig made some of the finest German dolls manufactured. They began making dolls sometime in the late 1860's or early 1870's and continued until the 1930's. Simon & Halbig made a great many heads for almost all the major doll makers of their time. They also supplied heads for the French trade. They made entire dolls, all bisque, flange necked dolls, turned shoulder heads and socket heads.

In 1895 Simon left the firm (retired or deceased) and Carl Halbig took over as single owner. Their dolls are marked with the full name or just the initials: S.H. or S.&H.

All prices are for dolls with no damage to the bisque heads and only minor scuffs to the body. They are well dressed, wigged and have shoes. These dolls should be ready to place into a collection.

Child: 1889 to 1930's. Open mouth and composition body. 719, 739, 749, 939, 949: 16" – $750.00; 20" – $1,000.00; 25" – $1,500.00; 30" – $2,200.00. 130, 540, 550, 1009, 1039, 1040, 1078, 1079, etc.: Allow

extra for flirty eyes: 12" – $350.00; 15" – $425.00; 18" – $500.00; 22" – $650.00; 26" – $750.00; 30" – $975.00; 33" – $1,250.00; 36" – $1,600.00; 40"-42" – $2,500.00 up.

Child: 1889 to 1930's. Open mouth and kid body. 1009 with fashion style kid body: 18" – $600.00; 23" – $800.00; 25" – $1,000.00. 1010, 1040, 1080, etc.: 16" – $450.00; 21" – $525.00; 25" – $700.00; 30" – $950.00. 1250, 1260: 15" – $350.00; 18" – $450.00; 21" – $550.00; 24" – $725.00.

Characters: 1910 and after. Wig or molded hair, glass or painted eyes and with open, closed or open/closed mouths. On jointed composition body: *IV:* 19" – $6,000.00. 120: 14" – $1,200.00; 22" – $2,300.00. 150: 15" – $5,800.00; 18" – $7,900.00; 22" – $9,000.00. *151:* 16" – $5,000.00; 22" – $7,800.00. *153:* 16" – $6,000.00. *600:* 14" – $425.00; 18" – $725.00; 21" – $825.00. *718, 719:* 16" – $1,800.00; 20" – $2,200.00. *720, 740:* Kid body, closed mouth. Bisque lower arms. Head and body in perfect condition: 10″ – $450.00; 16″ – $1,000.00. *740:* 10″ – $450.00; 16″ – $1,000.00; 20″ – $1,600.00. *749:* Closed mouth, jointed body. Head and body in perfect condition: 16″ – $1,500.00; 20″ – $4,900.00. *905, 908:* 14″ – $1,500.00; 17″ – $2,500.00. *939:* Composition body: 17″ – $1,800.00; 20″ – $2,400.00; 25″ – $3,000.00. *949:* 17″ – $1,300.00; 20″ – $1,800.00; 25″ – $2,500.00. *939* Kid Body: 17″ – $1,400.00; 20″ – $1,900.00; 25″ – $2,500.00. *949* Kid Body: 17″ – $1,100.00; 20″ – $1,500.00; 25″ – $2,100.00. *939* Composition body. Black: 17″ – $2,200.00; 20″ – $2,800.00; 25″ – $3,400.00. *949* Composition body. Black: 17″ – $1,700.00; 20″ – $2,200.00; 25″ – $2,900.00. *950* Kid Body: 10″ – $450.00; 14″ – $625.00; 18″ – $1,200.00. *1249* Santa: 16″ – $725.00; 20″ – $895.00; 26″ – $1,000.00. *1279:* 16″ – $1,000.00; 21″ – $1,800.00; 25″ – $2,400.00; 30″ – $3,200.00. *1299:* 17″ – $900.00; 21″ – $1,000.00. *1338:* Composition body, open mouth: 18″ – $1,100.00; 24″ – $2,200.00; 30″ – $3,200.00. *1339* Character face, open mouth, jointed body. Nicely dressed and perfect condition: 18″ – $1,100.00; 24″ – $2,200.00; 30″ – $3,200.00. *1358,* Black doll: 17″ – $4,500.00; 21″ – $5,400.00; 24″ – $6,000.00. *1388* Lady doll: 21″ – $8,200.00; 26″ – $13,000.00. *1428:* 20″ – $1,600.00. *1478:* 16″ – $5,000.00. *1488:* 16″ – $2,000.00; 20″ – $3,900.00.

Character Babies: 1909 to 1930's. Wigs or molded hair, painted or sleep eyes, open or open/closed mouths and on five-piece bent

22″ Marked: 1159, S&H DEP 8. Germany. On jointed lady body with slim arms and legs. Open mouth, sleep eyes, original wig. Courtesy Arthur Rouliette. 22″ – $1,800.00.

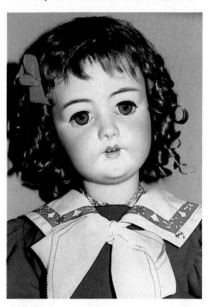

39″ Marked: Simon Halbig 1079 DEP. Socket head on bisque shoulder plate marked: Simon Halbig Germany. Kid jointed body with bisque lower arms, sleep eyes/lashes, open mouth with four teeth. Courtesy Frasher Doll Auctions. 39″ – $2,400.00.

26″ Marked: Simon and Halbig 1009 with large sleep eyes, open mouth. Fully jointed composition body. Courtesy Turn of Century Antiques. 26″ – $1,000.00.

limb baby body or toddler body: *1294:* 15″ – $525.00; 18″ – $625.00; 22″ – $725.00; 25″ – $850.00. *1294* With clockwise mechanism in head: 25″-26″ – $2,000.00. *1299* With open mouth: 10″ – $350.00; 16″ – $600.00; Toddler: 16″ – $750.00; 18″ – $900.00. *1428,* Toddler: 12″ – $1,250.00; 16″ – $1,450.00; 20″ – $1,850.00. *1428 Baby:* 12″ – $800.00; 16″ – $1,100.00; 20″ – $1,500.00. 1488 Toddler: 17″ – $3,200.00; 20″ – $3,600.00. *1488 Baby:* 17″ – $2,100.00; 20″ – $2,200.00; 24″ – $3,000.00. *1489 Ericka:* 19″ – $2,200.00; 21″ – $3,000.00; 25″ – $3,800.00. *1498* Toddler: 16″ – $2,000.00; 20″ – $3,600.00. *1498* Baby: 16″ – $1,400.00; 20″ – $2,400.00.

Walker: Key wound: 1039: 16″ – $995.00; 18″ – $1,100.00; 20″ – $1,400.00. 1039 Walking and kissing doll: 18″ – $750.00; 22″ – $995.00.

Miniature Dolls: Tiny dolls with open mouth on composition jointed or five-piece body with some having painted-on shoes and socks: Fully jointed body: 8″ – $365.00; 10″ – $425.00. Five-piece body: 8″ – $300.00; 10″ – $395.00.

Little Women Type: Closed mouth and fancy wig: 1160: 6″ – $300.00; 9″ – $375.00.

Ladies: Ca. 1910. Open mouths, molded lady style body, slim arms and legs: 1159, 1179: 18″ – $1,500.00; 22″ – $1,800.00; 25″ – $2,200.00.

Ladies: Ca. 1910. With closed mouths, slim limbs and adult style composition body: 1303: 15″ – $4,000.00; 18″ – $5,400.00. 1469: 15″ – $1,400.00; 18″ – $2,600.00.

18″ Marked: S&H 1249 DEP. Germany 7. Some are marked with their name "Santa" also. Jointed body, open mouth and sleep eyes. Courtesy Frasher Doll Auctions. 18″ – $800.00.

31″ Marked: S&H 1279 DEP. Germany 14½. Jointed body, sleep eyes/lashes, open mouth with four teeth. Character face. Courtesy Frasher Doll Auctions. 31″ – $3,100.00.

10" Marked: 1299/Simon & Halbig/3½. Set eyes, open mouth with two upper teeth. Dimples low on cheeks. All original on five-piece baby body. Courtesy Henri and John Startzel. 10" – $350.00.

Right: 18" Pale satin bisque marked: Simon Halbig, 42, made in Germany, 99/10. Open mouth, flutter tongue, sleep eyes/lashes and on five-piece baby body. Left: 18" Toddler marked: H Germany 12/J.D.K./220. Sleep eyes, open mouth and jointed at wrist toddler body. Courtesy Joanna Brunken. 18" – $700.00; 18" J.D.K. 220 – $2,700.00.

20" Twins marked: 1294 Simon Halbig. Toddler bodies, sleep eyes and open mouths with two upper teeth. Courtesy Frasher Doll Auctions. 20" – $685.00 each.

25" Simon and Halbig doll with mold number 1339. Open mouth and a much more character face than appears in photograph. The nose is quite full at the nostrils and she is on a fully jointed composition body. Courtesy Dora Barton. 18" – $1,100.00; 24" – $2,200.00; 30" – $3,200.00.

S.F.B.J.

22½" Marked: SFBJ 1159. Lady doll with flirty eyes, walks, head moves and arm raises to blow kisses. May be original gown. Courtesy Turn of Century Antiques. 23" – $1,700.00.

14" Doll by S.F.B.J. marked: 227. Set "jewel" eyes, open mouth with tiny teeth and on body with one-piece arms and legs. (five-piece body). Courtesy Frasher Doll Auctions. 14" – $1,400.00.

The Societe Francaise de Fabrication de Bebes et Jouets (S.F.B.J.) was formed in 1899 and known members were Jumeau, Bru, Fleischmann & Blodel, Rabery & Delphieu, Pintel & Godchaux, P.H. Schmitz, A. Bouchet, Jullien and Danel & Cie.

The director was Fleischmann and at the beginning of World War I, he was deported and his properties taken from him because he was an alien (Germany). By 1922 S.F.B.J. employed 2,800 people. The Society dissolved in the mid-1950's. There are a vast amount of "dolly" faced S.F.B.J. dolls, but also some are extremely rare and are character molds. Most of the character dolls are in the 200 series of mold numbers. Marks:

S.F.B.J.
239
PARIS

Child: Sleep or set eyes, open mouth and on jointed composition body. No damage and nicely dressed in the French style. 60: 14" – $465.00; 20" – $600.00; 24" – $750.00. 301: 8" – $200.00; 14" – $575.00; 18" – $800.00; 22" – $975.00; 28" – $1,200.00; 32" – $1,800.00.
Jumeau-type: 16" – $900.00; 20" – $1,150.00; 24" – $1,600.00; 28" – $2,000.00.
Closed mouth: 16" – $1,200.00; 20" – $1,600.00; 24" – $2,000.00; 28" – $2,400.00. S.F.B.J. Lady: Mold 1159. Open mouth and adult body: 22" – $1,600.00.
Character: Sleep or set eyes, wigged or with molded hair and some may have flocked hair over molded. Composition body. Nicely dressed and ready to display. No damage at all to head and only minor scuffs to body: 211: 16" – $4,700.00. 226: 16" – $1,700.00; 21" – $1,900.00. 227: 16" – $1,800.00; 21" – $2,000.00. 230: 23" – $1,800.00. 233: 14" – $1,600.00; 17" – $3,000.00. 234: 16" – $2,500.00; 21" – $2,900.00. 235: 16" – $1,700.00; 21" –

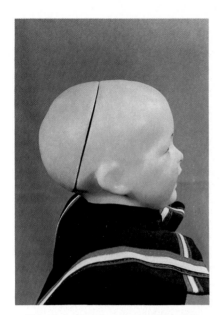

Side view of 15″ marked: SFBJ, 242.

15″ Marked: SFBJ 242 Paris. Has open mouth with round hole. Set "jewel" eyes and back of head opens and contains a rubber bladder. Comes with flocked hair or wig. (refer to *Doll Values, Vol. 1*, page 264). Courtesy Henri and John Startzel. 15″ – $3,000.00.

$1,900.00. *236* Toddlers: 12″ – $1,200.00; 16″ – $1,500.00; 20″ – $1,900.00; 25″ – $2,300.00; 27″ – $2,600.00. *236* Baby: 16″ – $1,200.00; 21″ – $1,600.00; 25″ – $2,000.00. *237:* 16″ – $1,800.00; 21″ – $2,000.00. *238:* 16″ – $2,600.00; 21″ – $3,000.00. *238* Lady: 22″ – $3,500.00. *239*(Poubout): 14″ – $3,700.00; 17″ – $4,300.00. *242:* 17″ – $3,200.00. *247:* 16″ – $2,200.00; 21″ – $2,800.00. *248:* Very pouty, glass eyes: 14″ – $3,200.00; 17″ – $4,000.00. *251* Toddler: 16″ – $1,200.00; 20″ – $1,800.00; 26″ – $2,400.00. *251* Baby: 10″ – $850.00; 16″ – $1,200.00. 21″ – $1,500.00. *252* Toddler: 16″ – $3,500.00; 20″ – $5,500.00; 26″ – $8,000.00. *252* Baby: 10″ – $2,000.00; 16″ – $2,400.00. 257: 16″ – $1,800.00. *266:* 20″ – $1,700.00.

Googly: Mold 245: No damage and nicely dressed: 14″-15″ – $5,000.00.

Kiss-Throwing & Walking Doll: Composition body with straight legs, walking mechanism and when walks, arm goes up to throw kiss. Head moves from side to side. Flirty eyes and open mouth. In working condition, not damaged, bisque head without any damage, nicely dressed in French styles and ready to display: 21″-22″ – $1,500.00.

33″ Marked: S.F.B.J. Paris and uses the Jumeau molds. Sleep eyes, open mouth and on jointed body. Courtesy Frasher Doll Auctions. 33″ – $2,400.00.

S.F.B.J.
SKOOKUM INDIAN DOLLS

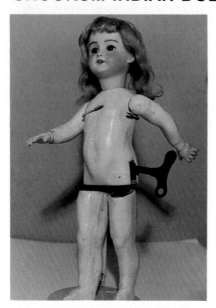

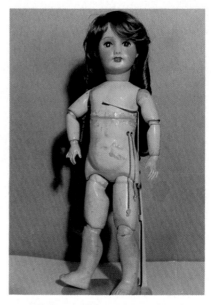

16″ S.F.B.J. 301 key wind walker. Sleep eyes, open mouth and papier mache/composition body with one-piece arms and legs with jointed wrists. Courtesy Turn of Century Antiques. 16″ – $1,000.00.

20″ S.F.B.J. 301 with painted bisque head, sleep eyes with tin eyelids, open mouth and has pull string ''MaMa-PaPa'' talker bellows. Upper part of both legs accidently turned backward. Courtesy Turn of Century Antiques. 20″ – $1,500.00.

SKOOKUM INDIAN DOLLS

Skookums Indians and heads still in original box. Courtesy Turn of Century Antiques. 12″ – $55.00; 18″ – $135.00; Box of Heads – $125.00.

138

Face mask with wig, wool blanket forms body that is stuffed with twigs and leaves or grass. Wood dowel legs and wooden feet. Paper label on feet. 4" – $18.00; 6" – $25.00; 12" – $55.00; 15" – $110.00; 18" – $135.00; 22" – $185.00; 30" – $325.00; 36" – $595.00.

Squaw with Baby: 15" – $125.00; 18" – $200.00; 22" – $325.00.
Portrait Chief: 15" – $125.00; 18" – $200.00; 22" – $325.00.
Sitting Squaw: 8" – $100.00.

SNOW BABIES

Snow Babies were made both in Germany and Japan and can be of excellent to very poor in quality from both countries. Snow Babies have a "pebbles" covering fired-on like clothes. Many are unmarked. The features are painted:
Single Figure: 1½" – $55.00; 3" – $75.00-100.00.
Two Figures together: 1½" – $100.00-125.00; 3" – $150.00-195.00.
Three Figures Together: 1½" – $125.00-175.00; 3" – $175.00-225.00.
One Figure On Sled: 2"-2½" – $125.00.
Two Figures On Sled: 2"-2½" – $145.00.
Three Figures On Sled: 3" – $165.00; 6" – $200.00.
Jointed: Shoulders and hips: 5" – $300.00 up.
Shoulder Head: Cloth body and china limbs: 7"-9" – $350.00.
Rare Snow Babies: On sled in glass "snow scene": $145.00 up. With Bear: $165.00. Musical Base: $125.00. With Snowman: 3" – $150.00. Laughing Child: 3" – $95.00 up. Snow Bear with Santa: $250.00. With Reindeer: $125.00.

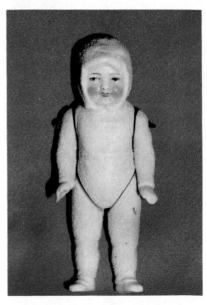

5½" All bisque Snow Baby. Textured bisque and wire pin jointed at shoulders and hips. Courtesy Frasher Doll Auctions. $300.00.

STEIFF

The Steiff Company was started by Margarete Steiff in 1894 and is still in business today. This German maker is better known for their animals than dolls. **Steiff Dolls:** Felt, velvet or plush with seam down the middle of the face. Button style eyes, painted features and sewn on ear. The dolls generally have large feet so they can stand alone. Prices are for dolls in excellent condition and with original clothes. Adults: 16"-17" – $700.00; 21"-22" – $950.00. Military Men: 17" – $1,000.00; 21" – $1,500.00. Children: 12" – $500.00; 15"-16" – $650.00; 18"-19" – $850.00. Made in U.S. Zone, Germany and has glass eyes: 12" – $600.00; 16" – $750.00.

Two early Steiff dolls with soft felt bodies. Wires joined inside bodies to permit limbs to be posed. Felt arms with stitched fingers, felt faces with center seam. Applied beard and brows. Both are original. Courtesy Frasher Doll Auctions. 16″ – $500.00.

Three Steiff Ca. 1957. 22″ "Lucki" and "Pucki". Pressed rubber heads, mohair beards, straw stuffed felt bodies and all are original. Courtesy Frasher Doll Auctions. 12″ – $90.00; 22″ – $200.00.

STEINER, JULES

Jules Nichols Steiner operated from 1855 to 1892 when the firm was taken over by Amedee LaFosse. In 1895 this firm merged with Henri Alexander (maker of Be'be' Phenix) and May Freres Cie (maker of Be'be' Mascotte), then in 1899 Jules Mettais took over the firm. In 1906 the company was sold to Edmond Daspres.

In 1889 the firm registered the girl with the banner and the words "Le Petite Parisien", and in 1892 LeFosse registered the trademark "Le Parisien". Marks:

J. STEINER   STE C3
BTE S.G.D.G.   J. STEINER
FIRE A 12   B. S.G.D.G.
PARIS

Bourgoin

"A" Series Steiner Child: 1885. Closed mouth, paperweight eyes, jointed composition body and cardboard pate. No damage, nicely dressed in French styles: 12″ – $2,000.00; 16″ – $3,000.00; 20″ – $3,400.00; 25″ – $4,200.00; 28″ – $5,000.00.

"A" Series Child: With open mouth, paperweight eyes and on jointed composition body. Nicely dressed in the French style and no damage: 16″ – $1,200.00; 20″ – $2,300.00; 26″ – $3,400.00.

Bourgoin Steiner: 1870's. With "Bourgoin" incised or in red stamp on head along with rest of the mark. Closed mouth and paperweight eyes. Composition body. No damage in any way and nicely dressed in French style: 16″ – $3,600.00; 20″ – $3,900.00; 25″ – $4,800.00.

Wire-Eyed Steiner: Closed mouth with flat

13″ "A" Series. Marked: Steiner Paris Fre. A.7. Closed mouth, pierced ears and on jointed body with straight wrists. Courtesy Frasher Doll Auctions. 13″ – $2,100.00.

14″ "A" Series Steiner. Marked: Steiner Paris Fre. A.7. Closed mouth, pierced ears, on Steiner jointed body with straight wrists. Courtesy Frasher Doll Auctions. 14″ – $2,200.00.

14½″ "C" Series Steiner with wired eyes which operate from metal handle in back of head. Marks: Ste. C O and red stamp: Steiner B.S.G.D.G./Bourgoin. This particular doll has three-piece eyeballs with glass fused to porcelain base and each is incised: Steiner. Original wig. Courtesy Frasher Doll Auctions. 15″ – $3,400.00.

STEINER, JULES
TYNIE BABY
UNIS

glass eyes that open and close by moving wire that comes out the back of the head. Composition body. No damage, chips or breaks and nicely dressed in French styles. Marked: Bourgoin: 16" – $3,800.00; 20" – $4,200.00; 25" – $4,600.00; 38" – $6,000.00.

"C" Series: Ca. 1880. 16" – $3,600.00; 20" – $4,200.00; 25" – $4,600.00; 29" – $6,000.00.

"A" Series: Le Parisien: 1892. 16" – $3,000.00; 20" – $3,600.00; 25" – $4,400.00.

"C" Series Steiner: Ca. 1880. Closed mouth and paperweight eyes and on composition body. No damage and nicely dressed in French style: 16" – $3,500.00; 20" – $3,900.00; 25" – $4,500.00.

Mechanical Steiner: Key wound, kicks, cries, moves head and has two rows of teeth. In working order, not damaged and nicely dressed: 18" – $1,800.00.

Bisque Hip Steiner: Motschmann style body with bisque head, shoulders, lower arms and legs and bisque torso section. No damage anywhere and nicely dressed: 18" – $4,000.00.

Early White Bisque Steiner: With round face, open mouth with two rows of teeth. Unmarked. On jointed Steiner body. No damage and nicely dressed: 14" – $1,200.00; 18" – $2,600.00.

Tynie Baby. Designed by Bernard Lipfert and made for Horsman Dolls in 1924. Sleep eyes, closed mouth with pouty look and modeling of frown between eyes. Cloth body with composition or celluloid hands. Marks: 1924/E.I. Horsman, Inc./made in Germany. Some will be incised "Tynie Baby", also. No damage and nicely dressed. Bisque head: 14" – $650.00; Composition head: 13"-14" – $250.00; All bisque: 9" – $850.00.

17" Baby with bisque head, brown sleep eyes, painted hair and wide open mouth. Cloth body with delicate celluloid hands. Marks: Paris 272/Unis France with 71 on one side and 149 on other. Courtesy Turn of Century Antiques. 17" – $800.00.

"Unis, France" was a type of trade association, a type of "seal of approval" for trade goods to consumers from the manufacturers. This group of businessmen, who were supposed to watch the quality of French exports, often overlooked guidelines and some poor quality dolls were exported. Many very fine quality Unis marked dolls were also produced.

Unis began right after World War I and it is still in effect today. Two doll companies are current members, Poupee Bella and Petit Colin. There are other types of manufacturers in this group and they include makers of toys, sewing machines, tile, pens, etc. Marks:

71 (UNIS FRANCE) 149 <UNIS FRANCE>
301

60, 70, 71, 301: Bisque head with papier mache' or composition jointed body. Sleep or set eyes, open mouth. Not damaged and nicely dressed: 14" – $450.00; 17" – $525.00; 21" – $650.00; 24" – $750.00. Black or Brown: 14" – $525.00; 17" – $600.00.

Provincial Costume Doll: Bisque head, painted, set or sleep eyes, open mouth (or closed on smaller dolls). Five-piece body. Original Provincial costume. No damage and in very good condition: 6" – $175.00; 12" – $265.00; 14" – $295.00.

Black or Brown: 6" – $200.00; 12" – $325.00; 14" – $325.00. On fully jointed body: 12" – $300.00; 14" – $365.00.

Baby: Mold 272: Glass eyes, wide open mouth: 14" – $400.00; 17" – $800.00.

20" Unis France 301 and 79-149. Also has an E, followed by an R in a circle and then T. On French jointed body, tin eyelids, open mouth. Courtesy Turn of Century Antiques. 20" – $575.00.

8" Marked: UNIS 60 Paris. Five-piece body, painted on boots, closed mouth, sleep eyes and original, with paper sticker. 1911. Courtesy Frasher Doll Auctions. 8" – $250.00.

WAGNER & ZETSCHE WAX

Richard Wagner and Richard Zetsche made dolls, doll's heads and doll's shoes. They operated in Ilmenau, Thur, Germany between 1870's and the 1930's. They used a blue paper label on the shoulder (inside) with the initials W & Z which is in heavy interwoven script, as well as block printed letters. They exported both kid and cloth bodies. The majority of the turned head dolls where the head has been removed to examine the Wagner & Zetsche label are unmarked. Marked heads have also been found on the W & Z bodies and some of the head makers are Simon & Halbig, Kestner and Heinrich Handwerck.

Turned Head Dolls: Can have solid dome or cut open pate, set, paperweight or sleep eyes, cloth or kid body with bisque lower arms. Eyebrows are flat on the underside. Large sizes may have applied ears. No damage with only minor damage or repair to body and nicely dressed. Closed mouth: 16" – $700.00; 20" – $950.00; 24" – $1,000.00.

Open Mouth: 20" – $495.00; 24" – $750.00; 28" – $900.00.

Harald: (also marked with WZ) celluloid type material: 15" – $245.00.

WAX

Poured Wax: Cloth body with wax head, arms and legs. Inset glass eyes and hair is embedded into wax. Very nicely dressed or in original clothes, no damage to wax, but wax may be slightly discolored (evenly all over): Not rewaxed: 15" – $900.00; 18" – $1,000.00; 21" – $1,250.00; 24" – $1,500.00.

Waxed Over Papier Mache' or Composition: Cloth body with wax over papier mache' or composition head and with wax over composition or wood limbs. Only minor scuffs with no chipped out places, nicely dressed: Early Dolls: 12" – $350.00; 16" – $595.00. Later Dolls: 12" – $150.00; 16" – $300.00.

12" Wax over papier mache' with glass eyes, human hair wig, cloth body with leather arms, original clothes. Courtesy Henri and John Startzel. 12" – $350.00 up.

21" Poured wax baby. Wax arms and legs with cloth torso. Inset glass eyes and head is bald. Courtesy Frasher Doll Auctions. 21" – $1,250.00.

18" Montanari-type wax with inset glass eyes, cloth body and composition arms and legs, which should be wax. Original wig. Courtesy Arthur Rouliette. 18" – $1,000.00.

20" Wax over composition. Glass eyes, mohair wig, cloth body with wax over composition lower arms and legs. May be original dress. Courtesy Frasher Doll Auctions. 20" – $365.00.

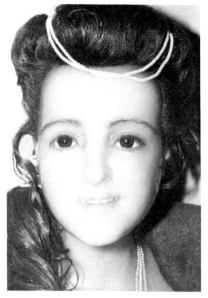

Lifesize poured wax. turned shoulder head, glass eyes and inset hair. On regular mannequin adult body. Date and maker unknown. Courtesy Frasher Doll Auctions. $700.00 up.

40" Poured wax. Mannequin child with inset glass eyes and inset human hair. Swivel head is fitted over wood neck piece and body is cloth and composition. Date and maker unknown. Courtesy Frasher Doll Auctions. 40" – $1,000.00 up.

WAX
WELLINGS, NORAH
WISLIZENUS, ADOLPF

Pumpkin Head: Molded or wigged and glass eyes: 14" – $200.00; 17" – $325.00; 21" – $450.00.

Bonnet Molded On: 1860-1880. May have mohair or human hair glued over molded hair, glass eyes: 14" – $750.00; 18" – $1,400.00.

Wax With Wig: 1850's-1900's. Not modeled as "pumpkin" heads but regular hair styles, open or closed mouth, glass eyes: 17" – $325.00; 21" – $385.00; 25" – $450.00.

Slit-Head Wax: 1830-1860's. Human hair embedded into slit down center of head. Glass eyes: 17" – $425.00; 21" – $500.00.

WELLINGS, NORAH

Norah Wellings' designs were made for her at the Victoria Toy Works in Wellington, Shropshire, England. These dolls were made from 1926 into the 1960's. The dolls are felt, velour and velvet as well as other fabrics. They will have a tag on the foot: Made in England by Norah Wellings. **Child:** All fabric with stitch jointed hips and shoulders and have a molded fabric face with oil painted features. Some faces are of papier mache' with a stockinette covering. All original felt and cloth clothes, clean condition: Painted eyes: 14" – $200.00; 17"

– $350.00; 21" – $500.00; 23" – $625.00. Glass Eyes: 14" – $285.00; 17" – $475.00; 21" – $600.00.

Mounties, Black Islanders, Scots and Other Characters: These are most commonly found. Must be in same condition as child dolls: 8" – $45.00; 11" – $85.00; 14" – $125.00; 17" – $185.00. Glass Eyes: 14" White – $150.00; 14" Black – $175.00.

Babies: Same description as "child" and same condition: 14" – $285.00; 17" – $475.00; 21" – $595.00.

WISLIZENUS, ADOLPF

The Adolpf Wislizenus doll factory was located in Walterhausen, Germany, and the

heads he used were made by Bahr & Proschild, Ernst Heubach of Koppelsdorf and Simon & Halbig. The company was in business starting in 1851. The marks on the dolls will be: A.W.

Child: Ca. 1890's into 1900. Bisque head on jointed composition body, sleep eyes and open mouth. No damage and nicely dressed: 16" – $325.00; 21" – $385.00; 24" – $450.00.

Baby: Bisque head in perfect condition and on five-piece bent limb baby body. Nicely dressed: 16" – $350.00; 20" – $475.00; 25" – $650.00. Mold 115: 12" – $450.00; 16" – $600.00.

Left: 23" Marked: 28 A.W. Special Germany. Sleep eyes, open mouth with four teeth and on jointed body. Right: 28" Marked: S&H 1250 DEP. Shoulder head on kid body. Bisque lower arms, set eyes and open mouth. Courtesy Frasher Doll Auctions. 23" – $450.00; 28" S&H – $800.00.

26″ Marked: Special 62. Sleep eyes, open mouth with four teeth, jointed body. Made by Adolpf Wislizenus. Courtesy Frasher Doll Auctions. 26″ – $600.00.

MODERN SECTION & INDEX

ADVANCE DOLL CO.
MADAME ALEXANDER-ALEXANDER-KINS

18" "Wanda Walker" all hard plastic. Key wind walker with plastic shoes and rollers. Head turns and arms move up and down. Original. Made by Advance Doll Co. Courtesy Frasher Doll Auctions. 18" Walker – $85.00; 24" Walker & Talker – $125.00.

MADAME ALEXANDER-ALEXANDER-KINS

Alexander-kins: All hard plastic, sleep eyes, jointed at shoulders, neck and hips. Can be 7½" or 8". Marks: "ALEX", on backs and full name "ALEXANDER" after 1977. TAGS: "Alexander-Kins", "Madame Alexander, etc.", specific name of doll, or "Wendy-Kins". 1953: Straight leg, non-walker. All solid, heavy hard plastic. 1954: Straight leg, non-walker and straight leg walker. 1955: Straight leg walker. 1956-1965: Bend-knee walker. 1973 to Date: Straight leg non-walker, light weight. 1973-1975: Marked: "Alex". 1976 to Date: Marked: "Alexander". 1978: Face change to smaller painted mouth. 1981 to Date: Very pale color. *Prices for mint, tagged dolls with original box.*

Alexander-Kin/Wendy-Kins: Short dresses, no pinafores – $125.00 up. Dirty, hair messy, no shoes – $35.00-50.00. Pinafore/dresses with hats – $225.00 up. Dirty, hair messy, no tag or shoes – $60.00. Brides: 1953-54 – $600.00 up; 1955 – $350.00 up; 1970's – $45.00 up. Dirty and played with – $25.00-100.00. Groom – $450.00 up. Dirty – $100.00. Ballgowns –

$600.00 up. Fading, tag gone, hats or hair flowers gone – $125.00. Ballerinas: 1950's – $250.00 up; 1960's – $150.00 up; Dirty – $50.00-75.00. Guardian Angel – $1,000.00 up; Fading, halo or harp missing – $200.00. Nurse: In white – $800.00; Dirty – $100.00. In blue/white – $550.00; Dirty, Baby missing – $90.00. Special long gowns: Melanie – $1,400.00 up; Dirty – $200.00. Aunt Pitty Pat – $1,400.00 up; Dirty – $200.00; Aunt Agatha – $1,400.00 up; Dirty – $200.00; Cousin Grace – $1,400.00 up; Dirty – $200.00. Quiz-kin: Has buttons in back to move head – $400.00 up; Played with and not mint – $150.00. Story Princess – $1,400.00 up; Soiled, tiara missing – $200.00.

International (discontinued): Africa – $350.00-450.00; Soiled – $150.00. Amish boy or girl – $450.00-550.00; Soiled – $200.00. Argentine boy – $450.00-550.00; Soiled – $200.00. Bolivia $425.00-525.00; Soiled – $175.00. Cowboy or girl – $500.00-600.00; Soiled – $225.00. Ecuador – $400.00-500.00; Soiled – $150.00. English Guard – $500.00-600.00; Soiled –

$225.00. Eskimo – $500.00-600.00; Soiled – $225.00. Hawaii – 450.00-550.00; Soiled – $200.00. Greek boy – $350.00-450.00; Soiled – $150.00. Indian boy or girl – $450.00-550.00; Soiled – $200.00. Korea – $425.00-525.00; Soiled – $200.00. Morocco – $400.00-500.00; Soiled – $150.00. Miss U.S.A. – $400.00-500.00;

Soiled – $150.00. Peruvian boy – $475.00-575.00; Soiled – $225.00. Spanish boy – $350.00-450.00; Soiled – $150.00. Vietnam – $425.00-525.00; Soiled – $175.00. Bend Knee Internationals – $85.00-150.00. Straight leg – S.A.. Storybook Dolls with Bend Knees – $85.00-125.00. Straight leg – S.A.

8″ "First Communion" 1957. Completely mint and original and has original box. Courtesy Doll Cradle. Mint in box – $800.00; Near mint – $600.00.

A rare version of the 1963 Southern Belle sold with cluster of flowers on bonnet, rather than feather plume. Wrist tag says "Southern Belle". Courtesy Margaret Mandel. $600.00.

8″ Alexander-kin #500. Basic doll sold as shown with wardrobe purchased separately. Bend knee walker. 1956-1964. Courtesy Doll Cradle. $150.00.

Two discontinued Internationals. He is "Peruvian Boy" 1965 and 1966. Can be on a bend knee walker or just have bend knees. She is "Bolivia" made from 1963 to 1966. Can be on bend knee walker or on just a bend knee doll. Courtesy Green's Museum, Chatsworth, GA. Girl – $425.00; Boy – $475.00.

MADAME ALEXANDER-BABIES

12" "Little Genius" mint and original in original box. Cloth and composition with sleep eyes and closed mouth. Courtesy Turn of Century Antiques. $250.00.

17" Little Genius. Composition head, hands and legs with cloth body. Molded, painted hair and sleep flirty eyes. Original tagged clothes. Courtesy Turn of Century Antiques. $185.00.

"Kathy" 1954-1956. Came with molded hair and rooted hair. All vinyl, sleep eyes. Came in sizes: 11", 15", 17", 19", 23" 26". Courtesy Doll Cradle. 11" – $85.00; 15" – $100.00; 17" – $145.00; 19" – $155.00; 23" – $170.00; 26" – $185.00.

7" "Fischer" Quintuplets. 1964. Little Genius head on vinyl bodies, original in tagged blanket. Courtesy Frasher Doll Auctions. $350.00.

Prices are for mint dolls.

Baby McGuffey: Composition: 20" – $175.00; Soiled – $65.00.

Bonnie: Vinyl: 19" – $150.00; Soiled – $55.00.

Cookie: Composition: 19" – $265.00 up; Soiled – $85.00.

Genius: Vinyl, flirty eyes: 21" – $150.00-200.00; Soiled – $65.00.

Genius, Little: 8" – $165.00 up; Soiled – $60.00.

Happy: Vinyl: 20" – $275.00; Soiled – $95.00.

Honeybun: Vinyl: 23" – $150.00; Soiled – $55.00.

Kathy: Vinyl: 19" – $150.00; 26" – $185.00; Soiled – $50.00-65.00.

Kitten, Littlest: Vinyl: 8" – $185.00 up; Soiled – $70.00.

Mary Mine: 14" – $165.00; Soiled – $60.00.

Pinky: Composition: 23" – $175.00 up; Soiled – $65.00.

Precious: Composition: 12" – $135.00 up; Soiled – $45.00.

Princess Alexandria: 24" – $150.00 up; Soiled – $55.00.

Pussy Cat: Black. 14" – $145.00; Soiled – $50.00.

Rusty: Vinyl: 20" – $450.00; Soiled – $135.00.

Slumbermate: Composition: 21" – $400.00 up; Soiled – $125.00.

Sunbeam: Vinyl: 16" – $165.00 up; Soiled – $60.00.

Sweet Tears: 9" – $100.00; With layette – $165.00 up; Soiled – $35.00-50.00.

Victoria: 20" – $195.00; Soiled – $75.00.

MADAME ALEXANDER-CISSETTE

First prices are for mint dolls. Second prices are for soiled, dirty or faded clothes, tags missing or hair messy. High heel doll, all hard plastic. Made from 1957 to 1963 as "Cissette", but used as other dolls later. Clothes are tagged: "Cissette", 10"-11". In

MADAME ALEXANDER-CISSETTE

Left to Right: "Gold Rush" 1963 and "Klondike Kate" 1963. Both use the Margot/Cissette doll. Both original with tags. "Queen" Portrette also original. Courtesy Frasher Doll Auctions. Gold Rush – $1,600.00; Klondike Kate – $1,600.00.

Street Dresses – $175.00-250.00 – $75.00-95.00. In Ballgowns – $325.00 up-100.00. Ballerina – $175.00-250.00 – $75.00-100.00.

Gibson Girl: $1,400.00 up-250.00.

Jacqueline: $475.00-125.00.

Margot: $450.00; 100.00.

Portrettes: Agatha: 1968 – $525.00-165.00. Godey: 1968-1970 – $525.00-165.00. Jenny Lind: 1969-1970 – $600.00-185.00. Melinda In Turquoise: 1968 – $550.00-175.00. Melinda In Pink Lace: 1969 – $525.00-165.00. Melanie: 1970 – $525.00-165.00. Queen: 1972-1974 – $525.00-165.00. Renoir In Navy: 1968 – $525.00-165.00. Renoir In Aqua: 1970 – $550.00-175.00. Scarlett: 1968-1973 – $525.00-165.00. Southern Belle: 1968-1973 – $525.00-165.00. Sleeping Beauty – $525.00-165.00. Wigged: In Case – $600.00 up-195.00.

11" 1969 Portrette "Jenny Lind" using the Cissette doll. Original in box. Courtesy Frasher Doll Auctions. $600.00.

MADAME ALEXANDER-CISSETTE
MADAME ALEXANDER-CISSY

10" "Cissette" in 1957. Sunsuit and carries matching purse. Courtesy Frasher Doll Auctions. $175.00 up.

"Cissette" in street dress with hat. All original. Courtesy Jay Minter. $175.00 up.

MADAME ALEXANDER-CISSY

First prices are for mint dolls. Second prices for played with, soiled, messed up dolls. High heel feet, vinyl arms jointed at elbows. 1955-1959. Clothes tag, "Cissy". 21" tall.

Ballgown: $350.00 up-125.00.
Bride: $350.00-125.00.
Flora McFlimsey, Miss (vinyl head): 15" – $450.00 up-185.00.
Queen: In white or gold: $550.00 up-150.00.
Portrait (Godey, etc.): – $475.00 up-195.00.
Scarlett: $650.00 up-200.00.
Street Dressed: $245.00 up-85.00 up.

21" 1957 "Cissy". Hard plastic with vinyl arms jointed at elbows. Original and tagged. Courtesy Frasher Doll Auctions. $245.00 up.

155

MADAME ALEXANDER-CLOTH DOLLS
MADAME ALEXNADER-COMPOSITION DOLLS

First prices are for mint dolls. Second prices for poor condition, dirty or played with dolls or untagged. The Alexander Doll Company made cloth and plush dolls and animals and also oil cloth baby animal toys in the 1930's, 1940's and early 1950's. In the 1960's there were a few, such as "Funny", "Muffin" and "Good or Bad Little Girl".

Animals: $200.00 up-75.00 up.
Dogs: $300.00-100.00.
Alice in Wonderland: 16″ – $500.00-150.00.
Clarabelle Clown: 19″ – $185.00-70.00; 29″ – $250.00-95.00; 49″ – $400.00 up-200.00.
David Copperfield: 16″ – $500.00 up-150.00 up.

Eva Lovelace: $450.00 up-135.00 up.
Funny: $95.00-20.00.
Good or Bad Little Girl: 16″ – $150.00-70.00.
Little Shaver: 7″ – $200.00-80.00; 10″ – $275.00-95.00; 16″ – $365.00 up-165.00.
Little Women: 16″ – $450.00 up-185.00.
Muffin: 14″ – $95.00-30.00; 19″ – $150.00-70.00.
So-Lite Baby or Toddler: $300.00-100.00.
Susie Q or Bobby Q: 16″ – $600.00 up-200.00 up.
Tiny Tim: $450.00 up-135.00 up.
Teeny Twinkle: $465.00 up-150.00 up.

MADAME ALEXANDER-COMPOSITION DOLLS

First prices are for mint dolls. Second prices for cracked, crazed, dirty or soiled clothes or tags gone.
Alice In Wonderland: 9″ – $195.00-60.00;

18″ Dr. Defoe is shown with the Dionne Quints. All are composition and original except the stethoscope added. Courtesy Florence Phelps. Dr. – $600.00 up; Quints – $1,000.00 up.

14″ – $265.00-80.00; 20″ – $475.00-125.00.
Babies: (Genius, McGuffey, etc.). 11″ – $125.00-35.00; 22″ – $200.00-75.00.
Baby Jane: 16″ – $700.00 up-200.00.
Brides-Bridesmaids: 7″ – $150.00-45.00; 9″ – $195.00-75.00; 15″ – $275.00-85.00; 21″ – $425.00-100.00.
Dionne Quints: 8″ – $150.00 up-50.00; Set of five – $1,000.00. 11″ – $225.00-90.00; Set – $1,600.00. 14″ – $300.00-125.00; Set – $1,800.00. 16″ – $400.00 up-150.00; Set – $2,200.00. 19″ – $450.00 up-175.00; Set – $2,500.00.
Dr. Defoe: 14″-15″ – $600.00 up-200.00.
Flora McFlimsey: (Marked Princess Elizabeth). Freckles. 15″ – $425.00 up-150.00; 22″ – $550.00 up-200.00.
Internationals/Storybook: 7″ – $165.00-55.00; 11″ – $265.00-85.00.
Jane Withers: 13″ With closed mouth – $675.00 up-150.00; 17″ – $675.00 up-150.00; 21″ – $850.00 up--225.00.
Jeannie Walker: 13″ – $325.00-100.00; 18″ – $475.00-175.00.
Karen Ballerina: (And other composition ballerinas): 15″ – $350.00 up-100.00.
Kate Greenaway: (Marked Princess Elizabeth): 14″ – $400.00 up-125.00; 18″ – $525.00 up-200.00.
Little Colonel: 9″ – $225.00 up-125.00;

13" (Closed mouth) – $375.00 up-200.00; 23" – $625.00 up-300.00.

Margaret O'Brien: 15" – $450.00 up-175.00; 18" – $525.00 up-225.00; 21" – $800.00 up-300.00.

Marionettes: Tony Sarg: 12" – $275.00-85.00; Disney: 12" – $300.00-95.00.

McGuffey Ana: (Marked Princess Elizabeth): 13" – $350.00 up-125.00; 20" – $575.00 up-175.00.

Portrait Dolls: 1939-1941, 1946: 21" – $1,200.00 up-400.00 up.

Princess Elizabeth: 13" (Closed mouth) – $350.00-145.00; 18" – $450.00-150.00; 24" – $500.00-175.00.

Scarlett: 9" – $300.00-125.00; 14" – $400.00-150.00; 18" – $600.00-200.00; 21" – $1,200.00-300.00.

Sonja Henie: 17" – $475.00-150.00; 20" – $550.00-175.00; Jointed waist: 14" – $375.00-135.00.

Three Pigs: 11" – $400.00 each-150.00; Set of three – $1,400.00.

Special Girl: 22"-23" – $385.00 up-150.00.

Wendy Ann: 11" – $325.00-125.00; 15" – $400.00 up—150.00; 18" – $450.00 up-165.00.

7½" "Carmen" 1936. Marked: MME. Alexander. All composition, painted eyes, shoes and socks. All original. Courtesy Frasher Doll Auctions. $125.00.

9" "Wendy Ann Bride" 1942. All composition with painted eyes and in tagged gown. Head piece/veil missing. Courtesy Frasher Doll Auctions. $175.00.

14" "Sonja Henie" marked: (on body) Wendy-Ann/MME. Alexander/New York. Tagged costume. All composition. Courtesy Frasher Doll Auctions. 14" – $325.00 up.

MADAME ALEXANDER-COMPOSITION DOLLS
MADAME ALEXANDER-HARD PLASTIC

13" "Wendy Ann". All composition with sleep eyes. Mint in original clothes and with original hair set. Courtesy Florence Phelps. 11" – $325.00 up.

"Kate Greenaway" with orange-yellow mohair wig and all original. Head marked: Princess Elizabeth, clothes tagged: Kate Greenaway. Courtesy Jay Minter. 14" – $400.00; 18" – $525.00 up.

MADAME ALEXANDER-HARD PLASTIC

First prices are for mint dolls. Second prices are for soiled, dirty, played with or untagged dolls.

Alice In Wonderland: 14" – $300.00-95.00; 17" – $400.00 up-125.00; 23" – $550.00 up-200.00.

Annabelle: 15" – $350.00-100.00; 18" – $450.00-125.00; 23" – $550.00-200.00.

Babs: 20" – $425.00-100.00.

Babs Skater: 18" – $550.00-200.00; 21" – $575.00-200.00.

Binnie Walker: 15" – $150.00-50.00; 25" – $400.00-125.00.

Ballerina: 14" – $285.00 up-95.00.

Cinderella: 14" – $550.00-200.00; 18" – $650.00-250.00.

Cynthia: (Black doll): 15" – $575.00 up-250.00; 18" – $625.00 up-275.00; 23" – $700.00 up-350.00.

Elise: 16½" Street dress – $275.00-95.00; Ballgown – $350.00 up-125.00.

Bride: $265.00-100.00.

Fairy Queen: 14½" – $450.00 up-200.00; 18" – $500.00-225.00.

Glamour Girls: 18" – $550.00 up-265.00.

Godey Lady: 14" – $650.00-200.00; Bride – $650.00-200.00.

Man/Groom: $700.00-250.00.

Kathy: 15" – $350.00-100.00; 18" – $500.00-125.00.

Kelly: 12" – $450.00-125.00; 16" – $295.00-95.00.

Lady Churchill: 18" – $700.00-200.00.

Lissy: Street dress, 12" – $265.00-100.00; Bride – $275.00-100.00; Ballgown – $325.00-165.00; Ballerina, 12" – $325.00-145.00; Bridesmaid – $325.00-185.00.

Lissy Classics: Such as McGuffey Ana, Cinderella, etc.: $1,100.00 up-450.00 up.

Little Women: 14" – $285.00-100.00; Set of five – $1,300.00.

Little Women: 12" (Lissy) – $285.00-

14" Margaret face unknown Madame Alexander doll. Ca. 1950-1955. Original clothes and wig. Wig is lambs' wool that is dark brown with reddish tints. Dress is pink satin and tagged. Shoes and socks may be replacements. Courtesy Richard Boss. Mint – $650.00; Fair – $300.00.

17" "Maggie Walker" all hard plastic. Sleep eyes and in tagged original outfit. Courtesy Frasher Doll Auctions. 17" – $425.00 up.

16½" "Elise Ballerina" 1957. Plastic and vinyl with jointed knees and ankles. Tagged. Courtesy Frasher Doll Auctions. $350.00.

12" "Kelly" of 1959. Uses the "Lissy Doll" all hard plastic and original. Courtesy Doll Cradle. $450.00.

MADAME ALEXANDER-HARD PLASTIC

12" "Lissy" 1956-1958. Jointed knees and elbows. All hard plastic. Came in this window style box with wardrobe in 1957. Courtesy Doll Cradle. $650.00 up.

15" "Marme" of Little Women. Ca. 1948-1949. All hard plastic using the Margaret doll. Original and tagged. Courtesy Frasher Doll Auctions. $285.00 up.

100.00; Laurie – $300.00-95.00.

Little Women: 8" Straight leg walker – $200.00 up-85.00; Bend knee walker – $125.00 up-70.00.

Maggie: 15" – $350.00-100.00; 17" – $500.00-125.00; 23" – $600.00-150.00.

Maggie Mixup: 8" – $450.00 up-175.00; 16½" – $350.00 up-125.00; 8" Angel – $1,200.00 up-300.00 up.

Margaret O'Brien: 14½" – $465.00 up-150.00; 18" – $650.00 up-250.00; 22" – $850.00 up-350.00.

Margaret Rose: Princess: 14" – $425.00 up-150.00; 18" – $450.00 up-175.00.

Mary Martin: Sailor suit: 14" – $600.00 up-200.00; 17" – $700.00 up-250.00.

Nina Ballerina: 14" – $275.00-100.00; 17" – $350.00-125.00.

Peter Pan: 15" – $475.00-150.00.

Polly Pigtails: 14" – $450.00-145.00; 17" – $550.00-165.00.

Prince Charming: 14" – $650.00-185.00; 18" – $700.00-200.00; 21" – $750.00-200.00.

Prince Phillip: 17" – $500.00-165.00; 21" – $600.00.

MADAME ALEXANDER-HARD PLASTIC
MADAME ALEXANDER-PLASTIC & VINYL DOLLS

Queen: 18" – $650.00 up-200.00.
Shari Lewis: 14" – $325.00-100.00; 21"
– $425.00-125.00.
Sleeping Beauty: 16¼" – $450.00-150.00;
21" – $600.00-200.00.
Story Princess: 15" – $450.00-150.00.
Violet, Sweet: 18" – $425.00 up-100.00.

Wendy (Peter Pan): 14" – $325.00-100.00.
Wendy Ann: 14½" – $275.00 up-100.00;
17" – $300.00 up-100.00; 22" – $350.00
up-125.00.
Winnie Walker: 15" – $200.00-75.00; 18"
– $275.00-85.00; 23" – $300.00-95.00.

8" "Beth and Jo" from the 1956 "Little Women" set. Bend knee walkers, all hard plastic.
Courtesy Margaret Mandel. $125.00 each.

MADAME ALEXANDER-PLASTIC & VINYL DOLLS

First prices are for mint dolls. Second prices for soiled, dirty, played with or untagged dolls.
Barbara Jane: 29" – $325.00-125.00.
Caroline: 15" – $350.00-100.00; In riding habit – $400.00-150.00.
First Ladies: First set of six dolls – $1,300.00; Second set of six dolls – $1,100.00; Third set of six – $800.00.
"Fischer Quints": Hard plastic head, vinyl body: Set of five – $350.00.
Gidget: 14" – $500.00-200.00.
Granny, Little: 14" – $300.00-125.00.

Jacqueline: 21" In ballgown – $900.00-300.00; Street dress – $650.00-175.00; Riding habit – $800.00-225.00; 10" – $475.00-125.00.
Janie: 12" – $365.00-175.00.
Joanie: 36" – $425.00-185.00; Nurse – $450.00-200.00.
Jenny Lind (and cat): 14" – $525.00-200.00.
Katie (Black): 12" – $450.00-200.00.
Katie (FAO Swartz): 12" – $1,000.00-300.00.
Leslie (Black): 17" Ballgown – $450.00-

16″ "Edith, the Lonely Doll" which also came in 22″ size. Completely original, with hair in original set. Has earrings. 1958. Uses the "Marybel" doll. Courtesy Doll Cradle. $325.00 up.

"Kelly" using the "Marybel" doll. Came in 16″ and 22″ sizes. 1958-1959. All vinyl, rooted hair and sleep eyes. All original. Courtesy Doll cradle. 16″ – $295.00; 22″ – $325.00.

24″ "Chatterbox", 1962. Hard plastic with vinyl head. In tagged, original romper suit. Replaced shoes. Courtesy Frasher Doll Auctions. $275.00.

12″ "Smarty" 1962. All vinyl with sleep eyes and rooted hair. Original in box. Courtesy Frasher Doll Auctions. $385.00 up.

175.00; Ballerina – $350.00-125.00; Bride – $350.00-100.00; Street dress – $375.00-125.00.

Madame Doll: 14″ – $450.00-175.00.

Madelaine: 18″. Jointed knees, elbows and wrists – $400.00 up-200.00.

Marlo Thomas: 17″ – $550.00-225.00.

Marybel: 16″ – $225.00-95.00; In case – $285.00-115.00.

Mary Ellen: 31″ – $450.00-200.00.

Melinda: 14″ – $350.00-150.00; 16″ – $350.00-150.00.

Michael With Bear: (Peter Pan set) 11″ – $400.00-125.00.

Mimi: 30″ – $450.00 up-175.00 up.

Peter Pan: 15″ – $425.00-125.00.

Polly: 17″ – $325.00-125.00.

Rozy: 12″ – $400.00-175.00.

Smarty: 12″ – $385.00-175.00.

Sound of Music Liesl: 10″ – $250.00-125.00; 14″ – $225.00-100.00.

Louisa: 10″ – $300.00-125.00; 14″ – $275.00-125.00.

Brigitta: 10″ – $225.00-100.00; 14″ – $225.00-100.00.

Maria: 12″ – $275.00-125.00; 17″ – $325.00-150.00.

Marta: 8″ – $185.00-85.00; 11″ – $175.00-75.00.

Gretl: 8″ – $185.00-85.00; 11″ – $175.00-75.00.

Friedrich: 8″ – $185.00-85.00; 11″ –

$225.00-100.00; Small set – $1,650.00; Large set – $1,650.00.

Timmie Toddler: 23″ – $175.00-95.00; 30″ – $225.00-100.00.

Tommy: (FOA Swartz) – $1,200.00-400.00.

Wendy of Peter Pan: 14″ – $300.00-95.00.

17″ 1974 "Elise Ballerina". Vinyl and plastic. Mint and tagged. Courtesy Frasher Doll Auctions. $125.00.

MADAME ALEXANDER-PORTRAITS

Prices are for mint dolls. The 21″ Portrait dolls are many and varied. All have the "Jacqueline" face and all will be marked 1961 on the heads as the same molds are being used as they were when "Jacqueline" was first introduced in 1961. Depending upon the individual doll: 21″ – $425.00-800.00.

Coco: 1966. 21″ Portraits – $2,400.00-700.00; Street dress – $2,300.00-700.00; Ballgowns (other than portrait series) – $2,300.00-700.00.

21″ 1977 "Godey" Portrait. Marked: 1961, on head. All original. Courtesy Frasher Doll Auctions. $350.00.

MADAME ALEXANDER-PORTRAITS
AMERICAN CHARACTER DOLL COMPANY

21" 1978 "Gainsborough". Marked: 1961, on head. All original. Courtesy Frasher Doll Auctions. $350.00.

AMERICAN CHARACTER DOLL COMPANY

15" "Sweet Sue" that is marked: A.C., on head. All hard plastic and original in lavender jumper and pale yellow organdy blouse. 15" – $100.00 up.

First prices are for mint dolls. Second for dirty, soiled, redressed or poor condition. The American Character dolls are very collectible. All are above average in quality of materials and clothes. Dolls marked: American Doll and Toy Co. are also American Character dolls, as this name was used from 1959 to 1968 when the entire firm went out of business. Early dolls will be marked: Petite.

Annie Oakley: 17" – $150.00-65.00.
Betsy McCall: 8" – $95.00 up-30.00; 14" – $125.00-65.00; 36" – $250.00-100.00.
Butterball: 19" – $150.00-50.00.
Cartwright, Ben, Joe or Hoss: 8" – $60.00-25.00.
Chuckles: 23" – $165.00-85.00; Baby, 18" – $95.00-40.00.
Composition Babies/Cloth Bodies: Marked: A.C.: 14" – $65.00-25.00; 22" – $85.00-35.00. Marked: Petite: 14" – $75.00-30.00; 22" – $125.00-45.00.
Cricket: 9" – $16.00-4.00.
Hedda - Get-Betta: 21" – $75.00-30.00.
Miss Echo, Little: 30" – $135.00-70.00.
Petite Marked Girls: 14" – $125.00-50.00; 20" – $165.00-85.00.

AMERICAN CHARACTER DOLL COMPANY

30" "Sweet Sue". Hard plastic and vinyl with sleep eyes, rooted hair. Has wrist tag and original box. Courtesy Frasher Doll Auctions. 30" – $295.00 up.

"Toddles Baby" all vinyl bent leg baby with rooted hair. Sleep eyes and completely original. Open mouth/nurser. Also came as toddler in sizes 22" and 28". Courtesy Doll Cradle. 16" – $85.00 up; 22" – $125.00 up.

Marked A.C.: 14" – $75.00-30.00; 20" – $125.00-50.00.
Popi: 12" – $16.00-4.00.
Puggy: Frown face marked Petite: 13" – $425.00-125.00.
Ricky, Jr.: 13" – $55.00-22.00; 20" – $85.00-40.00.
Sally: Composition: 14" – $135.00-80.00; 16" – $150.00-80.00; 18" – $200.00-90.00.
Sally Says: Plastic/vinyl: 19" – $85.00-35.00.
Sweet Sue/Toni: Hard plastic: 15" – $100.00-45.00; 18" – $150.00-55.00; 22" – $165.00-60.00; 24" – $185.00-70.00; 30" – $295.00-125.00. Vinyl: 10½" – $50.00-22.00; 17" – $95.00-45.00; 21" – $145.00-60.00; 30" – $295.00-125.00. Groom: 20" – $165.00-80.00.
Tiny Tears: Hard plastic/vinyl. 8½" – $45.00-15.00; 13" – $95.00-45.00; 17" – $145.00-65.00. All vinyl: 8" – $25.00-8.00; 12" – $45.00-20.00; 16" – $75.00-35.00.
Toodles: Baby: 14" – $65.00-20.00. Tiny: 10½" – $85.00-18.00. Toddler with "follow me eyes": 22" – $125.00-40.00; 28" –

11" Marked: Dream Baby, on back. All composition. All original. Sleep eyes and molded hair. Courtesy Dora Mitzel. 11" – $85.00 up.

AMERICAN CHARACTER DOLL COMPANY

$200.00-85.00. Child with "follow me eyes": 22" – $125.00-40.00; 28" – $200.00-85.00. Black: 22" – $225.00-100.00. Toodle-Loo: 18" – $125.00-40.00.

Tressy: 12½" – $22.00-8.00. Whimette: 7½" – $20.00-6.00. Whimsey: 19" – $95.00-40.00.

18" "Wheeler the Dealer" dressed as a river boat gambler and has a card up his sleeve, green visor cap and painted on mustache. Courtesy Marlowe Cooper. $95.00.

18" "Girl Devil" all original painted features and deep red rooted hair. Courtesy Marlowe Cooper. $100.00.

21" "Sampson the Strongman" and "Astronaut" Whimsies. He has rooted mustache and hair on his chest. The "Astronaut" is 18" and boots and gauntlets are painted on. Painted very large green eyes. Courtesy Marlowe Cooper. $95.00 each.

19" "Zero the Hero" and "Tillie the Talker". Whimsies. 1960-1961. All vinyl with painted features. Courtesy Marlowe Cooper. $95.00 each.

ANNALEE MOBILTEE DOLLS
ARRANBEE DOLL COMPANY

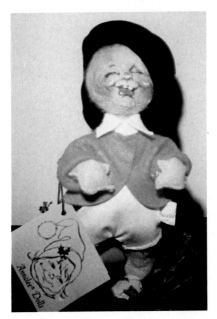

10″ "Go Go Girl" by Annalee. Ca. 1966. All felt, painted features. Wire throughout body allows doll to be posed. Also came in 24″ and has matching boy. (Author). 10″ – $100.00; 24″ – $350.00.

7″ All felt with painted features. Glued on hair, felt clothes and tagged: Annalee Mobiltee Dolls Inc/Meredith, N.H. 1957/1984. Courtesy Genie Jinright. 7″ – $95.00.

ARRANBEE DOLL COMPANY

First prices are for mint dolls. Second prices are for crazed, dirty, soiled or dolls in poor condition. The Arranbee Doll Company was started in 1922 and purchased by the Vogue Doll Company in 1959. The molds were still used with the name Arranbee (R&B) until 1961. Arranbee had the Armand Marseille firm of Germany make bisque head babies for them in the 1920's, and called them "My Dream Baby" using the mold numbers 341 and 351. (See bisque section under "Armand Marseille for prices).

Babies: Composition/Cloth bodies: 16″ – $55.00-30.00; 22″ – $85.00-45.00.

Bottle Tot: Has celluloid bottle molded to celluloid hand: 18″ – $125.00-45.00.

Debu-Teen: Composition girl with cloth body: 14″ – $150.00-55.00; 18″ – $185.00-60.00; 21″ – $225.00-100.00.

Dream Baby: Composition: 14″ – $115.00-45.00; Vinyl/cloth: 16″ – $75.00-35.00; 26″ – $145.00-60.00.

Kewty: Composition/molded hair: 10″ – $45.00-15.00.

Littlest Angel: All hard plastic: 10″ – $45.00-12.00; Vinyl head: 10″ – $35.00-12.00. Red hair, freckles: 10″ – $60.00-25.00.

Miss Coty: Vinyl: 10″ – $45.00-18.00.

My Angel: Plastic/vinyl: 17″ – $35.00-10.00; 22″ – $55.00-20.00; 36″ – $125.00-45.00.

Nancy: Composition: 12″ – $145.00-40.00; 17″ – $185.00-45.00; 19″ – $185.00-50.00; 23″ – $200.00; 60.00.

Nancy Lee: Composition: 14″ – $125.00-45.00; Hard plastic: 14″ – $125.00-40.00.

Nancy Lee: Unusual eyebrows/vinyl: 15″ – $95.00-32.00.

ARRANBEE DOLL COMPANY

Nancy Lee: Baby, painted eyes and looks as if crying: 15″ – $50.00-20.00.

14″ ''Debuteen'' composition with cloth body, glued on wig, sleep eyes and all original. Childhood doll of owner Margaret Mandel. 14″ – $150.00.

10″ ''Littlest Angel'' by Arranbee Dolls. All hard plastic, jointed knee walker. All original with original box. Courtesy Doll Cradle. 10″ – $45.00.

Nanette: H.P.: 14″ – $125.00-30.00; 17″ – $160.00-40.00; 21″ – $225.00-50.00; 23″ – 275.00-60.00.
Sonja Skater: Composition: 18″ – $140.00-45.00; 21″ – $175.00-60.00.
Taffy: Looks like Alexander's ''Cissy'': 23″ – $60.00-25.00.

22″ ''Little Angel''. Ca. 1940's. Cloth body with composition limbs and head, glued on wig. Sleep eyes. All original. Marked: R. & B., on head. Courtesy Jeannie Mauldin. 22″ – $100.00.

17″ ''Cinderella''. All hard plastic with glued on wig. Clear glass slippers with silver buckles. Marks: R&B, on head. Courtesy Maureen Fukuskima. 17″ – $260.00.

First prices are for mint dolls. Second for dolls in poor condition, dirty, soiled or not original.

Alfred E. Newman: Vinyl head: 20″ – $95.00-45.00.

Captain Kangaroo: 19″ – $85.00-30.00; 24″ – $125.00-50.00.

Christopher Robin: 18″ – $75.00-25.00.

Daisy Mae: 14″ – $95.00-40.00; 21″ – $125.00-50.00.

Emmett Kelly (Willie the Clown): 24″ – $95.00-40.00.

Lil' Abner: 14″ – $110.00-45.00; 21″ – $135.00-50.00.

Mammy Yokum: Molded hair: 14″ – $125.00-60.00; 21″ – $150.00-70.00.

Mammy Yokum: Yarn hair: 14″ – $100.00-40.00; 21″ – $135.00-50.00.

Pappy Yokum: 14″ – $125.00-60.00; 21″ – $150.00-70.00.

11″ "Mickey" by Effanbee and marked with name and company. All vinyl and original with molded on sailor cap. 13″ "Mammy Yokum" all vinyl and marked: B.B. Clothes tagged: Al Capp Dog Patch Family. Exclusive license Baby Berry Toy N.Y.C. all original. Courtesy Frasher Doll Auctions. 11″ Mickey – $95.00; 13″ Mammy – $100.00.

22″ Baby is unmarked. Very good detailed modeling. Sleep eyes/lashes, deeply molded hair. All vinyl and open/closed mouth. All original with Teddy bear. Box: Belle Doll and Toy Corp. Brooklyn, N.Y. Style B-23. Price on box is $7.98. Ca. 1950's. Courtesy Dora Mitzel. 22″ – $45.00 up.

BETSY McCALL

First prices are for mint dolls. Second for soiled, dirty, played with and not original dolls.

8″ All hard plastic, jointed knees. Made by American Character Doll Co. 8″ Street dress – $95.00 up; Ballgown – $100.00 up.

14″ "Betsy McCall" all vinyl sleep eyes and original (blue hat has faded to grey). Marked: McCall/1958/Corp., in circle. Jointed waist. Made by American Character. Courtesy Phyllis Houston. 14″ – $125.00.

11½″ Brown sleep eyes, reddish rooted hair. Unmarked. Made by Uneeda: 11½″ – $55.00-20.00.

13″ Made by Horsman in 1975 although doll is marked: Horsman Dolls, Inc. 1967, on head. 13″ – $35.00-15.00.

14″ Vinyl with rooted hair and medium high heel feet. Made by American Character. 14″ – $125.00-65.00.

8″ "Betsy McCall" in 1957-1960 "Cotillion Gown". $125.00.

8″ "Betsy McCall' in "Sugar and Spice" of 1957-1960. $125.00.

"Sugar and Spice" of 1960-1961 for 8″ "Betsy McCall". $125.00.

14″ Vinyl head, rooted hair. Hard plastic marked P-90 body. Made by Ideal Doll Co. 14″ – $125.00-45.00.

22″ Unmarked. Has extra joints at waist, ankles, wrists and above knees. Made by Uneeda. 22″ – $150.00-60.00.

29″ Marked: McCall 1961. Has extra joints at ankles, waist, above knees and wrists. Made by Uneeda. 29″ – $200.00-95.00.

29″ Marked: B.M.C. Horsman 1971 – $125.00-50.00.

36″ Girl. Marked: McCall Corp. 1959. Made by Ideal Doll Co. 36″ – $250.00 up-100.00.

36″ Boy. Sandy McCall. Marked same as girl. Made by Ideal Doll Co. 36″ – $350.00-165.00.

1957-1958 ''Birthday Party'' for 8″ Betsy McCall. $95.00 up.

8″ Betsy McCall in ''Sun 'N Sand'' of 1957-1961. $95.00 up.

''Sweet Dreams'' set of 1957-1961 for Betsy McCall. $65.00 up.

This outfit for 8″ Betsy McCall is called: ''Co-ed'' and ran from 1957-1961. $95.00 up.

BETSY McCALL
BUDDY LEE

1960 "Bride" on 8" Betsy McCall. $90.00 up.

"April Showers" rain gear of 1959 for 8" Betsy McCall. $85.00 up.

BUDDY LEE

Right: 13" "Buddy Lee". All composition with painted features and hair, jointed only at shoulders. Original. Left: 12" "Fanny Brice's Baby Snooks". 1938. Marked on head. Composition head, body, hands and feet with arms and legs of flexible metal cable. Courtesy Frasher Doll Auctions. 13" Buddy Lee – $225.00 up; 13" Hard plastic – $175.00 up; 12" Baby Snooks – $250.00.

Original dolls by Xavier Roberts Incorporated as Original Appalachian Artworks in September 1978. The Birth Certificates have a blue border.

"Helen" Blue: The very first edition less than 1,000 – $4,000.00.

"A" Blue Edition: Number in edition was 1,000: Preemie and called: "SP" Preemie – $1,500.00 up.

"B" Red Edition: Birth Certificates have red border and these were first to also have adoption papers. (Nov. 1978) – $1,500.00 up.

"C" Burgundy Edition: Jan. 1979. Number in edition was 5,000. Registration number has the prefix "C" and they also were first to use three-part adoption papers – $1,000.00 up.

"D" Purple Edition: Birth Certificate has purple border. Number in edition was 10,000 which were gone by November 1979 – $900.00.

"X" Christmas Edition: 1979. Snow white yarn hair and red costumes. Edge of certificate is leaves and berries. Number in edition 1,000 "X" prefix on registration number – $1,500.00.

"E" Bronze Edition: This was last of the personally signed limited edition of 1979. Bronze border on Birth Certificate and these babies were sent a Birthday Card from Babyland General. Number in edition was 15,000. This edition started in Dec. 1979 – $900.00.

Signed Preemies Edition: April, 1980, and number was 5,000. This was first of the Preemies and these babies are hand signed – $850.00.

Celebrity Edition: 1980. Number in edition was 5,000. All came dressed in jeans and T-shirt which states: "I'm a Little T.V. Celebrity". This was after the Little People were on the T.V. program "Real People". All are hand signed – $650.00.

Christmas Edition: 1980. Number in edition 2,500 and all are hand signed. Birth Certificate has green leaves and red berries border. Babies have white hair and red velveteen outfits – $850.00.

Grand Edition: 1980 and can still be adopted at Babyland General Hospital. Number in edition is 1,000. These Cabbage Patch dolls are dressed in evening attire in

Two boys from the Turquoise Edition. Left: "Watson Joel" and Right: "Horace Lee". Both hair styles discontinued. Courtesy Frasher Doll Auctions. $175.00.

Original Xavier Roberts Rose Edition. "Sheli Qyiana" freckles and green eyes. The boy is "Baxter Joseph". Courtesy Frasher Doll Auctions. $150.00.

CABBAGE PATCH

Xavier Roberts Ivory Edition. "Wanda Lane" marked: Xavier Roberts '85. Courtesy Frasher Doll Auctions. $150.00.

"Hugh Rolph" a 1981 New Ears Edition baby from Babyland General, made and designed by Xavier Roberts. Courtesy Lani Pettit. $250.00.

tuxedos, satins, mink and diamonds. Each are signed – $1,000.00.

New Ears Edition: 1981. First babies with ears. Number in edition is 15,000 and these are still available from Babyland General Hospital. This is the first group of babies to have the Xavier Roberts signature STAMPED rather than personally signed and is therefore the first "unsigned" edition. Boys have blue and girls have pink Birth Certificates – $250.00.

Unsigned Edition: 1980-1981. Number in edition was 73,650. This was first STAMPED rather than personally signed with the Xavier Roberts signature of the Little People – $250.00.

Preemie Edition: 1981. Number in edition is 10,000 and these are still available from Babyland General Hospital. This second Preemie edition began in May 1981. Dressed in pastel christening gowns and caps. These babies are STAMPED and not personally signed: Official name of the edition is "PRII" – $150.00.

Standing Edition: 1981. 23″ tall and will stand by themselves. Number in edition is 5,000 and they are still available from Babyland General Hospital. These are STAMPED and not signed personally by Xavier Roberts – $250.00 up.

Ears Edition: 1982 (Preemies). Number in edition is 5,000 with them still available from Babyland General Hospital. Lavender border on Birth Certificate and babies are STAMPED with signature and official name is "PE" Edition – $140.00-150.00.

Unsigned Edition: 1982. Number in edition was 21,000 and by Jan. 1984 this edition was adopted out. These are STAMPED and not personally signed and official name is "U" Edition – $200.00.

Cabbage Patch Edition: 1982. Prior to this edition the babies were called Little People. Edition was numbered at 2,500. This edition was adopted out by mid-1983. There are 10 names used in this edition with a variation of each second name of the 10. For example: Otis L. with the second name differing (beginning with L) for each baby. Edition is STAMPED and have "Cabbage Patch Kids" some place on clothes – $600.00 up.

Christmas Edition: 1982. Number in edition is 1,000. Ribbon border with green leaves and berries on Birth Certificate. The bald head and with-hair babies were used and all are dressed in red. They are STAMPED and HAND SIGNED in red. This is first year the name Cabbage Patch appears on the registration and adoption papers – $1,200.00.

Cleveland Green Edition: Number in edition is 2,000. Began in Jan. 1983 and babies were STAMPED and were all adopted out by Feb. 14, 1983. The Birth Certificates and registration papers have green border – $600.00.

"KP" Darker Green Edition: Number in edition was 2,000 and began in Feb. 1983 and were all adopted out by spring 1983. STAMPED in green with Xavier Roberts name – $800.00.

"KPR" Red Edition: Number in edition is 2,000 which began in June 1983 and all were adopted out by July 1983. STAMPED. All papers have a red border – $800.00.

"KPB" Burgandy Edition: Number in edition was 10,000 and these were STAMPED. All papers have a burgundy border. Began in Aug. 1983 and all adopted out by Dec. 1983 – $375.00.

Oriental Edition: Number in edition was 1,000. These Cabbage Patch dolls have Oriental looking features and adoption papers have pagoda roofs in yellow on them. Dressed in Oriental style clothes. This was first of the International Series. Began in Mar. 1983 and all adopted by Aug. 1983. STAMPED – $1,000.00.

American Indian Edition: Number in edition was 1,000. These began in June 1983 and were all adopted by Oct. 1983. STAMPED. Skin tones are brown and each is dressed in Indian outfits. 500 girls and 500 boys – $1,000.00.

Hispanic Edition: Number in edition was 1,000. STAMPED. The papers have red roses and the name Cabbage Patch Kids in green in the center top of papers. Edition adopted out in 1983 – $950.00.

KPZ Edition: (1983 or 1984) Bronze border. Edition of 30,000 – $250.00 up.

Champagne Edition: Number in edition was 2,000. This edition was to celebrate the Fifth Anniversary of the Cabbage Patch. This entire edition was personally SIGNED

by Xavier Roberts. The girls wear lilac with lace trimmings and the boys have lavender short pants. Each has lavender eyes and champagne light beige hair. This edition began in July 1983 and all were adopted out by Feb. 1984 – $1,500.00.

Christmas Edition: 1983. The STAMPED edition was numbered at 1,000. Light blonde hair, dressed in reds. All adopted by spring 1984 – $995.00.

"KPP" Purple Edition: Number in edition was 20,000. Papers all have purple borders. STAMPED. These began in Dec. 1983 and were all adopted out by April 1984 – $450.00.

Sweetheart Edition: Number in edition was 1,500 and they were STAMPED. These were available as a couple and dressed in coordinated outfits that were red and white. They were all adopted by Feb. 1984 – $1,000.00.

Bavarian Edition: Number in edition was 1,000 and they were STAMPED. These were the fourth in the International Series and were all adopted in a two-week period after they were introduced on March 1, 1984. All have blonde hair and blue eyes and are dressed in the Bavarian style – $1,000.00.

World Class Edition: Number in edition was 2,500 and they are STAMPED. Dressed in the Olympic style with running suits, white shorts, head bands and a World Class designed medal on red/white/blue ribbon around neck. First available in May 1984 and edition was adopted rapidly – $650.00.

KPF Edition: 1984. Turquoise border. Edition of 30,000 – $175.00.

KPG Edition: 1984. Coral Border. Edition of 30,000 – $125.00.

KPH Rose Edition: 1984. Edition of 40,000 – $150.00.

KPI Ivory Edition: 1985. Edition of 45,000 – $150.00.

KPJ Gold Edition: 1985. Edition of 50,000 – $130.00-150.00.

Emerald Edition: 1985. Edition size unknown – S.A.

Coleco Cabbage Patch Dolls: 1983: Black signature stamped. Boxes undated on front. Have powder scent. Bald babies – $85.00; Pacifiers – $95.00; Freckles – $125.00; Bald Black Babies – $85.00; Black boys –

CABBAGE PATCH
CAMEO DOLL COMPANY

$75.00; Regular boys or girls – $80.00; Red hair boys (fuzzy) – $80.00. **1984:** Green signature stamped. Boxes marked 1984 on front. Regular boys or girls – $65.00; Preemies – $55.00; Black Preemie – $65.00; Orange Hair – $85.00; Pacifier – $75.00. **1985:** Blue signature stamped. 1985 on front of boxes. Some 1984 dolls are in 1985 boxes and some 1985 dolls are in 1984 boxes. Twins: Regular boys or girls – $95.00; Preemies – $50.00; Black boys or girls – $55.00; Pacifiers – $55.00; Glasses – $85.00; One Tooth – $65.00. **1986:** Red signature stamped: Most issues still available.

Foreign: Germany, Canada, Spain, etc. Freckles – $55.00; Pacifiers – $50.00; Regular boys or girls – $55.00.

CAMEO DOLL COMPANY

Baby Bo Kaye: Celluloid head with cloth body: 15"-16" – $450.00-550.00.
Baby Bo Kaye: Bisque head, molded hair, open mouth: 17"-18" – $2,200.00.
Baby Bo Kaye: Composition/cloth. Mint condition: 18" – $550.00; Light craze and not original: 18" – $350.00.
Baby Mine: Vinyl/cloth. Sleep eyes. Mint condition: 16" – $100.00; Slight soil and not original: 16" – $55.00.
Betty Boop: Composition head. Mint condition: 12" – $450.00; Light craze and few chips: 12" – $275.00.
Champ: Composition/freckles. Mint condition: 16" – $525.00; Light craze, not original: 16" – $400.00.

Giggles: Composition, molded loop for ribbon. Mint: 11" – $250.00; 14" – $425.00; Light craze: 11" – $150.00; 14" – $250.00.
Ho-Ho: Plaster in excellent condition: 4" – $45.00; Vinyl in excellent condition: 4" – $15.00.
Joy: Composition. In mint condition: 10" – $265.00; 15" – $350.00; Slight crazing: 10" – $150.00; 15" – $275.00.
Kewpie: See Kewpie section.
Little Annie Rooney: Composition. Mint and original: 16" – $625.00; Slight craze and not original: 16" – $400.00.

8½" ''Pete The Pup'' by Cameo. Composition head, segmented wood body and marked by label on front. Courtesy Frasher Doll Auctions. 8" – $165.00.

27" ''Scootles''. All vinyl with sleep eyes, molded hair and fully jointed. All original. Courtesy Frasher Doll Auctions. $225.00.

Margie: Composition. Mint and original: 6″ – $165.00; 10″ – $225.00; Slight craze and not original: 6″ – $75.00; 10″ – $100.00.

Miss Peep: Pin jointed shoulders and hips. Vinyl. Mint and original: 1960's: 18″ – $45.00; Black: 18″ – $65.00; Slightly soiled and not original: 18″ – $28.00; Black: 18″ – $35.00.

Miss Peep, Newborn: Plastic and vinyl. Mint and original. 18″ – $60.00; Slight soil and not original: 18″ – $25.00.

Peanut, Affectionately: Vinyl. Mint and original: 18½″ – $90.00; Slight soil and not original: 18½″ – $40.00.

Pete The Pup: Composition. Mint: 8″ – $165.00; Slight craze: 8″ – $100.00.

Pinkie: Composition. Mint and original: 1930's. 10″ – $275.00; Slight craze: 10″ – $125.00; Vinyl and plastic, 1950's – $75.00; Slight soil and not original – $35.00.

Scootles: Composition. Mint and original: 8″ – $235.00; 12″ – $350.00; 15″ – $450.00. Light craze and not original: 8″ – $100.00; 12″ – $225.00; 15″ – $285.00. Composition. Sleep eyes: Mint: 15″ – $485.00; 21″ – $675.00 up. Slight craze: 15″ – $300.00; 21″ – $425.00; Composition. Black. 15″ – $600.00 up. Vinyl. Mint and original. 14″ – $85.00; 19″ – $145.00; 27″ – $225.00; Lightly soiled and not original. 14″ – $45.00; 19″ – $65.00; 27″ – $95.00.

Right: 20½″ Marked: Century Doll Co. Composition shoulder head, cloth body and composition limbs, sleep eyes and open mouth. Left: 27″ "Norma Talker" marked: Effanbee. Hard plastic head, open mouth and sleep eyes. Original. Courtesy Frasher Doll Auctions. 20″ – $185.00; 27″ – $85.00.

Left: 10½″ "Miss Ginger" by Cosmopolitan Doll Co. marked: Ginger. Rigid vinyl with swivel waist, soft vinyl head with rooted hair, sleep eyes and wears tagged outfit. Right: 8″ "Betsy McCall" by American Character. Courtesy Frasher Doll Auctions. 10″ – $50.00; 8″ Betsy (ballgown) – $125.00 up.

COSMOPOLITAN
CREATE

8½" "Little Miss Ginger" in tagged original clothes. Boots may not be original. Rooted hair and sleep eyes. Vinyl. Courtesy Karen Stephenson. 8½" – $40.00 up.

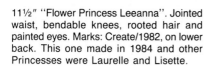

11½" "Flower Princess Leeanna". Jointed waist, bendable knees, rooted hair and painted eyes. Marks: Create/1982, on lower back. This one made in 1984 and other Princesses were Laurelle and Lisette.

12" "Prince Leslie" with molded yellow hair, with green leaves molded and painted eyes. Painted on leotards with removable shoes. Marks: Create/1984, on lower back. Other boys were Lancelot and Lawrence. $18.00.

DELUXE TOY COMPANY
DISNEY

All prices are for mint dolls. Deluxe Reading, Deluxe Topper, Topper Corp., Topper Toys, Deluxe Toy Creations are all the same company with the "parent" company being Deluxe Toys. None of the above named remain in business.

Deluxe Toy Company specialized in dolls that "do things", or as referred to as mechanical dolls. The quality of their dolls was good to excellent. Most dolls are fully marked with the name of the company and the date. They made regular dolls as well as the mechanical and almost all the dolls from these firms are becoming very desirable and also hard to find.

Baby Brite: Two buttons in stomach to move head and arms: 14" – $18.00.

Baby Boo: Battery operated: 21" – $30.00.

Baby Catch A Ball: Battery operated. Metal bracelets at wrists: 18" – $35.00.

Baby Magic: Button in stomach operated arms and mouth: 18" – $45.00.

Baby Peek and Play: Battery operated. Jointed wrist, hides eyes: 18" – $25.00.

Baby Tickle Tears: Painted eyes. Arms make mouth pout: 14" – $25.00.

Bikey: Battery operated. Rides bike, jointed knees: 11" – $12.00.

Bonnie Bride: Button on shoulder makes arm toss bouquet and legs walk: 22" – $25.00.

Dawn Series: 6" Girls: White – $6.00; Black – $10.00; Majorettes – $18.00; Models – $18.00; Floral Stand & Doll – $12.00; Boys: White – $12.00; Black – $14.00.

Go Go's: 6½" – $9.00 up.

Lil' Miss Fussy: Battery operated. Cries and kicks: 18" – $25.00.

Party Time: Battery operated. Blows balloons and noise makers: 18" – $25.00.

Penny Brite: 9" – $8.00.

School Girl Writing Doll: Battery operated. Arms move in all directions. 16" – $30.00.

Smarty Pants: Battery operated talker: 19" – $30.00.

Susie Cutie: Press stomach and arms and mouth move: 7" – $9.00.

Susie Homemaker: Jointed knees: 21" – $25.00.

10" "Jiminy Cricket" and 12½" "Pinnochio" all composition and painted on shoes. Felt clothes. Both made by Knickerbocker Toy Co. Courtesy Frasher Doll Auctions. 10" – $285.00; 12½" – $250.00.

20" "Small World" plastic mask face with painted features. All cloth body and limbs. "Jewel" glued to middle of forehead. Original. 20" – $95.00.

DISNEY
DOLL ARTIST

13" "Snow White" shown with 8" Seven Dwarfs by Knickerbocker. All are mint and original. All composition with painted features. Courtesy Florence Phelps. Dwarfs (mint) – $185.00 each; Snow White – $300.00 up.

DOLL ARTIST

All prices are for mint dolls.
Clear, Emma: Blue scarf: 20" – $350.00; Chinas: 20" – $250.00; 26" – $325.00; Danny Boy: 20" – $350.00; Lady Guenevere: 20" – $200.00; "Parian": 16" – $185.00 up; Washington, George & Martha: 20" – $900.00 up pair.
Kane, Maggie Head: Caldonia: 14" –

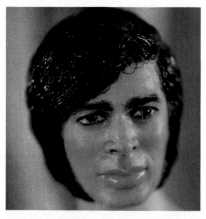

Wax Portrait Doll "Diana, the Princess of Wales". Designed and created by Paul Crees. Courtesy Joanna Stout of Scarlett O's., Humble, Texas. Value unknown.

17" "Englebert Humperdinck" by N.I.A.D.A. artist Pat Robinson. All bisque with intaglio eyes. Modeled hair and eyebrows. 1972. Courtesy Frasher Doll Auctions. 17" – $400.00 up.

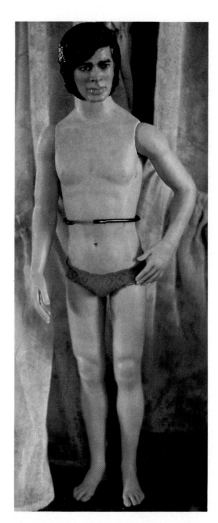

Right: 10″ ''Theresa Tonty'' by N.I.A.D.A. artist, Pat Robinson. Painted features and cloth body. Left: 11″ German boy by Gerbruder Heubach marked: Heubach in square, 6692. Courtesy Frasher Doll Auctions. 10″ – $125.00; 11″ Heubach – $400.00.

Shows body and limbs of 17″ ''Englebert Humperdinck'' by artist Pat Robinson. 1972. 17″ – $400.00 up.

$125.00; Marigold: 14″ – $200.00; Nicodemus: 13″ – $125.00; Peach Blossom: 14″ – $200.00; Uncle Ned: 15″ – $150.00.
Wilson, Lita: Cinderella: 16″ – $250.00; Girls: 16″ – $200.00; Boys: 16″ – $250.00.
Wick, Faith: Originals of late 1970's – $650.00 up.

Original character dolls designed and made by Faith Wick. Late 1970's. Courtesy Faith Wick. $650.00 each up.

DOLL ARTIST

11" Wax doll by N.I.A.D.A. artist Anne Parker called "Edwardian Lady" with painted features and dressed in period costume of 1902. Courtesy Frasher Doll Auctions. $265.00.

13½" Wax "Gibson Girl" by artist Sheila Wallace. Painted features. Courtesy Frasher Doll Auctions. $225.00.

Part of the "Gone with the Wind" dolls designed and created by Phyllis Juhlin Park. Scarlett, Rhett, Bonnie Blue, Ashley and Melanie. $185.00 each up.

17½" "Jenny Lind" china by Emma Clear. Cloth body with china limbs. Courtesy Frasher Doll Auctions. 18" – $300.00.

Right: 18" Blue Scarf by Emma Clear. Glass eyes, molded hair and scarf and bisque limbs. Cloth body. Left: 17" German shoulder head with bisque lower arms and kid body marked: L.4. Courtesy Frasher Doll Auctions. 18" – $300.00; 17" – $385.00.

EEGEE DOLL COMPANY

The name of this company is made up from the name of the founder, E.G. Goldberger. Founded in 1917, the early dolls were marked: E.G., then later, E. Goldberger and now Eegee.

Andy: Plastic/vinyl teen boy: 12" – $22.00.

Annette: Teen type: 11½" – $25.00.

Annette: Plastic and vinyl, walker legs: 25" – $32.00; 28" – $40.00; 36" – $60.00.

Baby Luv: Cloth/vinyl. Marks: B.T. Eegee: 14" – $40.00.

Baby Susan: Name marked on head: 8½" – $10.00.

Baby Tandy Talks: Foam body, rest vinyl. Pull string talker – $45.00.

Ballerina: Foam body and limbs. Vinyl heads. 1967: 18" – $35.00.

Ballerina: Hard plastic/vinyl: 20" – $45.00.

Boy Doll: Molded hair, all vinyl: 13" – $35.00; 21" – $45.00.

Composition, sleep eyes, open mouth girls: 14" – $85.00; 18" – $100.00.

Debutante: Vinyl head, rest hard plastic/jointed knees: 28" – $85.00.

Dolly Parton: 1980: 12" – $16.00.

Flowerkins: Plastic/vinyl. Marks: F-2, on head. 16" – $45.00.

Gemmette: Teen type: 14" – $18.00.

Georgette and Georgie: Cloth and vinyl. Redheads: 22"-23" – $35.00 each.

Gigi Perreaux: Hard plastic/early vinyl head: 17" – $200.00.

Granny: from "Beverly Hillbillies". Old lady modeling, grey hair. Painted or sleep eyes: 14" – $55.00.

Miss Charming: All composition Shirley

EEGEE DOLL COMPANY
EFFANBEE DOLL COMPANY

Temple look-a-like: 19″ – $185.00 up. Pin – $10.00.

Miss Sunbeam: Plastic/vinyl. Dimples: 17″ – $45.00.

Musical Baby: Has key wind music box in body: 17″ – $18.00.

My Fair Lady: All vinyl, jointed waist: 10½″ – $28.00; 19″ – $60.00.

Posey Playmate: Foam and vinyl: 18″ – $16.00.

Susan Stroller: Hard plastic/vinyl: 20″ – $45.00; 23″ – $55.00; 26″ – $65.00.

Tandy Talks: Plastic/vinyl, freckles, pull string talker: 20″ – $60.00.

19″ "My Fair Lady" with doll by Eegee. Clothes designed by Mollye Goldman of International Doll Co. for Eegee. All vinyl with jointed waist, sleep eyes. Doll is unmarked. Courtesy Debra Ekart. $60.00 up.

Shows layers of slip on 19″ "My Fair Lady" doll by Eegee.

EFFANBEE DOLL COMPANY

First prices are for mint dolls. Second prices for soiled, dirty, played with dolls or composition, crazed or cracked.

American Children: All composition. Painted or sleep eyes. Closed mouth girl: 18″ – $800.00-400.00; 21″ – $1,000.00-500.00; Closed mouth boy: 15″ – $800.00-400.00; 17″ – $1,000.00-500.00; Open mouth: 15″ – $600.00-300.00; 18″ – $675.00-300.00; 21″ – $800.00-400.00.

Anne Shirley: All composition: 15″ – $200.00-95.00; 21″ – $275.00-100.00; 27″ – $400.00-165.00.

Babyette: Cloth/composition: 12½″ – $165.00-85.00.

Babykin: All composition: 9″-12″ – $165.00-85.00; All vinyl: 10″ – $45.00-20.00.

Baby Cuddleup: Vinyl coated cloth body, rest vinyl. Two lower teeth. 1953: 20″ – $60.00-30.00.

Baby Dainty: Composition/cloth: 15″ – $150.00-85.00.

Baby Evelyn: Composition/cloth: 17″ – $165.00-85.00.

Baby Tinyette: Composition: 8″-9″ –

$165.00-60.00; Toddler: 8″-9″ – $165.00-60.00.

Betty Brite: All composition, fur wig, sleep eyes: 16″-17″ – $225.00-75.00.

Bi-Centennial: Boy and girl (Pun'kin): 11″ – $125.00 each-40.00.

Bridal Sets: 1970's – 4 dolls. White – $185.00-100.00; Black – $300.00-150.00.

Bright Eyes: Composition/cloth. Flirty eyes. 18″ – $200.00; 22″-23″ – $265.00-150.00.

Brother or Sister: Composition hands and head. Yarn hair and painted eyes: 12″ – $145.00-45.00; 16″ – $175.00-60.00.

Bubbles: Composition/cloth. 16″ – $200.00-95.00; 20″ – $250.00-100.00; 26″ – $350.00-150.00.

Button Nose: Composition: 8″-9″ – $165.00-60.00; Vinyl/cloth: 18″ – $50.00-20.00.

Candy Kid: All composition. White: 12″ – $225.00-70.00; Black – $285.00-85.00.

Carolina: Made for Smithsonian: 1980: 12″ – $65.00-30.00.

Charlie McCarthy: Composition/cloth: 19″-20″ – $250.00-100.00.

Cinderella: All hard plastic: 16″ – $195.00-95.00.

Composition Dolls: Molded hair, all composition, jointed neck, shoulders and hips. Painted or sleep eyes. Open or closed mouth. Original clothes, all composition in perfect condition. Marked: Effanbee: 1930's: 9″ – $95.00-40.00; 15″ – $150.00-65.00; 18″ – $195.00-85.00; 21″ – $225.00-95.00.

Composition Dolls: 1920's. Cloth body, composition limbs, open or closed mouth, sleep eyes. Original clothes and composition in perfect condition: Marked: Effanbee: 18″ – $150.00-65.00; 22″ – $185.00-75.00; 25″ – $225.00-90.00; 27″-28″ – $300.00-125.00.

Right: 12″ Black "Baby Grumpy" toddler. Marked: Effanbee Dolls Walk/talk/sleep. Composition shoulder head, cloth body and composition limbs. Painted features. All original. Left: 14″ Merrythoughts "Golliwog" Doll. Ca. 1950. Cloth with metal eyes and in original minstrel outfit. Merrythought tag on bottom of foot. Courtesy Frasher Doll Auctions. 12″ – $225.00 up; 14″ Golliwog – $175.00.

30″ Marked: Effanbee/Marilee/copyr. Doll. Composition shoulder head, arms and legs with cloth body. All original. 20″ All celluloid boy marked with Turtle Mark, molded hair and painted eyes. All original. Courtesy Frasher Doll Auctions. 20″ – $200.00; 20″ Celluloid – $185.00; 25″ – $365.00; 30″ – $485.00.

EFFANBEE DOLL COMPANY

30" "Mae Starr" composition shoulder head and limbs, cloth body and original wig. Redressed. Marked: Mae Starr Doll. Has record player in torso. Courtesy Frasher Doll Auctions. $425.00.

15" "Petite Sally" and so marked. Composition swivel head, shoulder plate and limbs with cloth body. Sleep eyes. Maybe original shoes and socks. 15" Marked: Effanbee Baby Dainty. Composition shoulder head, arms and legs with cloth body. Painted eyes and all original with Effanbee pin. Courtesy Frasher Doll Auctions. 15" Sally – $135.00; 15" Baby Dainty – $150.00.

Left: 21" American Children Series. Made by Effanbee and designed by Dewees Cochran. Painted eyes, human hair in braids. Right: 21" American Children Series with sleep eyes. Both are marked: Effanbee American Children, on heads. Anne Shirley, on back. Courtesy Frasher Doll Auctions. 21" – $1,000.00.

Currier & Ives: Plastic/vinyl: 12" – $50.00-25.00.

Disney Dolls: Cinderella, Snow White, Alice in Wonderland and Sleeping Beauty: 1977-1978: 14" – $150.00-65.00.

Emily Ann: 13" Puppet, composition – $125.00-45.00.

Dydee Baby: Hard plastic/vinyl: 15" – $100.00-45.00; 20" – $175.00-70.00.

Fluffy: All vinyl: 10" – $35.00-10.00; As Girl Scout: 10" – $45.00-10.00; Black – $45.00-10.00.

Grumpy: Cloth/composition: 12" – $165.00-65.00; 14" – $175.00-70.00; 18" – $250.00-95.00; Black: 12" – $225.00-85.00; 14"-15" – $285.00-95.00.

Historical Dolls: All composition: 14" – $450.00 up-125.00; 21" – $1,200.00-500.00.

Honey: All hard plastic: 14" – $150.00-50.00; 18" – $175.00-55.00; 21" –

21" "Barbara Ann" of American Children Series. All composition, sleep eyes, human hair wig, open mouth. Courtesy Frasher Doll Auctions. 21" – $800.00.

21" American Children Series. Made by Effanbee and designed by Dewees Cochran. Doll on left has sleep eyes and other two have painted eyes. All have human hair wigs. Courtesy Frasher Doll Auctions. 21" – $1,000.00.

16" "Patsy Joan" marked: Effanbee Patsy Joan, on body. All composition, sleep eyes, molded hair and all original. Courtesy Frasher Doll Auctions. $300.00.

26" "Patsy Ruth" and 22" "Patsy Lou". All composition sleep eyes. 26" re-dressed and 22" all original. Courtesy Frasher Doll Auctions. 26" Original – $500.00; 26" Redressed – $350.00; 22" – $375.00.

EFFANBEE DOLL COMPANY

$250.00-100.00; 24″ – $285.00-125.00. **Honey:** All composition: 14″ – $175.00-70.00; 20″ – $245.00-100.00; 27″ – $350.00-125.00.

Ice Queen: Skating Outfit. All composition, open mouth: 17″ – $675.00-250.00. **Lambkin:** Composition/cloth character baby: 16″ – $275.00-125.00.

15″ "Patricia" and marked: Effanbee/-"Patricia". All composition with sleep eyes, original wig, clothes and pin. Courtesy Glorya Woods. $250.00.

10″ "George and Martha Washington", marked: Effanbee Patsyette Doll, all composition and completely original. Painted eyes. Courtesy Frasher Doll Auctions. Mint with button – $200.00 each; Original, but soiled – $135.00 each; Not original & crazed – $85.00 each.

11″ "Portrait" doll of all composition, sleep eyes and all original. Courtesy Frasher Doll Auctions. $175.00.

14″ "Colonial Prosperity" 1711. Painted eyes and all original. Part of Historical Series. Courtesy Frasher Doll Auctions. 14″ – $450.00 up; 21″ – $1,200.00.

14″ Historical Series "Louisiana Purchase" 1804. All composition, painted eyes. Marked: Effanbee Anne Shirley. Courtesy Frasher Doll Auctions. 14″ – $450.00 up; 21″ – $1,200.00.

Historical Series dolls. Rear: Indian 1607, Primitive Indian 1492, Pioneer American Spirit 1720, Monroe Doctrine 1816 and Post War Period 1868. All composition, painted eyes and original. Courtesy Frasher Doll Auctions. 14″ – $450.00 up; 21″ – $1,200.00.

Limited Edition Club Dolls: 1975, Precious Baby – $450.00; 1976, Patsy – $350.00; 1977, Dewees Cochran – $175.00; 1978, Crowning Glory – $200.00; 1979, Skippy – $285.00; 1980, Susan B. Anthony – $150.00; 1981, Girl with Watering Can – $150.00; 1982, Princess Diane – $135.00; 1983, Sherlock Holmes – $145.00; 1984, Bubbles – $85.00.

Little Lady: All composition: 15″ – $175.00-70.00; 18″ – $200.00-80.00; 21″ – $245.00-85.00; 27″ – $400.00-125.00; Cloth body/yarn hair: 21″ – $200.00-75.00; Majorette: 14″ – $185.00-75.00.

Lovums: Composition/cloth: 15″-16″ – $200.00-85.00; 22″ – $275.00-100.00.

Mae Starr: Composition/cloth. Record player in torso: 30″ – $425.00; 125.00.

Marionettes: Composition/wood: 14″ – $125.00-65.00.

Martha and George Washington: 1976: 11″ – $200.00-85.00.

Mary Ann or Lee: Composition/cloth and all composition: 16″ – $165.00; 18″ – $195.00-85.00; 20″ – $225.00-95.00; 24″

19″ Effanbee's "Majorette" and "Charlie McCarthy". Both are composition and original. Courtesy Turn of Century Antiques. 19″ – $275.00; Charlie – $250.00.

– $250.00-100.00.

Mary Jane: Plastic/vinyl, walker and freckles: 31″ – $165.00-80.00.

Mickey: Composition/cloth. Flirty eyes: 18″

EFFANBEE DOLL COMPANY

14" "Suzanne" and both marked on head: Effanbee Suzanne: all composition, sleep eyes and both are original. Courtesy Frasher Doll Auctions. 14" – $200.00.

11" "Anne Shirley". All are composition with original wigs and clothes. 15" Majorette, 17" in dress and 21" in gown. All have sleep eyes and are fully marked. Courtesy Turn of Century Antiques. 15" – $250.00; 17" – $200.00; 21" – $245.00.

– $200.00-95.00; 22"-23" – $265.00-100.00.

Mickey: All vinyl. Some with molded hats: 11" – $95.00-30.00.

Pat-O-Pat: Composition/cloth, painted eyes. Press stomach and pats hands: 13"-14" – $100.00-40.00.

Patricia: All composition: 14" – $250.00-100.00.

Patsy: All composition: 14" – $250.00-100.00; Composition/cloth: 14" – $275.00-100.00.

Patsyette: 9" – $190.00-80.00.

Patsy Ann: 19" – $300.00-125.00; Vinyl: 15" – $95.00-40.00.

Patsy Joan: 16" – $300.00-125.00.

Patsy, Jr.: 11" – $225.00-80.00.

Patsy Lou: 22" – $375.00-150.00.

Patsy Mae: 30" – $500.00-175.00.

Patsy Ruth: 26"-27" – $500.00-175.00.

Patsy, Wee: 5"-6" – $300.00-100.00.

Polka-Dottie: 21" – $150.00-80.00.

Portrait Dolls: All composition: 12" – $175.00-55.00.

Prince Charming: All hard plastic: 16" – $225.00-125.00.

Rootie Kazootie: 21" – $165.00-55.00.

Rosemary: Composition/cloth: 14" – $165.00-80.00; 22" – $225.00-100.00; 28" – $325.00-125.00.

Skippy: All composition: 14" – $300.00-100.00.

Sugar Baby: Composition/cloth. Sleep eyes, molded hair or wig: 16"-17" – $200.00-80.00.

Sunny Toddler: Plastic/vinyl: 18" – $65.00-30.00.

Suzanne: All composition: 14" – $200.00-80.00.

Suzette: All composition: 12" – $150.00-50.00.

Sweetie Pie: Composition/cloth: 14" – $135.00-40.00; 19" – $185.00-65.00; 24" – $265.00-80.00.

Tommy Tucker: Composition/cloth. Flirty eyes: 18" – $200.00-95.00; 22"-23" – $265.00-100.00.

W.C. Fields: Composition/cloth: 22" – $695.00-200.00; Plastic/vinyl: 15" – $250.00.

16" "Honey" marked: Effanbee made in U.S.A. All hard plastic, sleep eyes. Original except shoes. Right: 14" "Toni" all hard plastic and original except shoes. Made by Ideal Doll Co. Courtesy Frasher Doll Auctions. 16" – $150.00; 14" – $125.00.

30" Marked: Electra. Composition head with molded hair with head band and painted eyes. Composition lower arms. Body and limbs stuffed cloth. Large metal button pin jointed. Courtesy Jeannie Mauldin. $185.00 up.

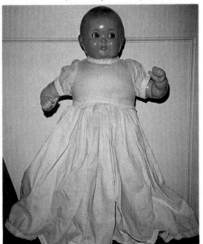

18" Brazilian Baby with cloth body, sleep flirty eyes, open mouth and all four fingers turned under on right hand. Marked on head. Ca. 1930. Composition head and limbs. Courtesy Genie Jinright. $95.00.

14" Scottish Girl marked: Pedigree England on head. Saran wig and dressed in wool tartans. Music box with key wind in back and plays "Auld Lang Syne". Courtesy Maureen Fukuskima. $125.00.

FOREIGN DOLLS

30" Early plastic with flirty sleep eyes. Completely original. Doll not marked. Box: AVA, Milano (Italy). Tag: Alberani/vecchioti/milano. Courtesy Doll Cradle. 30" Mint in box – $300.00 up; 30" Fair condition – $100.00.

14" "Bindi" all vinyl, rooted hair, sleep eyes/lashes, open/closed mouth with painted teeth. Dressed in aborigine "Lap Lap". Marks: Australia, on head. Courtesy Genie Jinright. $145.00.

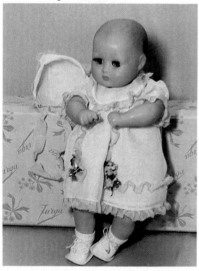

16" Rare baby of early plastic by Furga. Bent arms and curled fingers with slightly bent baby leg. Sleep eyes and painted hair. Completely original in original box. Courtesy Doll Cradle. 16" – $250.00 up.

Box design for large Italian doll. Courtesy Doll Cradle.

12" Plastic Googly with glued on floss wig, cork glued to feet and marked: made in Italy BREV. Original. $25.00.

23" Character Italian doll of all hard plastic, sleep flirty eyes, lashes, glued on wig. May be original clothes. Left: 22" Saucy Walker. Marked: Ideal Doll on head and body, flirty sleep eyes, all hard plastic and original. Courtesy Frasher Doll Auctions. 23" – $165.00; 22" Ideal – $95.00.

19" Doll purchased in Moscow, Russia in 1976. Plastic with sleep eyes. Original. Courtesy Diane Kornhauser. $65.00.

14" Tea Cosey purchased by owner in Odessa, Russia in 1973. Waxy plastic head and hands, stitched into dancing position. Painted features. Has quilted cotton underskirt for insulation. Courtesy Margaret Mandel. $45.00.

HASBRO

11″ G.I. Joe nurse. Green painted eyes/black lashes. Marks: Patent Pend./1967/Hasbro/made in Hong Kong. Tag on uniform: G.I. Nurse by Hasbro/Hong Kong. $200.00 up.

12″ "Eagle Eye G.I. Joe". Has extra joints at ankles, knees, elbow and wrists. Flocked hair, eyes move from side to side by lever on back of head. Scar on face. Marks: Hong Kong, on head. 1975/Hasbro/Pat. Pend./on lower back. Clothes not original. Courtesy Genie Jinright. $25.00 up.

Right: 15″ "Little Miss No Name". Plastic and vinyl. Large inset eyes, tear on cheek. Marks: 1965. Hasbro, on head. Original. Left: 13″ "Poor Pitiful Pearl". Vinyl, sleep eyes. Marked: 1963/WM Steig/Horsman Dolls, Inc. Courtesy Frasher Doll Auctions. 15″ – $65.00 up; 13″ – $25.00 up.

All prices are for mint dolls.
Adam: 1971. Boy of World of Love Series: 9″ – $12.00.
Aimee: 1972. Plastic and vinyl: 18″ – $40.00.
Defender: One-piece arms and legs. 1974: 11½″ – $10.00.
Dolly Darling: 1965: 4½″ – $6.00.
Flying Nun: Plastic/vinyl. 1967: 5″ – $20.00.
G.I. Joe: Flocked or molded hair, no beard. 1964: 12″ – $40.00 up; Black – $60.00 up. Flocked hair and beard: 12″ – $30.00 up. Eagle eyes. 1975: 11½″ – $25.00 up. Talking: 11½″ – $25.00 up. Foreign includes: Australian, Japanese, German, Russian – $95.00 up. Nurse: 11″ – $200.00 up.
Leggy: 10″ – $9.00.
Little Miss No Name: 1965: 15″ – $65.00.
Mama's and the Papas: 1967: $30.00 each.
Monkees: (Set of four). 4″ – $60.00.
Show Biz Babies: 1967: $25.00 each.
Storybooks: 1967: 3″ – $25.00-35.00.
Sweet Cookie: 1972: 18″ – $18.00.
That Kid: 1967: 21″ – $65.00.
World of Love Dolls: 1968: 9″ White – $8.00; Black – $10.00.

10″ Black "Baby Bumps" by Horsman. Ca. 1910. Composition and cloth with painted features and may wear original romper suit. 9½″ Black "Puss 'N Boots" by Freundlich Novelty Co. 1940's. All composition and original. Courtesy Frasher Doll Auctions. 10″ White – $135.00; 10″ Black – $185.00.

19″ Marked: E.I.H. Co. Inc. composition and cloth with tin sleep eyes/lashes, open mouth, dimples. 14″ Marked: Effanbee Baby Dainty. Painted features. Composition and cloth. In original tagged dress. Courtesy Frasher Doll Auctions. 19″ – $200.00; 14″ Baby Dainty – $150.00.

Left: 12″ "Campbell Kid" of 1940's. All composition painted features, molded hair and painted on shoes and socks. Not original. Right: 13″ "Campbell Kid" marked: E.I.H. Ca. 1911. Composition and cloth with painted features and hair. Not original. Courtesy Frasher Doll Auctions. 1940's, Original – $250.00; 1940's, Mint, but redressed – $100.00; 1911, Mint & original – $165.00; 1911, Fair condition – $75.00.

HORSMAN DOLL COMPANY

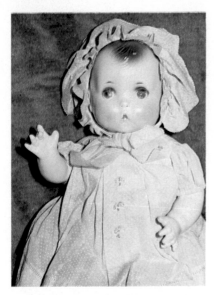

24″ Marked: Brother 1937 Horsman. Composition and cloth, molded hair, sleep eyes and small closed mouth. Original dress and bonnet. Courtesy Frasher Doll Auctions. 24″ – $150.00 up.

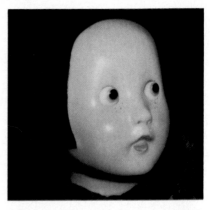

18″ "Ella Cinders" from comic strip by Bill Conselman and Charles Plumb called "Rags to Riches". Composition with cloth body. Painted features. Marks: 1925 MN S on head. Tag: Ella Cinders Trademark/Reg. U.S. Pat. Off. 1925. Metropolitan Newspaper Service. Courtesy Laura Cleghorn, $500.00.

22″ "Chubby Baby" marked: A Horsman Doll. Sleep, flirty eyes. Closed mouth and molded hair. Composition and cloth. Courtesy Frasher Doll Auctions. 22″ – $95.00.

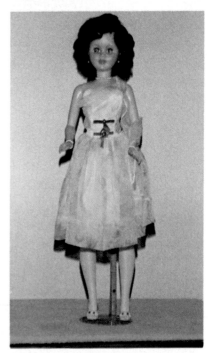

25″ "Jackie Kennedy". Blue sleep eyes, plastic and vinyl, rooted hair. High heel feet. Marks: Horsman/1961/J.K. 25/4. Courtesy Ann Wencel. $135.00.

First prices are for mint dolls. Second for dolls that may be crazed, cracked, soiled, dirty or not original.

Answer Doll: Buttons in back make head move. 1966: 10″ – $12.00-5.00.

Billiken: Composition head, slant eyes, plush or velvet body. 1909: 12″ – $300.00-100.00.

Baby Bumps: Composition and cloth. 1910: 11″ – $135.00-65.00; 16″ – $165.00-85.00; Black: 11″ – $185.00-85.00; 16″ – $225.00-100.00.

Baby First Tooth: Cloth and vinyl, cry mouth, one tooth, tears on cheeks: 16″ – $45.00-15.00.

Baby Tweaks: Cloth and vinyl. Inset eyes. 1967: 20″ – $32.00-16.00.

Bedknobs & Broomsticks: Came with plastic and tin bed. Doll has jointed waist, painted eyes: 6½″ – $28.00-6.00.

Betty: All composition: 16″ – $145.00-50.00; Plastic and vinyl: 16″ – $25.00-10.00.

Betty Jo: All composition: 16″ – $145.00-50.00; Plastic and vinyl: 16″ – $25.00-10.00.

Betty Ann: All composition: 19″ – $175.00-60.00; Plastic and vinyl: 19 ″ – $25.00-10.00.

Betty Jane: All composition: 25″ – $225.00-85.00; Plastic and vinyl: 25″ – $40.00-20.00.

Betty Bedtime: All composition: 16″ – $175.00-60.00; 20″ – $225.00-65.00.

Body Twist: All composition. Top of body fits down into the torso: 11″ – $150.00-50.00.

Bright Star: All hard plastic. Open mouth. 1952: 15″ – $95.00 up-40.00.

Brother: Composition/cloth: 22″ – $125.00 up-50.00; Vinyl: 13″ – $25.00-10.00.

Celeste Portrait Doll: In frame. Eyes painted to side: 12″ – $25.00-10.00.

Christopher Robin: 11″ – $32.00-10.00.

Child Dolls: All composition: 15″ – $125.00-50.00; 19″ – $175.00-65.00; All hard plastic: 14″ – $65.00 up-25.00; 18″ – $85.00 up-35.00.

Cindy: All hard plastic: 1950's. 15″ – $65.00 up-25.00; 17″ – $75.00 up-30.00; All early vinyl: 15″ – $35.00-15.00; 18″ – $45.00-20.00. Lady type: Swivel waist: 19″ – $45.00-20.00.

15″ "Fair Skin Doll". All vinyl. Rooted hair, sleep eyes and marked: Horsman/H14, on head and S-16, on bottom of feet. 1960. $65.00.

Cinderella: Plastic/vinyl. Painted eyes to side: 11½″ – $18.00-8.00.

Composition Dolls: 1910's to 1920's. Early all composition with painted or glass eyes. Molded hair or wig. Original or appropriate age clothing. Marks: E.I.H. and date (1911, 1913, 1915, etc.). Overall perfect condition: 10″ – $100.00-30.00; 16″ – $165.00-40.00; 20″ – $200.00-85.00.

Country Girl: 9″ – $12.00-5.00.

Crawling Baby: Vinyl. 1967: 14″ – $28.00-12.00.

Dimples, Baby: Composition/cloth: 14″ – $100.00-30.00; 20″ – $175.00-65.00; 24″ – $200.00-85.00. Toddler: 20″ – $185.00-75.00; 24″ – $225.00-95.00. Laughing, painted teeth: 22″ – $245.00-100.00.

HORSMAN DOLL COMPANY

10" "Super Flex Ruthie" by Horsman. All vinyl with one-piece body and limbs. Rooted hair and sleep eyes. All original in original box. Courtesy Doll Cradle. 10" in box – $35.00; 10" Re-dressed – $12.00.

Gold Medal Doll: Composition/cloth, upper and lower teeth: 21" – $100.00-40.00. Vinyl, molded hair: 26" – $150.00-65.00.
Ella Cinders: Comic character. Composition cloth: 14" – $285.00-100.00; 18" – $500.00-180.00.
Flying Nun: (Patty Duke). 1965: 12" – $45.00-20.00.
Hebee-Shebee: All composition: 10½" – $350.00-150.00.
Jackie Coogan: Composition/cloth: 14" – $425.00-185.00.
Jackie Kennedy: Marked: Horsman J.K. on head. Adult body. Plastic/vinyl: 1961. 25" – $135.00-50.00.
Jeanie Horsman: All composition: 14" – $135.00-50.00. Composition/cloth: 16" – $145.00-60.00.
JoJo: All composition: 12" – $145.00-60.00.
Life Size Baby: Plastic/vinyl: 26" – $150.00-70.00.
Lullabye Baby: Cloth/vinyl. Music box: 12" – $18.00-8.00; All vinyl: 12" – $12.00-5.00.
Mary Poppins: 12" – $25.00-10.00; 16" – $45.00-20.00; 26" – $100.00-50.00.
Mama Style Babies: Composition/cloth: 16"

Horsman's "Gretel" 1965 using the "Peggy Ann" doll. Plastic and vinyl, all original. Can be marked: Horsman Dolls Inc. T-11. or just Horsman Dolls, Inc. Courtesy Sheila Stephenson. 16" – $35.00.

– $100.00-30.00; 22" – $150.00-60.00. Hard plastic/cloth: 16" – $65.00-30.00; 22" – $90.00-40.00. Vinyl/cloth: 16" – $20.00-8.00; 22" – $30.00-15.00.
Peggy Pen Pal: Multi-jointed arms. Plastic/vinyl: 18" – $30.00-12.00.
Pippi Longstockings: Vinyl/cloth: 1972: 18" – $25.00-14.00.
Pipsqueaks: Four in set. 1967: 12" – $16.00 each-6.00.
Polly & Pete: Black dolls, molded hair: 13" – $150.00-45.00.
Poor Pitiful Pearl: 12" – $25.00-12.00; 17" – $45.00-20.00.
Peterkin: All composition, painted googly style eyes: 12" – $165.00-65.00.

Roberta: All composition. 1937: 14″ – $125.00-45.00; 20″ – $200.00-85.00.
Rosebud: Composition/cloth, dimples and smile. Sleep eyes and wig: 18″-19″ – $225.00-100.00.
Ruthie: All vinyl or plastic and vinyl: 14″ – $18.00-6.00; 20″ – $30.00-12.00.
Ruthie's Sister: Plastic and vinyl. 1960: 26″ – $65.00-30.00.

Sleepy Baby: Vinyl and cloth, eyes molded closed: 24″ – $35.00-15.00.
Tessie Talks: Plastic/vinyl: 18″ – $20.00-10.00.
Tuffie: All vinyl. Upper lip molded over lower: 16″ – $45.00-20.00.

HOWDY DOODY

Prices are for mint dolls.
Howdy Doody Doll: (not a puppet). Cloth body with composition head and hands: 17″ – $85.00; 23″ – $125.00.
Puppet: (mouth moves 7 limbs attached to strings): 14″ – $50.00; 20″ – $85.00.
Marionette: (mouth moves). Sleep eyes, cloth with hard plastic head and hands. Marked: Ideal Doll: 14″ – $50.00; 20″ – $75.00. All Vinyl: Molded in one-piece: 12½″ – $22.00; All vinyl: Jointed at shoulders, hips and neck: 14″ – $30.00. All cloth: Printed-on clothes and features: 16″ – $45.00.

HUMMEL

Hummel dolls are made by William Goebel in Germany. The all rubber dolls were made between 1948 and into the 1950's, with some being made as late as the 1960's. After 1964 the same molds were used to make the dolls in vinyl. Both models will have deeply molded hair and painted features. The dolls will be marked on the head, have tagged clothes and will have a paper tag (triangle shaped) attached to the wrist or around the neck.

First prices are for mint dolls. Second for checked, cracked, soiled or dolls that are not original. 12″ All rubber and original – $100.00-30.00. 12″ All vinyl and original – $125.00-45.00. 16″ All rubber and original – $150.00-65.00. 16″ All vinyl and original – $175.00-70.00. 10″ Vinyl baby – $85.00-30.00. 16″ Vinyl baby – $125.00-65.00.

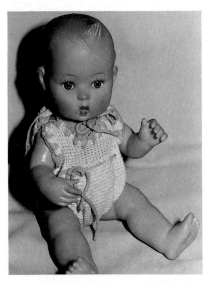

10″ All vinyl Hummel baby. Marked: V104 M.1. Hummel W. Goebel. Hard-to-find baby with molded hair, painted eyes and open/closed mouth with two molded upper teeth. Original romper. Courtesy Frasher Doll Auctions. 10″ – $85.00; 16″ – $125.00.

14″ "Mary Hoyer". All hard plastic, sleep eyes, mohair wig and original. Marked with circle on back. Courtesy Margaret Mandel. $300.00 up.

14″ "Mary Hoyer". All hard plastic and dressed in original outfit crocheted from Mary Hoyer pattern. Sleep eyes, mohair wig. Marked: Mary Hoyer Doll, in circle. Courtesy Margaret Mandel. $300.00 up.

The Mary Hoyer Doll Mfg. Co. operated in Reading, PA, from 1925. The dolls were made in all composition, all hard plastic and last ones produced were in plastic and vinyl. Marks: in a circle: "original Mary Hoyer doll" or "The Mary Hoyer Doll" embossed on lower back.

First price is for perfect doll in tagged factory clothes. Second is for perfect doll in outfits made from Mary Hoyer patterns. Third price is for re-dressed doll in good condition. (light crazing to composition). Composition Dolls: 14″ – $350.00 up-250.00 up-125.00. Hard Plastic Dolls: 14″ – $300.00 up-225.00 up-100.00. Plastic and vinyl: 14″ – $100.00-80.00-25.00.

14″ "Mary Hoyer". All hard plastic with Saran wig. Sleep eyes and marked: Mary Hoyer Doll, in circle on back. Original except socks added. Courtesy Esther Foss. $300.00 up.

12″ "Mary Hoyer". Brought from Mary Hoyer Co. from ad. Plastic with vinyl head and rooted hair. Sleep eyes. Marked: A.E.23, on head. Original. Courtesy Esther Foss. 12″ – $95.00.

23″ Marked: Hug Me/Kiddie Pal Dolly. Cloth and composition, tin sleep eyes, open mouth and molded hair. Made by Regal Doll Mfg. Co. Courtesy Frasher Doll Auctions. 23″ Mint & original – $185.00; 23″ Fair & re-dressed – $60.00.

IDEAL NOVELTY AND TOY COMPANY

First prices are for mint dolls. Second price for crazed, soiled, dirty or not original.

Baby Belly Button: Plastic/vinyl. 9" White – $8.00-4.00; Black – $15.00-8.00.

Baby Crissy: 24" White – $40.00-15.00; Black – 50.00-22.00.

Baby Snooks: and other "flexie". Wire and composition: 12" – $225.00-95.00.

Bam Bam: Plastic/vinyl or all vinyl: 12" – $12.00-5.00; 16" – $20.00-9.00.

Batgirl: and other Super Women: Vinyl: 12" – $65.00-20.00.

Betsy McCall: Hard plastic/vinyl head: 14" – $125.00-40.00.

Betsy Wetsy: Composition head, excellent all rubber body – $95.00-10.00.

Betsy Wetsy: Hard plastic/vinyl: 12" – $55.00-20.00; 14" – $75.00-30.00; All vinyl: 12" – $20.00-8.00; 18" – $60.00-25.00.

Betty Big Girl: Plastic/vinyl: 30" – $145.00-70.00.

Bizzy Lizzy: Plastic/vinyl: 17" – $28.00-14.00.

Blessed Event: Called "Kiss Me". Cloth body with plunger in back to make doll cry or pout. Vinyl head with eyes almost squinted closed: 21" – $75.00-30.00.

Bonnie Braids: Hard plastic/vinyl head: 13" – $42.00-15.00.

Bonnie Walker: Hard plastic. Pin jointed hips, open mouth, flirty eyes. Mark: Ideal W-25: 23" – $60.00-25.00.

Brandi: of Crissy Family: 18" – $55.00-25.00.

Brother/Baby Coos: Composition head/-latex: 24" – $35.00-10.00. Hard plastic head/vinyl: 24" – $50.00-15.00.

Bye Bye Baby: Lifelike modeling: 12" – $90.00-40.00; 25" – $250.00-125.00.

Cinnamon: of Crissy Family: 12" – $50.00-25.00; Black – $90.00-40.00.

Composition Dolls: All composition girl with sleep eyes, sometimes will be flirty, open mouth, original clothes and excellent condition. Will be marked: Ideal and a number or Ideal in a diamond: 14" – $125.00-30.00; 18" – $185.00-50.00; 22" – $225.00-75.00.

Composition Baby: Composition head and limbs, cloth body and closed mouth. Sleep eyes, sometimes flirty, original and in excellent condition: 18" – $125.00-30.00; 22" – $150.00-50.00; 25" – $175.00-70.00.

Cricket: of Crissy Family: 18" – $30.00-15.00; Black – $55.00-25.00; Look-a-round – $30.00-15.00.

Crissy: 18" – $35.00-15.00; Black – $65.00-25.00; Look-a-round – $30.00-15.00.

Daddy's Girl: 42" – $750.00 up-275.00.

Deanna Durbin: All composition: 14" – $350.00-150.00; 17" – $450.00-165.00; 21" – $500.00-200.00.

Dianna Ross: Plastic/vinyl: 18" – $135.00-75.00.

Dina: of Crissy Family: 15" – $50.00-25.00.

Flossie Flirt: Cloth/composition. Flirty eyes: 22" – $95.00-40.00; Black – $150.00-70.00.

Giggles: Plastic/vinyl: 16" – $35.00-18.00; 18" – $50.00-25.00; Black: 18" – $125.00-65.00.

Goody Two Shoes: 18" – $65.00-25.00; Walking/talking, 27" – $125.00-45.00.

Harriet Hubbard Ayers: Hard plastic/vinyl head: 14½" – $125.00-35.00; 18" – $165.00-50.00.

Joey Stivic (Baby): One-piece body and limbs. Sexed boy. 15" – $35.00-15.00.

Judy Garland: All composition: 14" – $750.00-250.00; 18" – $950.00-300.00. Marked with backward 21: 14" – $165.00-75.00; 18" – $250.00-95.00.

Judy Splinters: Cloth/vinyl/latex, yarn hair, painted eyes: 18" – $85.00-20.00; 22" – $125.00-30.00; 36" – $200.00-75.00.

Kerry: of Crissy Family: 18" – $45.00-20.00.

King Little: Composition and wood: 14" – $175.00-70.00.

Kissy: 22" – $50.00-20.00; Black – $100.00-50.00.

Kissy: Tiny: 16" – $55.00-25.00; 22" – $60.00-30.00; Black – $100.00-50.00.

Little Lost Baby: Three-faced doll: 22" – $45.00-20.00.

Magic Lips: Vinyl coated cloth/vinyl. Lower teeth. 24" – $65.00-30.00.

Mama Dolls: Composition/cloth: 18" – $100.00-25.00; 23" – $150.00-45.00; Hard plastic/cloth: 18" – $45.00-20.00; 23" – $65.00-25.00.

Mary Hartline: All hard plastic: 15" – $150.00-60.00; 21"-23" – $225.00-95.00; All composition: 21" – $225.00-95.00.

Mary Jane or Betty Jane: All composition,

sleep or flirty eyes, open mouth. Mark: Ideal 18: 18″ – $185.00-60.00.

Mia: of Crissy Family: 15½″ – $40.00-20.00.

Miss Curity: Hard plastic: 14″ – $150.00-60.00; Composition: 21″ – $185.00 up-75.00.

Miss Ideal: Multi-jointed: 25″ – $95.00-40.00; 28″ – $275.00-100.00.

Miss Revlon: 10½″ – $65.00-20.00; 17″ – $65.00-28.00; 20″ – $90.00-45.00.

Mitzi: Teen type: 12″ – $45.00-18.00.

Patti Playpal: 30″ – $135.00-60.00; 36″ – $175.00-70.00.

Pebbles: Plastic/vinyl and all vinyl: 8″ – $12.00-5.00; 12″ – $20.00-9.00; 15″ – $30.00-15.00.

Penny Playpal: 32″ – $125.00-60.00.

Peter Playpal: 38″ – $235.00-100.00.

Pinocchio: Composition/wood. 11″ – $200.00-70.00; 21″ – $450.00-125.00.

Posey: Hard plastic, vinyl head, jointed knees. Marks: Ideal VP-17: 17″ – $60.00-20.00.

Sandy McCall: Boy: 36″ – $350.00-165.00.

Sara Ann: Hard plastic, marked P-90, Saran wig: 14″ – $150.00-50.00.

Saralee: Cloth/vinyl. Black: 18″ – $145.00-50.00.

Saucy Walker: 16″ – $65.00-20.00; 19″ – $85.00-30.00; 22″ – $95.00-40.00. Black: 22″ – $145.00-70.00. Vinyl head: 19″ – $75.00-25.00.

Shirley Temple: See that section.

Snoozie: Composition/cloth, molded hair, sleep eyes, open yawning mouth. Marks: B. Lipfert. 13″ – $125.00-40.00; 16″ – $165.00-60.00; 20″ – $200.00-85.00.

Snow White: All composition: 12″ – $400.00-135.00; 18″ – $400.00-135.00. Molded hair: 14″ – $175.00-85.00; 18″ – $400.00-135.00.

Sparkle Plenty: 15″ – $45.00-20.00.

Susy Play Pal: Fat, chubby, vinyl body and limbs. Marks: Ideal O.E.B. 24-3: 24″ – $95.00-35.00.

Tara: Grow hair. Black: 16″ – $25.00-18.00.

15″ "Toni". Marked: P-91 Ideal. All hard plastic, sleep eyes and nylon wig. 19″ Shirley Temple look-a-like. All composition sleep eyes, open mouth. Maybe all original. Unmarked. Courtesy Frasher Doll Auctions. 15″ – $125.00; 19″ – $165.00.

18″ "Snow White" by Ideal and body is marked: Shirley Temple 18. All composition, open mouth and sleep eyes. All original. Courtesy Frasher Doll Auctions. 18″ – $400.00.

IDEAL NOVELTY AND TOY COMPANY

Right: 26" "Baby Sally" by Ideal. Composition and cloth with molded hair, sleep eyes and open mouth and original clothes. Left: Horsman's "Brother" in original clothes. (See Horsman section). Courtesy Frasher Doll Auctions. 26" – $175.00.

18" and 21" "Deanna Durbin". All composition, sleep eyes and open mouths. Marked: Deanna Durbin Ideal Doll USA. Both are original and metal pin is original. Courtesy Frasher Doll Auctions. 18" – $450.00; 21" – $500.00.

15" "Judy Garland" as Dorothy in the Wizard of Oz. Marked: Ideal Doll. All composition. With large sleep eyes, open mouth. Original dress. Human hair wig has been rebraided and tied with yarn. Courtesy Frasher Doll Auctions. 15" Mint – $750.00; 15" Near mint – $600.00.

IDEAL NOVELTY AND TOY COMPANY

Left: 22" "Mary Lou". Marked: Ideal, in diamond, USA. All composition, sleep eyes, open mouth and all original. Right: 19" "Mary Ann" by Effanbee. Marked: Mary Ann, on head and on a Patsy Ann body. All composition. Wig combed out and replaced clothes. Courtesy Frasher Doll Auctions. 19" – $185.00; 22" – $225.00.

Right: 14" "Toni". Marked: P-90 Ideal. All hard plastic, sleep eyes and with nylon wig. All original. Left: 17" Effanbee's "Little Lady". All composition and re-dressed. Courtesy Frasher Doll Auctions. 14" – $125.00 up; 17" Original – $200.00; Redressed – $145.00.

16" "Mary Hartline". Marked: P-91 Ideal Doll. Sleep eyes with eyeshadow. Saran wig, all hard plastic and original. Courtesy Frasher Doll Auctions. $150.00 up.

IDEAL NOVELTY AND TOY COMPANY

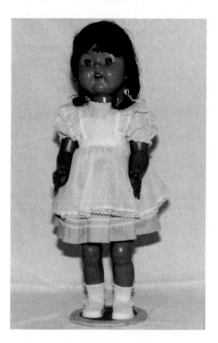

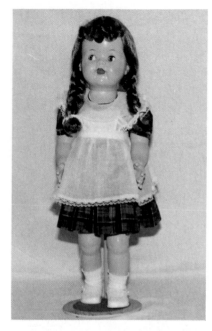

23″ "Saucy Walker". Rare black doll with original clothes except Pinafore replaced. Hard plastic, pin jointed walker. Sleep eyes and open mouth. Marked: Ideal Doll. Courtesy Doris Chandler. $145.00.

23″ "Saucy Walker" with flirty sleep eyes. Pin jointed walker. All hard plastic. Replaced pinafore. Courtesy Doris Chandler. $95.00.

23″ Ideal Doll that is cloth with vinyl face mask and in-set eyes, black yarn hair and has a crank when wound that plays "Rock-a-By Baby". Removable pinafore which has a tag: Ideal Doll, and is located on the side at the waist. Refer: MCD, Vol. 3, page 200. Courtesy Diane Kornhauser. 23″ – $35.00.

16″ "Saucy Walker". All hard plastic, pin jointed walker. Original. Courtesy Doris Chandler. $65.00.

IDEAL NOVELTY AND TOY COMPANY

Tammy: 9″ – $22.00-12.00; 12″ – $30.00-15.00; Black – $35.00-15.00; Grown-up: 12″ – $20.00-10.00.

Thumbelina: Kissing: 10½″ – $14.00-6.00; Tearful: 15″ – $20.00-10.00; Wake-up: 17″ – $22.00-10.00; Black – $40.00-15.00.

Tickletoes: Composition/cloth: 15″ – $95.00-35.00; 21″ – $145.00-50.00.

Tiffany Taylor: Top of head swivels to change hair color: 18″ – $50.00-20.00.

Tippy or Timmy Tumbles: 16″ – $35.00-15.00; Black – $50.00-25.00.

Toni: 14″ – $125.00-45.00; 21″ – $200.00-75.00; Walking – $185.00-60.00.

Tressy: of Crissy Family: 18″ – $45.00-20.00; Black – $55.00-25.00.

Velvet: of Crissy Family: 16″ – $35.00-15.00; Black – $65.00-25.00; Look-a-round – $30.00-15.00.

18″ "Miss Revlon". Marked: Ideal Doll. vinyl and rigid vinyl, sleep eyes, jointed waists and high heel feet. Both original. Courtesy Frasher Doll Auctions. 18″ – $65.00 up.

19″ "Princess Mary" of 1954. Hard plastic with vinyl head, sleep eyes, rooted hair. Pin hip jointed walker. Original gown. Courtesy Debra Ekart. $75.00.

Shows body construction on 19″ pin jointed walker.

IDEAL NOVELTY AND TOY COMPANY
KENNER

12" "Tammy" in tagged outfit with dog. Painted features and marked: Ideal Toy Corp. B5-12. Courtesy Sheila Stephenson. 12" – $30.00.

12" "Tammy" in tagged nurses outfit. Missing sneaker-type shoes. Plastic and vinyl. Marked: Ideal Toy Corp. B5-12. Courtesy Sheila Stephenson. 12" – $30.00.

KENNER

First prices are for mint dolls. Second price for played with and missing original clothes or accessories.

Baby Bundles: 16" – $16.00-7.00; Black – $20.00-10.00.

Baby Yawnie: Cloth/vinyl. 1974. 15" – $18.00-9.00.

Big Foot: All rigid vinyl: 13" – $18.00-7.00.

Butch Cassidy or Sundance Kid: 4" – $10.00 each-4.00.

Blythe: 1972. Pull strings change eye color and positions: 11½" – $25.00-10.00.

Charlie Chaplin: All cloth with walking mechanism: 1973: 14" – $50.00-25.00.

Cover Girls (Darcie, Erica, Dana, etc.): 12½" White – $18.00-9.00. Black – $20.00-10.00.

Crumpet: 1970. Plastic/vinyl: 18" – $25.00-10.00.

Dusty: 11½" – $20.00-7.00.

Gabbigale: 1972: 18" – $25.00-10.00; Black – $40.00-15.00.

Garden Gals: 1972. Hand bent to hold watering can. 6½" – $10.00-4.00.

Hardy Boys: 1978. Shaun Cassidy and Parker Stevenson: 12" – $20.00-8.00.

Jenny Jones and Baby: All vinyl. 1973: 9" Jenny and 2½" Baby – $20.00-7.00 set.

Skye: Black doll: 11½" – $22.00-8.00.

Sleep Over Dolly: and miniature doll: 17" – $35.00-10.00; Black – $40.00-15.00.

Star Wars: Large size figures: R2-D2, 7½" – $75.00 up-25.00; C-3PO, 12" – $75.00 up-25.00; Darth Vadar, 15" – $75.00-25.00;

5″ Sleep eyes "Strawberry Shortcake" marked: American Greeting/Made in Hong Kong, on head. Vinyl head with rooted hair and sleep eyes. Shown with plastic "Custard" her cat in original box. Made by Kenner in 1984 only. Box also contains strawberry-shaped sleeping bag. Sleep eyes – $20.00.

5″ "Blueberry" along with plastic "Cheesecake Mouse". Marks and description same as "Strawberry Shortcake". Has sleep eyes and rooted hair, also came with berry-shaped sleeping bag. Sleep eyes – $20.00.

KENNER

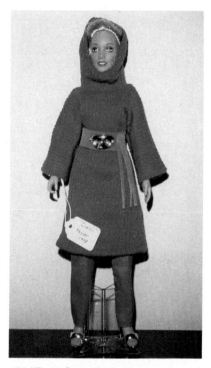

4½" Glamour Gals "Erin" in "Hawaiian Holiday" and "Erin" in "Golden Glitter". There were 42 different dolls in set, plus a great many different outfits. Marks: 8/CPG/82, on head. CPG 1981/Hong Kong, crossways on back. Rooted hair, jointed waist, bendable legs and has molded on panties. Made by Kenner. $9.00 each.

12" "Darci Cover Girl". Plastic and vinyl with jointed waist, painted features. Jointed at elbows, wrists and knees. Marks: 53/Hong Kong/G.M.F.G.I. 1978, on head. G.M.F.G.I. 1978/Kenner. Cin'ti. 0/47000 made in Hong Kong, on back. Original. Courtesy Genie Jinright. $20.00.

8¼" "Jawa" and 7½" "R2-D2". Both plastic and will be marked: Kenner. G.M.F.G.I. 1978. Courtesy Karen Heidemann. Jawa – $55.00; R2-D2 – $75.00 up.

Jawa, 8¼″ – $55.00-20.00; Stormtrooper, 12″ – $75.00 up-25.00; IG-88, 15″ – $95.00 up-45.00; Hans Solo, 12″ – $75.00-25.00.

Princess Leia: 11¼″ – $75.00 up-25.00; Luke Skywalker, 13½″ – $75.00-25.00; Chewbacca, 15″ – $75.00-25.00; Boba Fett, 13¼″ – $85.00 up-30.00; Obi-Wan Kenobi, 12″ – $80.00 up-28.00.

Steve Scout: 1974: 9″ – $15.00-6.00; Black – $18.00-9.00.

Sweet Cookie: 18″ – $20.00-9.00.

13″ "Boba Fett" and rare 1G-88. Both are original and will be marked G.M.F.G.I. 1978 Kenner. Courtesy Karen Heidemann. Boba Fett – $85.00 up; IG-88 – $95.00 up.

12″ Obi-Wan Kenobi. Plastic and vinyl. Painted features, molded hair and beard. Original. Marked: G.M.F.G.I. 1978. Kenner. Made in Hong Kong. Courtesy Karen Heidemann. $80.00 up.

KEWPIE

First prices based on mint dolls. Second for soiled, dirty, cracked or crazed and not original. (See front section for bisque Kewpies).

All Composition: Jointed shoulders only: 9″ – $75.00-30.00; 14″ – $125.00-48.00. Jointed hips, neck and shoulders: 9″ – $100.00-50.00; 14″ – $200.00-85.00; Talcum Powder Container: 7″-8″ – $150.00-60.00.

Celluloid: 2″ – $32.00-12.00; 5″ – $50.00-18.00; 9″ – $125.00-35.00; Black, 5″ – $125.00-25.00.

Bean Bag Body: 10″ – $25.00-12.00.

Cloth Body: Vinyl head and limbs: 16″ – $165.00-70.00.

Kewpie Gal: With molded hair/ribbon: 8″ – $35.00-15.00.

Hard Plastic: 8″ – $60.00-20.00; 12″ – $200.00-90.00; 16″ – $285.00-125.00.

Ragsy: Vinyl one-piece/molded clothes with heart on chest. 1964: 8″ – $60.00-28.00; Without heart. 1971: 8″ – $45.00-19.00.

Thinker: One-piece vinyl sitting down: 4″ – $9.00-4.00; Vinyl: jointed shoulders and hips: 9″ – $60.00-20.00; 12″ – $95.00-30.00; 14″ – $125.00-45.00; 27″ – $225.00-95.00. Not jointed: 9″ –

11″ "Kewpie". All composition with one-piece body, legs and head. Jointed at shoulders only. Red heart sticker on chest. Shown with 13″ Shirley Temple "Little Colonel". Courtesy Glorya Woods. 11″ – $85.00; 13″ Shirley – $475.00.

27″ "Kewpie". All vinyl in original clothes. 27″ "Baby Beautiful" by Ideal with brown sleep eyes, 19″ head circumference, cloth body. Composition head on composition shoulder plate, mohair wig and lower composition limbs. 1943. Courtesy Turn of Century Antiques. 27″ – $225.00 up; 19″ Ideal – $185.00.

"Kewpie Visits Tara" made exclusively for the Collector's United Gathering Doll Show in Atlanta, GA. Made by Jesco from original Cameo molds. The girl is from 1985 and boy from 1986. 1985 – $65.00; 1986 – $45.00.

$40.00-10.00; 12″ – $60.00-15.00; 14″ – $80.00-22.00.

Black: 9″ – $35.00-15.00; 12″ – $50.00-25.00; 14″ – $95.00-45.00; 27″ – $195.00-85.00.

Wards Anniversary: 8″ – $45.00-15.00.

All Cloth: (Made by Kreuger) All one-piece including clothes: 12″ – $125.00-70.00; 16″ – $165.00-80.00; 20″ – $385.00-125.00; 25″ – $685.00-250.00. Dress and bonnet: 12″ – $150.00-70.00; 16″ – $225.00-95.00; 20″ – $485.00-175.00; 25″ – $785.00 up-250.00.

Kewpie Baby: With hinged joints: 15″ – $125.00-60.00; 18″ – $145.00-65.00.

Kewpie Baby: With one-piece stuffed body and limbs: 15″ – $135.00-60.00; 18″ – $155.00-65.00.

13″ Klumpe Mailman. All felt with wired limbs so doll is posable. Painted features. 13″ – $125.00.

KLUMPE

Two all felt dolls made by Klumpe of Spain. All felt with posable limbs, painted features. Distributed by Effanbee Doll Co. Courtesy Ruth Lane. 8″ – $85.00; 13″ – $125.00.

8″ Nurse and Doctor made by Klumpe of Spain and distributed by Effanbee Doll Co. All felt with painted features. Courtesy Ruth Lane. 8″ – $85.00.

9″ and 8″ Klumpe dolls made in Spain and distributed by Effanbee Doll Co. All felt with painted features. Courtesy Ruth Lane. 8″-9″ – $85.00.

KNICKERBOCKER TOY COMPANY

All prices for mint dolls.

Bozo Clown: 14″ – $25.00; 24″ – $45.00.

Clown: Cloth: 17″ – $15.00.

Composition Child: Bent right arm at elbow: 15″ – $100.00 up.

Flintstones: 17″ – $45.00.

Levi Rag Doll: All cloth. 15″ – $16.00.

Little House On Prairie: 1978: 12″ – $15.00 each.

Lord of Rings: 5″ – $15.00.

Pinocchio: All plush and cloth: 13″ – $85.00.

Scarecrow: Cloth: 23½″ – $45.00.

Seven Dwarfs: Composition: 10″ – $185.00 up each.

Sleeping Beauty: All composition with bent right arm: 15″ – $125.00 up.

Snow White: All composition with bent right arm: 15″ – $125.00 up.

Soupy Sales: Vinyl, cloth, non-removable clothes: 13″ – $100.00.

Two-Headed Dolls: With vinyl face masks, one crying, other smiling: 12″ – $20.00.

Cinderella: With two bodies, one sad face, other with tiara: 16″ – $25.00.

L.J.N.
MAKER UNKNOWN

14½" "Boy George". Cloth body stitched jointed. Vinyl head, painted features, rooted yarn hair and has high top vinyl shoes. Marked: Sharpe-grade Ltd./L.J.N. Toys Ltd. 1984. Courtesy Genie Jinright. $35.00.

12" "Michael Jackson" in "American Music Awards" outfit. Vinyl and plastic with jointed knees, molded hair and painted eyes. Comes with snap together stand with his name across top. Marks: HJJ Productions/LJN Toys Ltd. $15.00.

Left: 17" Patsy-type unmarked. Right: 17½" Patsy look-a-like by Arranbee. Both have sleep eyes and are all composition. Larger doll has open mouth. Courtesy Turn of Century Antiques. $85.00 each.

25″ Unmarked composition and cloth, sleep eyes and open mouth with upper and lower teeth, molded hair. Not original. Courtesy Frasher Doll Auctions. $95.00.

22″ Unmarked baby of composition and cloth, sleep, flirty eyes and closed pouty mouth. Original mohair wig. Clothes not original. Courtesy Frasher Doll Auctions. $95.00.

14″ "Princess Spring, Summer, Fall, Winter" from the Howdy Doody show. Played by Judy Tyler for brief period and she was killed in car accident and the show returned to using a puppet for this part. All hard plastic, mohair wig and sleepy eyes. Marked: made in U.S.A., on back. Original Gown is ¾ length and has slippers with blue ties. Heavy painted features. Courtesy Florence Phelps. $250.00.

14″-15″ Left doll is dressed as teaching nun and is plastic and vinyl with sleep eyes. Right doll is dressed as nursing nun and is all hard plastic, sleep eyes and open mouth. This doll may have been made for Roberta Doll Co. or Valentine Doll Co. Courtesy Frasher Doll Auctions. $75.00.

MAKER UNKNOWN

18" Rabbit. Soft stuffed sateen cloth covered body and limbs with plush paws, feet and head. Molded face mask with wooden "carrot" in mouth. When carrot is turned a music box plays. Tag across chest: "Turn the Carrot and Hear Me Sing". Maker unknown. $45.00.

17" Marked: 3 on hips and 20 on head. Jointed neck, shoulders and hips. All vinyl with rooted hair and sleep eyes. Original. Souvenir style doll from Hawaii. Courtesy Sally Bethscheider. $50.00.

24" Marked: A. One-piece body and limbs. All vinyl and original. Sleep eyes and rooted hair. Courtesy Sally Bethscheider. $45.00.

24″ Marked: A, on head. All vinyl, one-piece body and limbs, sleep eyes, rooted hair and all original. Courtesy Sally Bethscheider. $45.00.

17″ Marked: P-23 on hip and A on head. One-piece body and limbs. Sleep eyes and rooted hair. Maybe original clothes. Courtesy Sally Bethscheider. $55.00.

6″ Trainer and Horse. Unmarked. Painted features and molded hair. Sold through National Catalog Co. in 1984. $35.00.

6″ Bareback Rider. All vinyl with rooted hair and painted features. Leg strap and bar attach doll to horse. Sold through National Catalog Co. 1984. $35.00.

MARX & CO.
MATTEL

17″ "Miss Seventeen" of 1961 shown with box and brochure showing clothes available for doll. $65.00 up.

17″ "Miss Seventeen". All plastic with inset scull cap, painted features and marked: US Patent 2925784/British Patent 804566/Made in Hong Kong. Box: Louis Marx & Co. 1961. Original with original stand. Courtesy Pat Parton. $65.00 up.

MATTEL

First prices are for mint dolls only. Second for dolls with clothes soiled, dirty and not original. M.I.B. stands for Mint In Box.
Allen: 12″ – $45.00 up-8.00.
Baby First Step: 18″ – $25.00-10.00; Talking – $35.00-12.00.
Baby Go Bye Bye: 12″ – $15.00-6.00.
Baby's Hungry: 17″ – $22.00-8.00.
Baby Pataburp: 13″ – $20.00-8.00.
Baby See 'N' Say: 17″ – $17.00-8.00.
Baby Secret: 18″ – $25.00-12.00.

Baby Small Talk: 11″ – $10.00-4.00; Black – $16.00-8.00.
Baby Tenderlove, Newborn: 13″ – $8.00-4.00.
Baby Walk 'N' Play: 11″ – $18.00-6.00.
Baby Walk 'N' See: 18″ – $18.00-9.00.
Barbie: #1: 11½″ M.I.B. – $500.00 up; Doll only – $250.00 up-100.00; #2: Same as #1 but no holes in feet – $600.00 up M.I.B.; Doll only – $325.00 up-125.00; #3: 1960 (still marked 1958 on body) – $110.00 up

#1 Barbie dressed in "Parisienne", The Stole is from "Enchanted Evening". Missing is gold purse and doll is on #2 Barbie stand. Courtesy Margaret Mandel. $500.00 up.

Bend knee Barbie in "American School Girl" haircut. Outfit is #1647, "Gold 'N Glamour" with mink fur trim. Brown gloves and shoes original. Courtesy Margaret Mandel. $150.00 up.

M.I.B.; Doll only – $50.00-20.00; #4: Soft, heavy material of new body does not turn light colored. Marked with Pat. Pend. mark. 1961 – $75.00 up M.I.B.; Doll only – $40.00-18.00; #5: Same as #4 but has one row of hair pulled through for bangs and bangs have a firm texture – $80.00 up M.I.B.; Doll only – $40.00-18.00; #6: First Bubblecut – $75.00 M.I.B.; Doll only – $35.00-15.00; #7: Hard hollow Pat. Pend. body. Rest as #6 – $75.00 M.I.B.; Doll only – $35.00-15.00; #8 & #9: 1962 and basically same as #7 – $65.00 M.I.B.; Doll only – $30.00-12.00; #10: Bubble cut with paler nails and lips. Midge marked body –

$50.00 M.I.B.; Doll only – $30.00-12.00; #11: Fashion Queen with molded Hair/band, plus wigs – $165.00 M.I.B.; Doll only – $60.00; #12: Swirl bangs (across forehead and to the side). Midge-marked body – $90.00 up M.I.B.; Doll only – $45.00-18.00; #13: Miss Barbie with sleep eyes. Midge-marked body – $450.00 M.I.B.; Doll only – $150.00-70.00; #14: Side part with head band – $350.00 up M.I.B.; Doll only – $250.00-70.00.

Color Magic Barbie: 1965 – $200.00 up M.I.B.; Doll only – $100.00-20.00.

Twist 'N' Turn Barbie: 1966 – $50.00 up M.I.B.; Doll only – $30.00-10.00.

MATTEL

Talking Barbie: $75.00 up M.I.B.; Doll only – $45.00-15.00.

Spanish Talking Barbie: $100.00 M.I.B.; Doll only – $55.00-20.00.

Barbie Items: Car-roadster – $265.00-80.00; Sports car – $125.00-60.00; Dune Buggy – $75.00-45.00; Clock – $40.00-10.00; Family House – $45.00-10.00; Watches – $20.00 to 40.00-10.00; Airplane – $200.00 up-75.00; Horse "Dancer" (Brown) – $50.00-25.00; Wardrobe – $35.00-10.00; #1 Barbie Stand: (round with two prongs): $50.00 up-20.00.

Bozo: 18" – $20.00-8.00.

Buffie (with Mrs. Beasley): 6" – $25.00-8.00; 10" – $50.00-15.00.

Capt. Lazer: 12½" – $45.00-12.00.

Casey: 11½" – $65.00 M.I.B.; Doll only – $35.00-12.00.

Casper The Ghost: 16" – $28.00-12.00.

Charming Chatty: 25" – $50.00 up-20.00.

Chatty Brother, Tiny: 15" – $18.00 up-9.00; Baby – $18.00 up-9.00.

Chatty Cathy: 20" – $45.00-10.00; Brunette/brown eyes – $55.00-15.00; Black – $100.00-40.00.

Cheerleader: 13" – $12.00-6.00.

Cheerful Tearful: 13" – $18.00-7.00; Tiny: 6½" – $10.00-5.00.

Cynthia: 20" – $25.00-10.00.

Dancerina: 24" – $25.00-8.00; Black – $40.00-15.00. Baby, not battery operated: $18.00-9.00; Black – $27.00-10.00.

Dick Van Dyke: 25" – $50.00-22.00.

Francie: 11½" – $60.00 up M.I.B.; Doll only – $30.00-10.00; Black – $200.00 M.I.B.; Doll only – $95.00-25.00.

Grandma Beans: 11" – $14.00-6.00.

Gorgeous Creatures: Mae West style body/animal heads: 1979 – $15.00 each-6.00.

Hi Dottie: 17" – $16.00-7.00.

Herman Munster: 16" – $22.00-10.00.

Hush Lil' Baby: 15" – $12.00-4.00.

Julia: 11½" Nurse – $55.00 up M.I.B.; Talking – $45.00 M.I.B.

"Twiggy" London's top teen model. Twist waist and bendable knees. Very short rooted hair and heavy painted features. 1967-1968. Courtesy Phyllis Houston. $75.00 up.

"Truly Scrumptious" in the two outfits she was released in. From movie "Chitty Chitty Bang Bang". 1968-1969. Courtesy Margaret Mandel. $225.00.

Lil Big Guy: 13″ – $8.00-4.00.
Kiddles: Mint in packages – $18.00-8.00; Storybook with accessories – $40.00-12.00; Jewelry – $10.00-3.00; Baby Liddle in Carriage – $30.00-10.00; Santa – $20.00-9.00.
Ken: Flocked hair – $60.00-10.00; Molded hair – $50.00-8.00.
Midge: 11½″ – $110.00 M.I.B.; Doll only – $45.00-15.00; Molded hair – $50.00 up M.I.B.; Doll only – $30.00-10.00.
Moon Mystic: 11½″ – $100.00-35.00.
Mother Goose: 20″ – $35.00-17.00.
Mrs. Beasley: Talking: 16″ – $20.00-10.00.
Peachy & Her Puppets: 17″ – $20.00-10.00.
Randy Ready: 19″ – $22.00-10.00.
Real Sister: 14″ – $20.00-10.00.
Rockflowers: 6½″ – $12.00 each-6.00.
Rose Bud Babies: 4″ – $16.00-8.00; 7″ – $22.00-10.00.
Saucy: 16″ – $65.00-25.00; Black – $85.00-40.00.
Scooby Doo: 21″ – $58.00-20.00.
Skediddles: 4″ – $15.00-8.00.
Shrinking Violet: 15″ – $55.00-18.00.
Singing Chatty: 17″ – $30.00-10.00.

"Tutti and Todd" with rooted hair, painted features and bendable limbs. All original, except dog added. Courtesy Margaret Mandel. She – $30.00 up; He – $35.00 up.

Lori 'N Rori #1133. One of the hard-to-find 1970 Pretty Pairs. Uses the "Tutti" mold, painted features, limbs bendable and comes with plush Teddy bear. Courtesy Margaret Mandel. $65.00 up.

16″ "Mork" cloth doll with pull string talking mechanism. Tag: Mattel. Copyright 1979 Paramount Pictures Corp. Mattel, Inc. Courtesy Jeannie Mauldin. $30.00.

MATTEL
MEGO

Sister Belle: 17″ – $28.00-9.00.
Skipper: $35.00 up-9.00; Black – $85.00
up-30.00; Grown-up – $15.00-5.00.
Skooter: 9½″ – $35.00-10.00.
Stacey Talking: $50.00 M.I.B.;
Sun Spell: 11½″ – $100.00-35.00.
Swingy: 20″ – $20.00-10.00.
Tatters: 10″ – $22.00-10.00.
Teachy Keen: 17″ – $20.00-8.00.
Teener: 4″ – $20.00 each-10.00.

Tinkerbelle: 19″ – $12.00-7.00.
Tippy Toes: 16″ – $25.00-9.00; Tricycle or
horse – $15.00-5.00.
Truly Scrumptious: 11½″ – $225.00
M.I.B.; Doll only – $100.00-35.00.
Tutti: 6″ – $30.00-9.00; Packaged sets –
$50.00 up.
Todd: 6″ – $35.00-10.00.
Twiggy: 11″ – $75.00-25.00.

MEGO

7″-8″ Wizard of Oz collection made by Mego in 1974. Will be marked: Mego
Corp/MCMLXXII/Pat. Pending/made in Hong Kong, on back and M.G.M. Inc., on heads,
or 1974 Mego Inc. on heads. Courtesy Sheila Stephenson. $10.00 up each.

Prices are for mint dolls.
Batman: Action figures: 8″ – $10.00.
Cher: 12″ – $12.00 up. Dressed in Indian
outfit – $20.00.
Dianna Ross: 12½″ – $25.00 up.
Dinah-Mite: 7½″ – $12.00; Black – $15.00.
Happy Days Set: Fonzie – $14.00; Others
– $9.00.
Joe Namath: 12″ – $48.00.
Our Gang Set: Mickey – $22.00; Others –
$12.00.
Planet of Apes: 8″ – $15.00 each.
Pirates: 8″ – $15.00 each.
Robin Hood Set: $15.00 each.

Sir Lancelot Set: 8″ – $15.00 each.
Star Trek Set: 8″ – $20.00.
Soldiers: 8″ – $9.00 each.
Sonny: 12″ – $12.00 up.
Starsky & Hutch: $10.00 each; Captain or
Huggy Bear – $15.00 each.
Super Women: Action figures: 8″ – $8.00
each.
Waltons: 8″ – $9.00 each.
Wizard of Oz: Dorothy: 8″ – $15.00; 15″
– $35.00 up each. Munchkin – $10.00 each.
Wizard – $15.00. Others: 8″ – $10.00; 15″
– $35.00 up each.

13" "Grow Hair Cher". Rare model of this doll. Bend knees and jointed at shoulders, waist, hips and wrists. Pull hair to lengthen and shorten by using key (shown over arm). Keyhole in center of back. Marks: 3906 AF/Mego Corp. 1975, on head. Mego Corp. 1975, made in Hong Kong, on lower back. Courtesy Genie Jinright. Grow hair – $20.00.

MOLLYE

Prices are for mint dolls.

Mollye Goldman of International Doll Co. and Hollywood Cinema Fashions of Philadelphia, PA, made dolls in cloth, composition, hard plastic and vinyl. Only the vinyl dolls may be marked with her name on the heads, the remainder will usually have a paper tag. She purchased undressed, unmarked dolls from various companies and designed clothes for them and they were sold under her name.

Airlines: Hard plastic: 14" – $125.00; 18" – $165.00; 23" – $200.00; 28" – $250.00.
Babies: All composition: 15" – $100.00; 21" – $175.00. Composition/cloth: 18" – $65.00; 23" – $95.00. All hard plastic: 14" – $85.00; 20" – $145.00. Hard plastic/cloth: 17" – $85.00; 23" – $145.00. Vinyl: 10" – $20.00; 15" – $30.00; 8½" – $12.00.
Cloth: Children: 15" – $95.00; 18" –

14" Mollye Dolls. All cloth and original. Oil painted mask face and yarn hair. Courtesy Frasher Doll Auctions. $65.00.

MOLLYE

$110.00; 24" – $135.00; 29" – $175.00. Young ladies: 16" – $135.00 up; 21" – $175.00 up. Internationals: 13" – $65.00; 15" – $95.00; 27" – $125.00 up.
Composition: Children: 15" – $95.00; 18" – $135.00. Young ladies: 16" – $175.00;

21" – $250.00. Jeanette McDonald: 27" – $450.00 up. Bagdad Dolls: 14" – $175.00 up; 19" – $325.00 up. Sultan: 19" – $400.00. Subu: 15" – $40.00.
Vinyl Children: 8" – $18.00; 11" – $25.00; 16" – $40.00.

18" "Airline Stewardess" by Mollye. All hard plastic, sleep eyes, glued on saran wig and original except shoes. These dolls will be marked: 14/made in U.S.A. and nude dolls were made by Desoto Doll Co. in Chicago and sold to Mollye to dress. Courtesy Bonnie Stewart. 18" – $165.00 up.

11" "Martha Washington". All composition, jointed at neck, shoulders and hips. Painted features and glued on wig. All original. Received by owner on Sept. 15, 1944 at birth of daughter, Judi. Clothes designed by Mollye and doll sold through Mollye International. Courtesy Genie Jinright. $45.00.

Right: Musical Ballerina by Mollye. Marked: 14 made in U.S.A. All hard plastic, sleep eyes, mohair wig and original costume. Mounted on musical base that plays "Stardust" as doll turns. Left: 20" "Sweet Sue" by American Character. All hard plastic and original except shoes are replaced. Courtesy Frasher Doll Auctions. 14" – $145.00; 20" – $145.00.

Left: 17" "Marion" by Monica Dolls Hollywood. All hard plastic, sleep eyes and rooted hair into hard plastic scalp. Unmarked. Right: 17" "Mary Hoyer". All hard plastic and original. Courtesy June Schultz. 17" – $300.00; 17" Hoyer – $250.00 up.

NANCY ANN STORYBOOK

Rear: 5½" "Rain, Rain Go Away" #170 and 5½" "Pretty as a Picture" #24. Both are all bisque. Front: 5½" "Jeannie" #161 and 5½" "Princess Rosanie". Both are all bisque. Courtesy Frasher Doll Auctions. $40.00 up each.

The painted bisque Nancy Ann dolls will be marked: Story Book Doll U.S.A. and the hard plastic dolls marked: Storybook Doll U.S.A. Trademark Reg. The only identity as to whom the doll represents is a tiny wrist tag with the doll's name on it. The boxes are marked with name of doll, but many of these dolls are found in the wrong boxes.

Bisque: 5" – $40.00; 7½"-8" – $45.00; Black – $75.00.
Plastic: 5" – $35.00; 7½"-8" – $40.00; Black – $65.00.
Bisque Bent Leg Baby: 3½"-4½" – $75.00.
Plastic Bent Leg Baby: 3½"-4½" – $60.00.

NANCY ANN STORYBOOK

Marked: Nancy Ann: All vinyl: 10½" – $55.00.
Muffie: All hard plastic: 8" Dress – $95.00 up; Ballgown – $125.00 up; Riding Habit – $125.00 up.
Nancy Ann Style Show Dolls: 17"-18" All hard plastic in ballgowns – $300.00 up.

5½" Bride and 6½" Groom. Both are all bisque with one-piece body and head. Painted features. Both original. Courtesy Frasher Doll Auctions. $40.00 up each.

8" "Muffie". Completely original in original box. Courtesy Doll Cradle. $95.00 up.

8" "Muffie" by Nancy Ann. All hard plastic, sleep eyes. Marks: Storybook Dolls/California/Muffie, on back. Original. Courtesy Dora Mitzel. $95.00 up.

NANCY ANN STORYBOOK
RAGGEDY ANN & ANDY

8" "Muffie". All hard plastic with sleep eyes. Original except Brides veil and one in pink nightgown and bonnet. Courtesy Frasher Doll Auctions. $95.00 up.

18" Nancy Ann style show doll. All hard plastic, glued on wig. Sleep eyes and unmarked. Courtesy Sheila Stephenson. $300.00.

RAGGEDY ANN & ANDY

First prices are for mint dolls. Second for played with, soiled, dirty and no clothes.

Designed by Johnny B. Gruelle in 1915 and is still being made. EARLY DOLLS by Johnny B. Gruelle will have black stamp on front "Patented Sept. 7, 1915". All cloth, brown yarn hair, tin button eyes (or wooden), painted lashes below eyes and no outline to white of eyes. Some are jointed by having the knees or the elbows sewn. Features on early dolls are painted on cloth: 15"-16" – $500.00 up-100.00; 23"-24" – $600.00 up-150.00.

Averill, Georgene Dolls: Red yarn hair, printed features and have cloth label sewn to side seam of body. Mid-1930's to 1963: 15" – $45.00 up-20.00.

Beloved Belinda: Black doll: 15" – $225.00 up.

Mollye Dolls: Red yarn hair and printed features. Will be marked in printed writing on front upper torso "Raggedy Ann and Raggedy Andy Dolls/Manufactured by Mollye Doll Outfitters": 15"-16" – $150.00-80.00; 22"-24" – $200.00-95.00.

Knickerbocker Toy Co.: Printed features, red yarn hair. Will have tag sewn to seam with name of maker. 1963-1982. 12" – $12.00-6.00; 17" – $20.00-10.00; 24" – $30.00-15.00; 26" – $42.00-20.00; 36" – $65.00-25.00.

Vinyl Dolls: 8½" – $9.00-3.00; 12" – $12.00-6.00; 16" – $17.00-8.00; 20" – $22.00-10.00.

Applause Dolls: Will have tag sewn in seam. These dolls are still available.

229

REMCO

5″ "Lily Munster". Vinyl head with rooted hair and plastic body and limbs. Jointed only at neck. Painted features. Copyright by Karo-Vue Productions and marked Remco 1964. Courtesy Kathy Gentry. $40.00.

15½″ "Little Orphan Annie". Plastic and vinyl, painted teeth, disc eyes. Original. Marked: Remco Inc. Copyright 1967, on head. Courtesy Jeannie Mauldin. $35.00.

REMCO

First prices are for mint dolls. Second for soiled, dirty and not original dolls.

Adams Family: Figures: 5½″ – $10.00 each-3.00 each.

Baby Crawalong: 20″ – $18.00-6.00.

Baby Grow A Tooth: 14″ – $24.00-8.00; Black – $35.00-12.00.

Baby Know It All: 1969: 17″ – $18.00-6.00.

Baby Laugh A Lot: 16″ – $15.00-7.00; Black – $30.00-15.00.

Baby Sad & Glad: 14″ – $20.00-12.00.

Dave Clark 5: 4½″ – $45.00. Set-20.00.

Heidi: 5½″ – $8.00-3.00; Herby: 4½″ – $12.00-5.00; Spunky (glasses): 5½″ – $14.00-5.00; Winking Heidi – $10.00-4.00.

Jeannie, I Dream Of: 6″ – $15.00-5.00.

Jumpsy: 14″ – $15.00-6.00; Black – $22.00-10.00.

Laurie Partridge: 19″ – $45.00-15.00.

L.B.J.: Portrait: 5½″ – $25.00-10.00.

Little Chap Family: Set of four – $175.00-50.00; Dr. John: 14½″ – $50.00-20.00; Lisa: 13½″ – $40.00-12.00; Libby: 10½″ – $30.00-10.00; Judy: 12″ – $30.00-10.00.

Mimi: Battery-operated singer: 19″ – $35.00-12.00; Black – $60.00-20.00; Outfits – $12.00 each.

Orphan Annie: Plastic and vinyl: 15″ – $35.00-14.00.

Tumbling Tomboy: 1969: 16″ – $15.00-6.00.

Rainbow and Computer: 1979: 8½″ – $35.00-10.00.

ROBERTA DOLL CO.
SASHA

"Roberta Ann". All original in original box. Made by Roberta Doll Co. Vinyl head with rooted hair, sleep eyes, one-piece vinyl body and limbs. Courtesy Doll Cradle. $65.00.

SASHA

The Sasha dolls were originated by Sasha Morgenthaler in Switzerland and were hand made by her from 1963 to 1965. Her original dolls are in the Zurich Museum. The dolls have been commercially made by the Trenton Co. in England since 1967 until spring of 1986 when the Trenton Co. went out of business (although a French firm was/is talking about taking over the making of the dolls). Sasha dolls were imported into the United States by Creative Playthings.

Sasha dolls are the same each year, except the clothes are different. For example: the 1973 Gregor (boy) is the same except he now wears pale denim pants instead of dark jeans and a roll neck sweater instead of a turtle neck. The babies were also slightly sexed and the Trenton Co. stopped this somewhere between 1974 and 1976. (Thank you for information to Nona Appleby, Victoria, Canada)

Prices have been very inflated on the Sasha dolls since the company went out of business and will settle down to a normal price range with time. 16" Sasha Limited Edition (5,000) in 1981 dressed in navy blue velvet and incised: #763 – $600.00 up. 1986: Dressed in sari from India – $1,000.00 up; Princess – $900.00 up. 1985: Prince – $600.00 up.

SASHA
SHINDANA

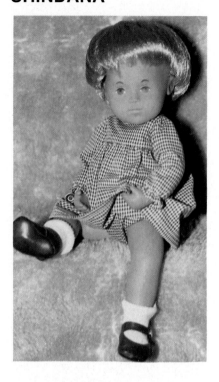

12″ Sasha Baby painted features, rooted hair and original. All babies were lightly sexed up to 1974-1976, all since then have not been sexed. Courtesy Shirley Merrill.

SHINDANA

Prices are for mint dolls.

Dolls will be marked: Div. of Operation Bootstraps, Inc. U.S.A./(year)/Shindana.

Shindana is no longer in business, but was the economic arm of Operation Bootstraps, a non-profit self-help business organization, whose goals were to establish business in the riot torn Watts (Los Angeles, Ca.) area right after 1968.

Baby Jamie: Plastic and vinyl. 1968: 13″ – $25.00.

Dr. J.: (Julius Erving): Full action figure. 1977: 16″ – $20.00.

Flip Wilson/Geraldine: All cloth, talker. 1970: 16″ – $20.00.

J.J.: All cloth talker. (Jimmy Walker). 15″ – $20.00; 23″ – $25.00.

Kim: Young lady in ballgown. 1969-1973: 16″ – $45.00.

Lea: Cloth/vinyl face mask and gauntlet hands. 1973: 11″ – $20.00.

Malaika: 1969 young lady: 15″ – $20.00.

O.J. Simpson: Full action figure: 9½″ – $20.00.

Rodney Allen Rippy: 1979 All cloth talker: 16¼″ – $20.00.

Tamu: Cloth/vinyl talker. 1969: 15″ – $25.00.

Wanda: 11½″ Nurse – $18.00; Ballerina – $15.00; Disco – $15.00; Airline Stewardess – $18.00.

Zuri: Sculptured hair baby. All vinyl. 1972: 11½″ – $25.00.

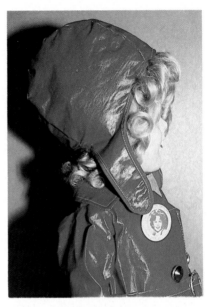

22" Shirley in rare aviator outfit from movie. "Bright Eyes". Imitation leather, brass buttons and belt buckle. Helmet and belt tagged: 22. Jacket tagged: Shirley Temple/Doll Dress/Reg. U.S. Pat. Off./Ideal Nov. & Toy Co., along with N.R.A. symbol. Courtesy Glorya Woods. $625.00 up.

Aviator cap and jacket from "Bright Eyes".

13" Shirley Temple in original trunk with tagged clothing. Jumpsuit-style outfit she is wearing is very rare. All composition. Ca. 1935. Courtesy Frasher Doll Auctions. $475.00 up.

Right: 18" Shirley Temple. Marked on head and body. All composition and original. Left: 18" Sonja Henie marked on head and in tagged outfit. All composition and original. Courtesy Glorya Woods. $500.00 up; 18" Sonja – $500.00 up.

SHIRLEY TEMPLE

16" Shirley Baby with flirty sleep eyes. Open mouth with upper and lower teeth. Cloth body. Composition head, shoulder plate and limbs. Courtesy Frasher Doll Auctions. $600.00.

Rear: 25" Shirley. Marked head and body. Flirty, sleep eyes. All composition and original in "Stowaway" two-piece outfit. Center Back: 19" Shirley 1957. Vinyl and original. Lower Left: 15" Shirley. All composition in original dress from "Our Little Girl" 1935. Baby: 19" marked on head. Composition and cloth molded hair, two upper and lower teeth. Right: 16" in dress from "Baby Take A Bow" 1936. Courtesy Frasher Doll Auctions.

15" 1950's Shirley Temple. Marked: Ideal Doll ST-15N. All vinyl. All original. Courtesy Dora Mitzel. $175.00.

All Composition: Marked on head or body or both. Made by Ideal Toy Company. Must have a Shirley Temple face and hairdo, as Ideal used the marked bodies for other dolls also. First prices are for mint and original dolls. Second prices for doll with light craze, clouded eyes and original clothes. Third price is for small cracks, badly crazed dolls and not originally dressed: Allow extra for outfits such as "Little Colonel", "Wee Willie Winkie", "Bluebird", etc. 11" – $600.00-400.00-85.00. 11" Cowgirl – $650.00-325.00-85.00. 13" – $475.00-300.00-85.00. 16" – $500.00-300.00-95.00. 18" – $500.00-325.00-95.00. 20" – $600.00-345.00-100.00. 22" – $625.00-400.00-120.00. 25" – $750.00-500.00-130.00. 25" Cowgirl – $800.00 up-595.00-150.00. 27"

12″ Shirley Temple 1950's. All vinyl, sleep eyes and rooted hair. All are original. Courtesy Frasher Doll Auctions. $125.00 each.

– $850.00-595.00-175.00. 27″ Cowgirl – $875.00 up-500.00-175.00.

Shirley Display Stand: Mechanical doll – $1,500.00.

Shirley at Organ: Mechanical doll – $1,500.00.

Hawaiian: Marked Shirley doll: 18″ – $650.00-400.00-120.00.

Baby: Marked Shirley Temple on head: (Price scale same as for dolls). 16″ – $600.00-325.00-95.00. 18″ – $625.00-400.00-120.00. 22″ – $700.00-425.00-130.00. 25″ – $785.00-450.00-140.00. 27″ – $825.00-500.00-140.00.

Vinyl of 1950's: Marked Ideal Doll and size number. Has set-in teeth. Allow more for flirty eyes in 17″ and 19″ sizes. 12″ M.I.B. – $150.00; Mint, not in box – $125.00; Dirty – $35.00. 15″ M.I.B. – $225.00; Mint, not in box – $175.00; Dirty – $85.00. 17″ M.I.B. – $275.00; Mint, not in box – $225.00; Dirty – $95.00. 19″ M.I.B. – $350.00; Mint, not in box – $300.00; Dirty – $100.00. 36″ M.I.B. – $1,400.00; Mint, not in box – $1,200.00; Dirty – $600.00. **1972:** Re-issue for Montgomery Wards –$165.00; Dirty – $45.00.

1973: Has box with many pictures of Shirley on it. Doll in red polka dot dress: 16″ M.I.B. – $100.00; Mint, no box – $75.00; Boxed outfits – $25.00 up.

16″ Shirley Temple. 1972. Vinyl and plastic in original box. Courtesy Frasher Doll Auctions. $165.00.

Pin: Old (1930's) doll pin – $75.00.

Statue: Chalk. In dancing dress: 7″-8″ – $28.00 up.

Japanese: Mold hair. All composition. 7″-8″ – $165.00.

STERLING DOLL CO.
TEDDY BEARS

Left: 29″ Marked: Sterling Doll Co. Inc. Painted hair, smiling open/closed mouth, painted eyes. Cloth body, composition football shoes and hands. Right: 29″ Swivel head marked: Elekta, Inc. N.Y. Cloth and composition, dressed in W.W.I. uniform. Courtesy Frasher Doll Auctions. 29″ – $200.00; Elekta – $185.00.

5″ Very rare Teddy Bear perfume bottle. Head comes completely off and has glass vial in body with glass stopper. Courtesy Turn of Century Antiques. $395.00.

Rear Left: 19½″ old bear. Rear Right: 26″ yellow mohair bear with glass eyes that light up. In tub is grey 18″ old bear with ears set in sides of head and standing is a 9″ old bear. Courtesy turn of Century Antiques. 26″ Yellow, eyes light up – $595.00; 19½″ – $185.00; 9″ – $350.00; In tub – $225.00.

First prices are for mint dolls. Second for soiled, poor wig, not original.

Terri Lee: 16″ Composition – $185.00-75.00; Hard plastic. Marked: Pat. Pend. – $195.00-85.00; Other – $150.00-50.00; Black – $325.00-100.00; Oriental –

16″ Black Terri Lee marked: Terri Lee Pat. Pending. Redressed. Courtesy Frasher Doll Auctions. $325.00.

"Jerri Lee" with rare platinum hair and all original "Terri Lee" in original outfit referred to as ballgown, Bridesmaid or ballerina. Marked: Terri Lee. Courtesy Margaret Mandel. She – $185.00 up; He – $195.00 up.

Painted bisque plastic "Terri Lee" with wire-like hair. All original. Courtesy Margaret Mandel. $185.00 up.

"Terri Lee" marked: Pat. Pend. All original and hair in original set. Courtesy Margaret Mandel. $185.00 up.

TERRI LEE

$350.00-100.00; Vinyl – $145.00 up-75.00;
Talking – $225.00 up-100.00.
Jerri Lee: 16″ Hard plastic –
$195.00-85.00; Black – $395.00-125.00;
Oriental –$425.00-125.00.
Tiny Terri Lee: 10″ – $110.00-40.00; Tiny
Jerri Lee: 10″ – $165.00-50.00.
Connie Lynn: 19″ – $300.00-100.00.
Gene Autry: 16″ – $500.00 up-125.00.
Linda Baby: (Linda Lee): 10″-12″ –
$150.00 up-75.00.

16″ Terri Lee marked on head and body.
Redressed. 10″ Tiny Terri Lee walker with
sleep eyes. Redressed. 10″ "Linda Baby".
All vinyl. Molded hair. Redressed. Courtesy
Frasher Doll Auctions. 16″ – $185.00 up;
10″ – $110.00 up; 10″ Baby – $150.00 up.

10″ Tiny Jerri Lee. Walker with sleep eyes.
Original with cowboy belt and guns (Tiny
Terri and Jerri Lee) added. Courtesy
Frasher Doll Auctions. $165.00.

17″ x 10″ x 7″ Terri Lee wardrobe. All
nautral wood. Painted trim on front with
Terri Lee name and initials. Sticker inside
door: T.M. Reg. U.S. Pat. Off. Scandia Toys
Los Angeles with emblem of a Viking Ship.
Plastic hangers read: Terri Lee Apple
Valley California. Ca. 1950. Courtesy Genie
Jinright. $95.00.

TERRI LEE
THREE-IN-ONE DOLL CORP.
TROLLS

So Sleepy: 9½" – $125.00-45.00.
Clothes: Ballgowns – $40.00 up-15.00; Riding outfits – $40.00-15.00; School dresses – $28.00-8.00; Skaters – $40.00-15.00; Coats – $20.00-6.00; Brownie Uniform – $20.00-6.00; Davy Crockett –

$40.00-15.00; 2 Pc. suits (Terri Lee) – $20.00-6.00; 2 Pc. suits (Jerri) – $25.00-9.00; Short pant suits – 40.00-15.00.
Mary Jane: Plastic walker Terri Lee look-a-like with long molded eyelids – $125.00-40.00.

THREE-IN-ONE

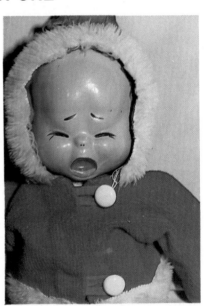

16" Three-faced Trudy. Ca. 1946. Mady by Three-in-One Doll Corp. Composition head, cloth body. Knot on top of head rotates faces. Smiling, sleeping and crying. Original. Courtesy Frasher Doll Auctions. 16" – $165.00.

TROLLS

5" Long Troll Turtle marked: DAM 1964. Ranks with Dam Alligator and Monkey as extremely rare. Courtesy Margaret Mandel. $55.00 up.

TROLLS
UNEEDA

Prices are for mint dolls.

Dam Things: 3″ – $9.00; 6″ – $20.00; 12″ – $20.00; 16″ – $30.00; 18″ – $52.00.

Uneeda: 3″ – $7.00; 6″ – $11.00.

Cloth Body/rest vinyl: 14″ – $38.00; 16″ – $65.00.

Unmarked: 3″ – $5.00; 6″ – $8.00; 12″ – $12.00.

Animals: Cow – $20.00; Large Cow – $65.00; Horse – $65.00; Giraffe – $65.00; Donkey – $65.00; Turtle – $55.00; Monkey – $55.00.

Two-Headed Troll: 6″ – $18.00; 12″ – $28.00.

Santa Claus Troll: 3″ – $16.00; 6″ – $20.00.

Grandpa & Grandma: 1977. 13″ – $25.00 each.

10″ Troll with tail and purchased in Norway in 1960. Originally cost $16.00 in 1960. Courtesy Diane Kornhauser. $45.00 up.

21½″ Troll purchased in Bermuda in 1980. Made in Norway and marked: Nyform. Courtesy Diane Kornhauser. $45.00 up.

UNEEDA

First prices are for mint dolls. Second for soiled, dirty, not original dolls.

Anniversary Doll: 25″ – $50.00-20.00.

Baby Dollikins: 21″ – $30.00-12.00.

Baby Trix: 16″ – $18.00-6.00.

Ballerina: Vinyl: 14″ – $20.00-7.00.

Blabby: $20.00-8.00.

Bare Bottom Baby: 12″ – $20.00-8.00.

Dollikins: 8″ – $12.00-5.00; 11″ – $18.00-6.00; 19″ – $25.00-12.00.

Fairy Princess: 32″ – $65.00-30.00.

Freckles: 32″ – $65.00-30.00.

Freckles Marionette: 30″ – $65.00-30.00.

Lucky Linda: (Lindbergh). Composition. 14″ – $225.00-95.00.

Pollyanna: 10½″ – $30.00-9.00; 17″ – $45.00-15.00; 31″ – $85.00-30.00.

Pri-Thilla: 12″ – $18.00-7.00.

Rita Hayworth: Composition: 14″ – $200.00-50.00.

Serenade: Battery-operated talker: 21″ – $35.00-12.00.

Suzette: 10½″ – $25.00-8.00; 11½″ – $25.00-8.00; 11½″ Sleep eyes – $30.00-9.00.

Tiny Teens: 5″ – $8.00.

31″ "PollyAnna" plastic and vinyl, rooted hair, sleep eyes/lashes and eye liner. Open mouth with painted teeth. Character from Walt Disney movie by the same name and starring Hayley Mills. Marks: Walt Disney Prod./Mfd. by Uneeda/J.F. 1960. Original. Courtesy Frasher Doll Auctions. $85.00.

"Toddles" Red Riding Hood. 1940's. All composition with painted eyes. Courtesy Petersen Collection. $225.00 up.

Ca. 1948-1950. Painted eyes, mohair wig and marked head and body. Courtesy Maureen Fukuskima. $250.00 up.

VOGUE DOLLS

Painted eyes, strung Ginny all original in sunsuit and cape. Mohair wig. Courtesy Karen Stephenson. $250.00 up.

Tiny Miss Series #41. 1952. Red Caracul wig. Painted lashes and marked on head and body. Courtesy Maureen Fukuskima. $275.00 up.

1952-1953. Bride. Strung doll and painted lashes. Courtesy Dora Mitzel. 1954 painted lash walker Bridesmaid. Courtesy Karen Stephenson. $250.00 up

First prices are for mint dolls. Second is for dirty, soiled, messed up wig, or not original dolls.

Baby Dear: 12" 1961 – $40.00 up-15.00; 17" – $65.00 up-20.00; 12" 1964 – $35.00-15.00.

Baby Dear One: 25" – $145.00-65.00.

Baby Dear Two: 27" – $165.00-85.00.

Brickette: 22" – $80.00-35.00.

Ginny: (Composition-see "Toddles") 8" Hard plastic. Allow more for special outfits. Strung. Painted eyes. Mark: Vogue Dolls – $185.00-250.00 up-85.00. Sleep eyes. Painted lashes. Strung – $200.00-75.00. Caracul wig (child, not baby) – $275.00-85.00; Painted lashes, sleep eyes, walker. Marks: Ginny/Vogue Dolls – $145.00 to $165.00-50.00. Molded lashes, walker: Ginny mark – $125.00 to 145.00-40.00. Molded lashes, jointed knee walker – $100.00 to 125.00-35.00.

Ginny Crib Crowd: Bent leg baby with caracul wig – $350.00 up-100.00.

Ginny Queen: $1,000.00 up.

Ginny: All vinyl, International – $22.00-8.00; Others – $28.00-10.00.

Ginny Clothes: Ballerina – $25.00 up; Ballgown – $30.00 up; Bride – $22.00; Riding Habit – $30.00 up; Skater – $25.00 up; Prince – $30.00 up; Hansel/Gretel – $30.00 up each; Clown – $30.00 up; Groom – $30.00 up; Majorette – $30.00 up; Skier – $28.00 up.

Ginny's Gym Set: $200.00 up.

Ginny's Pup: (Steiff) – $150.00 up.

Hug-A-Bye Baby: 16" – $22.00-8.00; Black – $28.00-10.00.

Jan: 12" – $45.00-15.00.

Jeff: 10" – $35.00-15.00.

Jill: 10" – $45.00-15.00.

Lil Imp: 11" – $35.00-15.00.

Love Me Linda: 15" – $30.00-12.00.

Star Bright: 18" – $40.00-20.00; Baby, 18" – $40.00-20.00.

Toddles: 8" "Ginny". All composition – $165.00 to 225.00 up-85.00.

Welcome Home Baby: 20" – $50.00-22.00.

Welcome Home Baby Turns Two: 24" – $65.00-28.00.

Wee Imp: 8" Red wig – $200.00-85.00.

Ca. 1952. Painted lash with dynel wig. Marked head and body. Courtesy Maureen Fukuskima. $200.00 up.

Frolicking Fables Series Ballerina. 1952. Painted lashes. Marked: Vogue, on head and Vogue Doll, on back. Courtesy Maureen Fukuskima. $200.00 up.

VOGUE DOLLS

"Ginny Queen". All hard plastic with sleep eyes/no molded lashes and all original. Courtesy Petersen Collection. $1,000.00 up.

Quilted blanket for "Ginny". Vogue tag on side and in original box. Courtesy Jay Minter. $20.00.

Other side of "Knit-Kit". Courtesy Jay Minter.

Debs. 1956 #6074. Molded lash walker. Marked: Vogue, on head and Ginny/Vogue Dolls Inc. Pat. No. Made in U.S.A., on body. Courtesy Karen Fukuskima. $125.00 - 145.00.

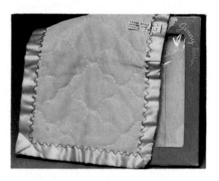

Vogue "Knit-Kit" with angora knitting yarn in pale blue to make sweater for Vogue dolls. Courtesy Jay Minter. $45.00 up.

244

10" "Jill" by Vogue. Original with original box. All hard plastic and sleep eyes. Marked: Vogue Dolls. Courtesy The Doll Cradle. $45.00.

25" Baby Dear One. Marked: 1963/E. Wilkins/Vogue Dolls. Sleep eyes and rooted hair. Courtesy Margaret Mandel. $145.00.

"Miss Ginny" by Vogue and first one issued. 15" Tall and doll is unmarked. Clothes tagged: Vogue Dolls Inc. Made in U.S.A.. Courtesy Karen Stephenson. $50.00.

VOGUE DOLLS
WONDERCRAFT

8″ "Ginny Goes Country" made exclusively for Shirley's Doll House in Wheeling, IL in 1985. Doll is vinyl and has sleep eyes. The pig and lamb are plastic. Comes with extra outfit. $60.00.

11″ "Bobbi-Mae" Swing and sway doll. Ca. 1940. by Wondercraft Co. N.Y. U.S.A. All composition with molded and painted clothes and features. Courtesy Frasher Doll Auctions. $165.00.

INDEX

NUMBERS AND SYMBOLS

LETTERS & SYMBOLS

Schroeder's Antiques Price Guide

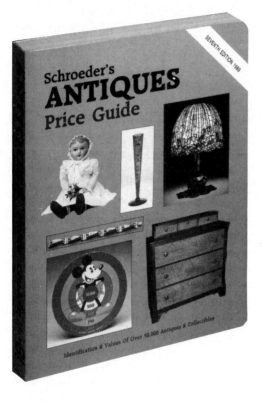

Schroeder's Antiques Price Guide has climbed its way to the top in a field already supplied with several well-established publications! The word is out, *Schroeder's Price Guide* is the best buy at any price. Over 500 categories are covered, with more than 50,000 listings. From ABC Plates to Zsolnay, if it merits the interest of today's collector, you'll find it in Schroeder's. Each subject is represented with histories and background information. In addition, hundreds of sharp original photos are used each year to illustrate not only the rare and the unusual, but the everyday "fun-type" collectibles as well. All new copy and all new illustrations make Schroeder's THE price guide on antiques and collectibles. We have not and will not simply change prices in each new edition.

The writing and researching team is backed by a staff of more than seventy of Collector Books' finest authors, as well as a board of advisors made up of well-known antique authorities and the country's top dealers, all specialists in their fields. Prices are gathered over the entire year previous to publication, then each category is thoroughly checked. Only the best of the lot remains for publication. You'll find the new edition of *Schroeder's Antiques Price Guide* the one to buy for factual information and quality.

No dealer, collector or investor can afford not to own this book. It is available from your favorite bookseller or antiques dealer at the low price of $12.95. If you are unable to find this price guide in your area, it's available from Collector Books, P.O. Box 3009, Paducah, KY 42001 at $12.95 plus $2.00 for postage and handling.